# on track ...

# Pink Floyd

## every album, every song

Richard Butterworth

sonicbondpublishing.com

Sonicbond Publishing Limited
www.sonicbondpublishing.co.uk
Email: info@sonicbondpublishing.co.uk

First Published in the United Kingdom 2022
First Published in the United States 2022

British Library Cataloguing in Publication Data:
A Catalogue record for this book is available from the British Library



ISBN 978-1-78952-242-6



Typeset in ITC Garamond & ITC Avant Garde
Printed and bound in England

Graphic design and typesetting: Full Moon Media

# on track ...

# Pink Floyd

## every album, every song

Richard Butterworth

sonicbondpublishing.com

# Acknowlegements

Finally, thanks to Roger, David, Rick, Nick, Syd and all the Floydians who, wittingly or not, helped me; and of course to my wonderful and ever-patient partner, Sue.

# Foreword

Author's caveat: spanning more than half a century, Pink Floyd product is sizeable enough. Larded with a reissue/remaster programme that seems to enjoy a relaunch every other year, it's massive. Therefore it's impossible to fulfil to the letter this book's remit of discussing literally every album, every track, while preserving enough bandwidth to dumb down the facts with my pithy and doubtlessly side-splitting observations. So I've limited reviews to Floyd's complete sequence of regular album releases, from *The Piper At The Gates Of Dawn* to *The Endless River*; the band's early singles; and the 2022 single 'Hey Hey, Rise Up'. Towards the end, I've covered authorised live albums, 'disappeared' pieces (such as 'Embryo') and compilations. However, way above the author's paygrade are bootlegs: for years, unauthorised recordings have been *betes noir* for Floyd and their management; until life-changing royalties permit me legal advisors who have actually studied law, my instinct is to let sleeping suits lie.

Reviews are of Pink Floyd records only, with no solo albums. I avoid digging too far into the infamous rift between Roger Waters and David Gilmour, and I'll certainly take no side in the hostilities. Sometimes the squabbling leaches into musical evaluation; in such cases, I'll touch upon it as necessary and move quickly on.

You might disagree with some (or all) of my thoughts on Pink Floyd. That's your prerogative. Except where stated, the opinions and analyses are the author's own, based on existing knowledge, extensive research and my emotional (rather than blindingly technical) responses to the music – which to these ears is how Pink Floyd ought to be appreciated anyway. However, appraisals of content whose meaning is allegorical or obscure can be subjective; I hope it goes without saying that your interpretations of Pink Floyd's words and music carry no less weight than mine.

# *on track ...*

# Pink Floyd

## Contents

# Introduction

May 1967. Two months or so before the release of Pink Floyd's first album, *The Piper At The Gates Of Dawn*. On BBC-TV's Sunday evening arts strand, *Look Of The Week*, Floyd are showcasing two tracks, 'Pow R. Toc H'. and 'Astronomy Dominé'. With live performances taped at London's Queen Elizabeth Hall, the programme is broadcast in the stark monochrome that precedes the arrival in Britain of colour television. The band are bathed in their light show, which makes as much sense on a black-&-white telly as world championship snooker, although a certain guttering malevolence suggests Floyd's show is part of some devilish candlelit ritual. If this really is the look of the week, viewers of nervous dispositions will probably be glad to make it to the Monday morning.

Despite the superbly atmospheric music and guitarist Syd Barrett's sinister 'windmilling' silhouettes, best remembered is the interview with two band members by an Austrian-born musicologist, Dr Hans Keller. A spit for Frank Zappa's Republican older brother, the learned PhD enquires of Barrett and bassist Roger Waters, 'Why does it got to be so terribly loud?', advising the young bucks that he is 'too much of a musician' to fathom what's going down here. Syd and Roger politely bat away Dr Keller's barely-contained disdain: 'I don't guess it has to be [so loud], but that's the way we like it', Roger replies equably, pointing out that, unlike for their interlocutor, the privilege of 'growing up in a string quartet' had somehow evaded them. After a few minutes of musicological arm-wrestling, Dr Keller is handed the judicial black cap and turns to the camera with a wilting dismissal: 'My verdict is that it is a little bit of a regression to childhood', the great man decrees. 'But, after all, why not?'

Dr Keller's haughty, patronising *froideur* spoke volumes about how the arts establishment perceived a younger generation's attempts to occupy space on its hallowed cultural high ground. You may carry on with your little games, he seemed to be saying, but leave the real Art to the grown-ups. The doctor's diagnosis was centred on two elements impossible to divorce from rock'n'roll: volume and repetition. Like a fatherly priest warning schoolboys off too many girlie mags, the academic also observed that continual exposure to such obscene decibel counts might render young minds 'unable to appreciate softer types of music.'

His predictable derision notwithstanding, Dr Keller was only doing his job: that of a pompous, middle-aged connoisseur of civilised standards keen to preserve the generation gap and, with it, the status quo. Meanwhile, Floyd happily did theirs by ramming the volume and repetition right up the string quartets of their elders and betters. For irrespective of the burgeoning sophistication of Floyd's music, their articulacy and intelligence, their relative lack of interest in singles chart success, even the fashionable satin and tat that comprised their 1967 wardrobe, Pink Floyd were, at heart, a garage band.

Ten years later, EMI tore up The Sex Pistols' box-fresh recording contract, playing squarely into the eager hands of the punks' publicity-hungry manager, Malcolm McLaren. In January 1977, Pink Floyd programmed the 17-minute

'Dogs' into the first side of their new LP, *Animals*: a set of connected discourses on society's winners and losers imagined as Orwellian anthropomorphs. In 1979, Floyd released the still more thematic *The Wall*, an expansive double-album, following this with the most complex and spectacular live performances ever mounted by a rock band.

Heroically long songs, operatic concept albums and lavish stage shows: in 1979, these were as good a way as any to return, with interest, the two fingers being stuck up at Pink Floyd and their ilk by the Pistols and theirs. In Floyd's apparent indifference to fashion, in going large despite the diktats of trendily minimalist scenesters, in their studied lack of interest even in talking to the press, the band's attitude felt … well, oddly punk-like.

In 1976, Nick Logan invited 'hip young gunslingers' to persuade the record-buying public that only his reinvented *New Musical Express* could launch the meteorite that would finally put paid to the dinosaurs of prog. Once Logan's sullen hirelings were training their catapults on anyone playing songs longer than the average punk's attention span, the old guard was ready for demob. In concert with the *NME* and prodded by the beady McLaren, Johnny Rotten's 'I Hate Pink Floyd' t-shirt was all it took to convince a lucrative floating market that side-long opuses were *so* last year. Even John Peel, once a committed Floyd fan, discovered overnight that 1976 was rock's Year Zero, and that a reductionist tsunami of three-minute, three-chord ranting was about to engulf the greatcoat-wearing classes and wash them away forever.

John Lydon later recorded how he'd been slapped down by McLaren for daring publicly to admit that his tastes in pop really ran to Hawkwind and Van der Graaf Generator. Punk, much of which (though certainly not all) was little more than pub-rock safety-pinned to heavy metal, raged for a year or so while prog retreated underground. Consigned to limbo and with post-punk unblushingly wearing many of its clothes, prog patiently waited for that recurring node in the pop-cultural cycle to crank back around and assure record buyers it was once again safe to venture near a 13/4 time signature.

But anyway, were Pink Floyd ever really prog? For several years, Floyd were probably the most genuinely progressive rock group in the world. If the only criteria for membership of Club Prog were song length and conceptual grandeur, Floyd would be winning on penalties against anyone with a Mellotron and a Gibson double-neck. Yet Floyd never comfortably aligned with prog's orthodoxies: dazzling technique, theatrical showmanship and flowery, magical-real lyrics were largely strangers in a Floydian universe gloomily strewn with dark matter. On stage, Floyd were relatively faceless; like everyone in 1967, they ponied around in scarves and silks, but a year later a thereafter-unchanging uniform of jeans and t-shirts lent Floyd the anonymity of their own road crew. And while Roger Dean's record covers for Yes, Gentle Giant and other prog behemoths depicted verdant, sci-fi Middle Earths inhabited by friendly alien lifeforms, Hipgnosis (a design company owned by Storm Thorgerson and Aubrey 'Po' Powell, Cambridge schoolmates of Waters and

Barrett) crafted for Floyd a series of high-touch visual puns, *trompe l'oeil* deceptions and surreal non-sequiturs. The sleeves delighted the eye and teased the brain; but, evoking neither cut-out ransom notes nor aerial views of Hobbiton, the imagery felt detached equally from punk and prog. Defiantly unclassifiable, Pink Floyd fell between the two.

Lyrically Floyd were far from the rococo allegories of Jon Anderson and Peter Sinfield. They also avoided prog's ostentatious displays of instrumental technique. Although Roger Waters' earliest songwriting efforts were awkward accounts of extra-terrestrial goings-on in the Cambridgeshire fens, the bassist would refine his lyrics to address the prosaically Earthbound basics of human existence, not to mention his own inner demons. While David Gilmour (guitar) and Richard Wright (keyboards) were gifted and excellent musicians, neither at first read notation. Waters and Nick Mason were feeling their respective ways into bass and drums for many months after the departure of Floyd's original lead guitarist. And the mercurial Syd Barrett's own playing was always less about technical skill than madcap, acid-fuelled inspiration.

During (The) Pink Floyd's residency at London's premier underground club, UFO, their music was raw, daring, undisciplined and often astoundingly violent. Their three-chord party-piece could run for half an hour, but 'Interstellar Overdrive', along with Floyd's other typically overdriven, primitively spacy conflations of Bo Diddley, The Rolling Stones and Stockhausen, suggested a sonic approach far removed from those of the earnest prophets of prog. Floyd's music post-Syd, while distanced from the tortuous complexities of ELP and Genesis, steadily became more structured and disciplined, its frameworks embellished by Wright's growing banks of keys and synths and newcomer Gilmour's yearningly emotive guitar.

It took Gilmour's arrival properly to establish Floyd's identity, despite the explorations of the Barrett era. Between 1965 and early 1968, Syd was the group's leader, characterful link to a flourishing underground and principal songwriter. His compositional instincts tended towards pastoral, whimsically English psychedelia deconstructed into lysergic freakouts. But as the guitarist's faculties evaporated in an acid-ravaged miasma – Rick Wright gamely tried his hand at Syd-style songwriting, with rather less success – the band stretched to still more epic experimentalism. Now Floyd were free to fly to extraordinary new realms and universes, their sense of adventure never as panoramic before or, arguably, since. As technical wizardry distributed the new sounds around cavernous auditoria with head-spinning facility, Floyd continued to weave sophisticated textures into often heart-wrenchingly beautiful themes, lengthy chord sequences and sometimes startling key changes. While Yes piloted carefully through the baroque, serpentine *Topographic Oceans* and King Crimson's Robert Fripp continued his career-long mission to tear fissures in music's space-time continuum, Pink Floyd were creating operatic substance from relatively little; if musical intricacy were present, it was entirely at the service of stately evocations of mood and emotion. Yet, for all the studio ethereality, the group's post-Barrett live performances could be astoundingly brutal, as languid originals such as Gilmour's 'Fat Old Sun' and Waters' 'Green Is The Colour' were transformed into eardrum-shattering 15-minute leviathans. With Roger and Nick shaping modest instrumental talents into a formidably powerful rhythm machine, this was amped-up audial ferocity easily the equal of anything punk would manage. (Listen to the slashing release of Gilmour's guitar solo at the end of 'Sheep', from 1977's *Animals*; any fears that Pink Floyd would buckle under punkish onslaught were palpably absurd). Floyd's sense of dynamics – of juxtaposing light with shade, pastoral serenity with sudden, scorching viciousness, of just how far to build musical tension before an explosively cathartic release – proved as unerring as it was uncanny.

Although rock'n'roll sensibilities were always present, gradually Stockhausen nosed ahead of Bo Diddley and the Stones. In came the free-jazz influences of Cecil Taylor and late-period Coltrane, Middle Eastern scales, the creative possibilities of atonal noise, silence and apparently random, often aggressive and sometimes profoundly new sounds. The collapsing of musical reserve initiated by Syd onstage was now studiously channelled into marathon sonic treks through the outer reaches: 'A Saucerful Of Secrets', 'Set The Controls For The Heart Of The Sun', 'Embryo', 'Careful With That Axe, Eugene', 'Cymbaline', 'Atom Heart Mother', 'Echoes'. And here lay the supreme irony: shorn of their one true psychedelic tourist, where else had Floyd to go but the stars? Yet even as they populated such songs – and, indeed, the firmly terrestrial *Dark Side Of The Moon* – with suitably otherworldly SFX and musique concrète, the band played down the inevitable accusations of 'space rock'. This seems disingenuous – Floyd once seriously considered majoring in sci-fi movie soundtracks – yet they had a point: 1971's 'Echoes' remains a Floyd touchstone, a stunning 23-minute odyssey through whatever heights (or depths) get you through the night. But exploratory as it is, the song also showcases how it's Roger's mounting talent for lyrically questioning the human condition that's now making landfall, not flying saucers in Mildenhall.

However conveniently Floyd's music may be categorised, it's long been fashionable to denounce the group's output from immediately after Syd's departure to before the release of *Dark Side Of The Moon*. Could this be due to the chorus of disapproval from three of its four creators, their crosshairs sited in particular on *Ummagumma* and *Atom Heart Mother*? Nick Mason's Saucerful Of Secrets, a 'self-tribute' band formed by Nick in 2019 expressly to perform Floyd songs dating from 1967 to 1972, indicates the drummer's fondness for that period. Nick has cited *A Saucerful Of Secrets* as his favourite Floyd album, yet his affection is not shared by Roger Waters. David Gilmour might have told *MOJO* in 2006 he thought the second album's title track was 'fantastic', but don't even get him started on *Ummagumma*. Before his death in 2008, Rick Wright largely agreed with his bandmates.

No one's more entitled than Roger, David and Rick to write off their own work. Less authoritative, perhaps, are the critics hitched to the band's proprietary disclaimers, marching an army of received wisdoms through the pages of biographies and magazines as allegedly solid evidence of Pink Floyd losing their way during a rudderless post-Syd era. For Floyd's inventiveness during this period, far from indicating a band hobbled by ennui, realised some truly astonishing music. Rick's 'Sysyphus', from *Ummagumma*, has been routinely monstered, not least by its composer. Yet on its arrival in November 1969, the four-part work represented perhaps the most startling fourteen minutes in contemporary rock. Gilmour's three-part 'The Narrow Way', from the same album and again trashed by its writer, was as clear a signpost to Floyd's direction of travel as anything the band were producing. The title suite from *Atom Heart Mother* delivered the emotional uplift of a Saturn 5, exploding any number of sage theories on where extended rock composition should be headed. Floyd may have baulked at the idea, but in its questing nature, this was rock music for space – outer *and* inner – as no one, not even they, would dare to attempt again. The delirious urge for these sonic hunter-gatherers to damn the torpedoes, to shut their eyes and think of England in case it all falls apart around their ears, was never more evident than *before* the arrival of their magnum opus. And in this music's suck-it-and-see insouciance, it was, oddly, the essence of punk.

Music as substantial as *Dark Side Of The Moon* rarely appears from a vacuum. Like prudent householders adapting knick-knacks squirrelled away in the attic, by 1972 Floyd had become masters of upcycling their own fragmented musical experiments. Just as 'Echoes' unified 24 disparate nuggets and effects they'd toyed with earlier, *Dark Side* merged elements which, for several years, Floyd had been shopping around soundtracks, studio sessions and a prodigious touring schedule.

That the final combination reaped such astronomical success needs little reminder. *Dark Side Of The Moon* might have lacked the audacity and naïve inquisitiveness of the earlier music, but the album indisputably represented Floyd's coming of age. With all four musicians pulling together towards a common goal and the musical direction tillered, never more confidently, by Gilmour and Wright, *DSOTM* also confirmed the maturity of Roger Waters as Floyd's lyricist and conceptual guide, a mantle he would wear for the rest of the 1970s.

In 1976 The Damned – unintentionally, to be fair – introduced 'gobbing' to punk's users' manual not long before Waters infamously hawked in the face of an obnoxious fan at a Floyd stadium gig. The bassist was tetchy at the best of times; his unearthly, teeth-bared vocal screams on 'Careful With That Axe, Eugene' suggested Roger was the only Floyd since Syd to possess a jot of onstage charisma. But over several years, the bassist became progressively angered by the artifice of fame and 'the incoherent scale of stadium events'. When in July 1977 he finally lanced the boil at Montreal's Olympic Stadium, the act was as punkish as anything in Rat Scabies' playbook.

By now, Floyd's uncertain status relative to Britain's pop-cultural tribes was mirrored by identity issues closer to home. Contradictory messages were skewering the public's notion of what the band stood for. After 1973's lunar eclipse of the planet's every other rock group, Floyd – especially the lifelong socialist Roger Waters – might have paused to reflect upon how comfortably their work's anti-establishment sentiments sat with such humungous personal wealth. Floyd were playing North American stadium shows before average audiences of 60,000, most fans apparently wanting nothing more than to get on down to rockaboogie Floyd faves like 'Money' and 'One Of These Days'. This appalled the now determinedly highbrow Waters. Concerned that his increasingly thoughtful work was falling upon the deaf ears of arrivistes, the bassist imagined a high, stage-wide wall that would safely partition the performers from the great unwashed seething in the arena beyond. *The Wall* proved to be another massive exercise in Floydian paradox: so furious was Roger over the metaphorical barrier between band and fans that he built a real one, and even higher. Those stage sets became ever more dramatic; Floyd shows, and those by Waters following his acrimonious walkaway in 1985, would continue to provide rich banquets for the senses – even if, for some, the feasts were a tad overcooked.

*The Wall* was the last of Pink Floyd's 1970s albums, completing a tetralogy increasingly dominated by Waters. As ever, the bassist was haunted by the foibles of humanity and, more directly, by his father and Syd Barrett. Gilmour's contributions were limited to a miserly, though brilliant three tracks, while fewer still were those of Mason and Wright; on *The Wall*'s earliest sleeves, neither even received a credit.

Coinciding with the personal hostilities, it seemed the band had reached the summit of their ambition. By the turn of the 1980s, Floyd were fractured and dissolute. Seen to be under-contributing, Wright was sacked, while Waters and Gilmour entered a period of mutually toxic enmity that would drag on for decades. Not long after 1983's woefully underrated *The Final Cut* (by Pink Floyd in name only and effectively a Roger Waters solo album) the bassist was gone, the game of thrones leaving Gilmour as legal custodian of the battered yet still wildly successful Pink Floyd brand. With Mason a co-director and Wright resuming duties as a salaried foot-soldier, the House of Gilmour would produce two Waters-free studio albums during the 1980s-90s, each followed by a high-grossing world tour, each preserved in a live album.

In 2005 Bob Geldof, seeking big names for the Hyde Park charity concert Live 8, wrangled Wright and Mason and brokered a brief reconciliation between Waters and Gilmour. The rumour mill spluttered into action: will they or won't they? Despite the short but glorious Live 8 set, bassist and guitarist swiftly quashed any idea of reform. A year later, the long-reclusive Syd Barrett died; then, in 2008, any lingering hopes of a full Floyd reunion were finally beached by Rick Wright's passing. In tribute to the keyboardist, in 2014 Gilmour used new material and various offcuts he'd made with Wright to assemble the mainly instrumental *The Endless River*. On Russia's invasion of Ukraine in 2022, Gilmour reconvened a Waters-free Floyd for a charity single.

Today, Pink Floyd's influence remains incalculable. Barrett's songwriting has informed the work of a galaxy of stars, from Blur and Bolan to Paul Weller and Paul McCartney. Listen to The Grateful Dead, Hawkwind, Velvet Underground, Jimi Hendrix, Nine Inch Nails, The Orb, Can, Tangerine Dream, Kraftwerk, Vangelis, Jean-Michel Jarre, neo-psych bands of 1990's 'second summer of love', avant-garde Industrialists such as Throbbing Gristle/Psychic TV, Faust and Einstürzende Neubauten – I could go on – and you'll hear the shards and splinters of Floyd's early experiments with dynamics, prepared instruments, atonal noise and ambient drones. For anyone since 1973 contemplating a suite of thematically-linked songs, the symphonic, architectural grace of *Dark Side Of The Moon* is the motherlode. Amazon, Ebay and YouTube are awash with peer homage sets and dubious new takes on PF favourites (*Jazz Side Of The Moon*, anyone?).

Floyd's music, in particular the guitar-playing of King of Feel David Gilmour, has been superficially easy plunder for tribute bands; only The Beatles' people have been obliged to collect royalties from more worldwide soundalikes. But Gilmour's warmth, expressiveness and intuitive flair for melody, and his command of bent and blue notes, vibrato and sustain, are deceptive. Few modern guitarslingers can bottle the undiluted *rightness* of a Gilmour solo; a single wasted note is a crime, his every phrase worth a thousand shredded by his lessers for the sake of showy bombast.

In 1977, to confess publicly a liking for Pink Floyd was as cool as wearing fifteen-inch loons and a perm to the Conservative Club disco. But in the third decade of the 21st century, it would be so nice to think that Roger Waters, David Gilmour and Nick Mason spend at least some of their average week fending off grateful musicians, all queueing to say 'thanks.'

## Syd Barrett and the first two singles

29 April 1967 saw stark evidence of the difficulties that would plague Pink Floyd for the next year: Syd Barrett took LSD.

Acid had been etching away at the guitarist's fragile nervous system since he began evangelising the lysergic experience in 1965. Now the drug was gaining the upper hand. Floyd were headlining the *14-hour Technicolour Dream*, a star-studded hippie beanfeast at Alexandra Palace to raise funds for the underground newssheet *IT*. As the rising sun pierced the Great Hall's stained glass window at 5 am on 30 April, Floyd at last occupied the stage. Due to a coinciding gig in the Netherlands, they'd arrived in north London only two hours earlier, everyone feeling bushed. But Syd's deportment suggested something darker than travel fatigue, as June Child, their management secretary (and future Mrs Marc Bolan) told Nick Mason for the drummer's memoir *Inside Out*: 'I found [Syd] in the dressing room and he was so … gone. We got him out to the stage … and Syd just stood there, his guitar round his neck and his arms just hanging down.'

At gigs, on TV shows and tours, Syd would be similarly indisposed; unpredictable, sometimes inert, his demeanour borderline catatonic. Yet things were different on the formation of The Pink Floyd Sound in 1965. Playful, charismatic, good-looking, at one with the heady spirit of the mid-60s English counterculture, Syd assumed a natural leadership of Roger Waters, Rick Wright and Nick Mason and proceeded to sculpt their music in his image. Word spread of these radical young practitioners of psychedelia with the fearless sonic alchemist at the controls. Eventually, it took shedloads of psychoactive drugs, and Syd's inability to cope with their consequences, to allow the emergence of Roger, Rick, Nick and, later, David Gilmour.

Enough has been written about the band's 1963 beginnings in London, Syd's promotion to lead guitarist in 1965 and his creation of the Pink Floyd name. At an early gig at the Marquee Club, ambitious LSE lecturer Peter Jenner (who'd pitched to manage The Velvet Underground but was pipped by Andy Warhol) noted Floyd's unusual take on traditional R'n'B. A deal followed, Jenner and Andrew King's Blackhill Enterprises shepherding Floyd around the capital's budding freak scene. In January 1967, UFO co-founder Joe Boyd and booking agent Bryan Morrison trooped Floyd into Sound Techniques to cut the first two sides, 'Arnold Layne' and 'Candy And A Currant Bun', alongside two lengthy instrumental jams, 'Interstellar Overdrive' and 'Nick's Boogie', earmarked for Peter Whitehead's film *Tonite Let's All Make Love In London* (the latter pieces, chaotic exemplars of Floyd's early enthusiasm, would be released in 1991 as a twelve-inch single and a CD EP). Advancing a modest £5,000, EMI signed The Pink Floyd shortly after.

### **'Arnold Layne'** 2.57 (Barrett) b/w **'Candy And A Currant Bun'** 2.48 (Barrett)

Recorded at: Sound Techniques, London, 29 January-1 February 1967
Produced by: Joe Boyd

Released: 10 March 1967
Highest UK chart position: 20

It's a measure of Pink Floyd's ambition that the band felt able to dismiss predictable mutterings over their risqué first single. 'Arnold Layne' was Syd's name for a Cambridge cross-dresser who delighted in stealing freshly-laundered women's underwear from washing lines. Possibly to curry favour with broadcasting regulators ahead of September's sinking of the pirates, Radios London and Caroline (though not, for once, the BBC) promptly banned Syd's quirky tale of everyday Fenland kinkiness.

Although 'Arnold Layne' was nicely produced by Joe Boyd, the relationship between the Bostonian and the band proved short-lived. To represent Floyd to the industry, Blackhill hired the well-connected Bryan Morrison Agency, who secured a deal with EMI at a time when the UK's biggest record label refused to use outside producers. Boyd's brief tenure in the studio with Floyd was therefore brought to an abrupt end. 'Arnold Layne' embodies Anglian psychedelia: a controversial song topic, downplayed by words couched in whimsy. Their singer's diction was carefully middle-class and a long way from the *faux*-American drawl that had characterised post-Elvis British pop singing. Such quaintness risked tipping into affectation; the studied soppiness of many songs by inferior artists in 1967 seeped onto more than one 7-inch that Floyd would release post-Barrett. Syd, however, was a natural wordsmith, easily capable of running with a poetic cue from classic fantasy writers such as A. A. Milne and Kenneth Grahame. And even if 'Arnold Layne' was mildly off-colour set against the sweet children's tales of Pooh and *The Wind In The Willows* – if there were any transgendered folk at Toad Hall, they weren't filching Mrs Toad's undies – Barrett's genius for unexpected rhyme, syntax, cadence and allegory invested his work with his own charm and innocence. It was a skill few more knowing contemporaries could manage.

'Arnold Layne' is soaked in reverb-drenched guitar and Farfisa organ: the two instruments which typify Pink Floyd's sound in these early days. With Boyd history, EMI wanted its own producer, Norman Smith, to redo the song and oversee all other Floyd studio work. Roger and Rick agreed with the suits – 'Normal' Smith being a consummate professional who'd engineered many Beatles records – but Syd refused to countenance another 'Arnold Layne' session.

On the B-side, Syd was 'fessing up: 'I'm high, don't try to spoil my fun', he sang. 'Too bad', EMI countered, demanding the line be excised from 'Candy And A Currant Bun' and unsurprisingly removing Syd's original title, 'Let's Roll Another One'. The more explicitly psychedelic of these first two sides, the song hints at what Pink Floyd had in mind for the blues form; in this case represented by Chester Burnett's 'Smokestack Lightnin''. Howlin' Wolf's famous riff is marinated in hallucinogenics, though, as Syd's arrangement slides around the distantly familiar theme.

Behind the composer's alternately fuzzed and reverbed guitar, ghostly background vocals sound like they've drifted in from Borley Rectory on a moonless night.

## **'See Emily Play'** 2.57 (Barrett) b/w **'Scarecrow'** 2.11 (Barrett)

'See Emily Play' recorded at Sound Techniques, London, 18-20 May 1967
Produced by: Norman Smith
Released: 16 June 1967
Highest UK chart position: 6

In its short existence, the Queen Elizabeth Hall, on London's South Bank, had become home to polite recitals by chamber quartets and jazz groups. On 12 May 1967, a houseful of hippies were overstimulated by a Floydian cacophony coming at them from every compass point of the small theatre. It was an outrage surely not lost on Dr Keller, then busy preparing the TV inquisition that would alert the world to this and other juvenile delinquency.

Floyd created this early adventure in quadraphonic sound with a contraption they'd seemingly made earlier from a Meccano set, a pair of knitting needles and a biscuit tin. Piloted by Wright as part of his growing squadron of electronic widgetry, the Azimuth Co-ordinator (actually an antediluvian surround-sound mixer commissioned by Floyd from EMI studio boffin Bernard Speight) allowed the keyboardist to pan an audio signal between up to six loudspeakers positioned around the hall. Thus were Floyd's happily stoned congregation transported to still higher states of bliss; one or more celebrants were even so taken by the gadget they quietly took it away for themselves shortly after the performance.

The dizzying effects of the Co-ordinator were a natural progression for a band now gathering a sizeable fanbase beyond the acid and soot of UFO and the Roundhouse. The QEH gig, dubbed *Games For May*, was probably the UK's first multimedia rock concert, featuring a light show, quadraphonic audio and numerous musique concrète effects both live and on tape. Since it had lent its name to the evening, naturally an early iteration of Pink Floyd's second single was included in the setlist. Only later was the song's name changed.

'See Emily Play' and its jaw-dropping slide-guitar intro rippled from every transistor radio in the land from 16 June 1967. It's devastating: a strange and beguiling soup of winningly sellable hooks baked into kaleidoscopic weirdness, a perfect combination of underground and hit parade. Few instruments go untreated: particularly noteworthy are Rick's and Syd's use of the Binson Echorec, a delay machine that was nearly as *Blue Peter*-ish as the Azimuth Co-ordinator. Syd obtains a startling glissando effect by combining the Echorec with his idiosyncratic bottleneck technique, achieved by sliding over his guitar strings either a plastic ruler (after Keith Rowe, of the free-music ensemble AMM, an early Jenner signing) or a Zippo lighter. As Rick's keyboards meet

Syd's 'mirrored' 1962 Fender Esquire, an elegant electronic dance ensues, shimmering away to a stunning middle-eight crescendo.

The eponymous young woman is very much of her time: 'Emily' floats through the song like an ethereal woodland spirit, a diaphanous cypher for the archetypal hippie 'old lady'. 'Emily could be anyone', Roger explained, adding in the argot of the time, 'She's just a hung-up chick'. Another source was more helpful, positively ID-ing UFO's own 'psychedelic schoolgirl', the Hon Emily Young. The daughter of author, politician and the 2nd Baron Kennet, Wayland Young, was supposedly eulogised by Syd after he espied the privileged poppet sleeping off an acid trip in woods near Cambridge.

The B-side, 'Scarecrow', was a straight lift from the forthcoming LP *The Piper At The Gates Of Dawn*, in which chapter see review.

# **The Piper At The Gates Of Dawn** (1967)

Personnel:
Syd Barrett: lead guitar, vocals
Roger Waters: bass guitar, vocals
Rick Wright: organ, piano, vocals
Nick Mason: drums, percussion
Produced at: Abbey Road Studios, London, by Norman Smith
Engineers: Pete Bown, David Harris
Released: 5 August 1967 (UK); 21 October 1967 (US, as ***Pink Floyd*** with alternate track listing)
Highest chart places: UK: 6, US: 131

On 21 February 1967, The Beatles were recording at EMI's Abbey Road Studio Two. The same day, Pink Floyd entered Studio Three to begin their maiden album. One month later, Norman Smith petitioned Beatles' producer George Martin for an audience. Though hesitant at first, Martin finally invited Floyd next door to gaze upon the Fabs as they worked on 'Lovely Rita' for *Sergeant Pepper*. 'We sat humbly at the back of the control room', Nick Mason recalled. 'After a suitable period, we were ushered out again ... They were God-like figures to us.'

The four young initiates must have lingered long enough to be anointed with transcendent Beatlejuice. For the eleven songs Floyd created, during more than 50 sessions between February and July, would comprise one of rock's finest debut albums. And more than any subsequent solo release, *The Piper At The Gates Of Dawn* would bottle the essence of Syd Barrett.

That cornerstone of children's fantasy, *The Wind In The Willows* (from which seventh chapter Syd appropriates *Piper*'s title) saturates the album. Kenneth Grahame's spirit bathes the songs in bucolic innocence, surrounding their principal author with a Pan-like aura. *The Piper At The Gates Of Dawn* (the title was nearly the dour *Projection*) testifies to Barrett's raging inventiveness of the time, an optimum snapshot of an unpredictable mindset. His delicate psyche might be bound for collapse, but here you'd never know it; at this supremely confident moment, Syd enjoys total control over whatever unlocks his restlessly fertile imagination.

The general mood is enchantingly pastoral, as English as a red pillar box, occasionally lifting off for stranger, more distant worlds; Syd as readily peers out beyond the solar system as he burrows impishly beneath clumps of Fenland toadstools. And if his words are smart and mischievous, his expressiveness rivalling his literary idols, the frameworks set up by the band are bold, unearthly and surprising. Musical restraints are loosened, the instrumentalists free to explore (at least within the limitations imposed by the ever-careful Smith) and dynamics are everywhere. Space exploration blends seamlessly with fireside familiarity; astronauts rub shoulders with elemental nature deities.

Making *Piper* had its headaches. Most were apparently endured by Smith. The straight-laced producer was later scathing: Waters 'wasn't a great bass player'; Wright was 'quietly arrogant'; Mason 'was just along for the ride'. Unsurprisingly Smith reserved his most damning criticism for the guitarist, whose acid consumption had soared during *Piper*'s sessions: 'Working with Syd was sheer hell', he told Barrett's biographers. 'There are no pleasant memories'. (Having made his bones on every Beatles record up to and including *Rubber Soul*, Norman would stoically return to work on Floyd's second and fourth albums, as well as recordings for labelmates The Pretty Things and Barclay James Harvest. But the producer also longed for pastures beyond the control booth; in June 1971, as Syd's old band lovingly assembled the towering 'Echoes', 'Hurricane' Smith was busily throwing shapes on *Top Of The Pops*, his slushy, self-penned single 'Don't Let It Die' riding number two on the UK chart).

*Piper*'s sleeve depicted Floyd themselves as pop stars. Resplendent in their Carnaby Street threads, the band were shot by photographer Vic Singh on a prism lens that multiplied its subject like a trippy kaleidoscope. The image was clichéd and dull; EMI's middle-aged groovers were probably chuffed, but the cover was unlikely to have been cheered by a band who preferred relative anonymity. Far more interesting was the reverse: what started life as an unpromisingly 1960s 'wacky popsters' publicity photo by Colin Prime was graphically reduced by Syd to a terrifyingly abstract, Rorschach-like silhouette. A quantum shift from gnomes, scarecrows and Granny Takes a Trip taffetas, this unnameable, Cthuloid entity could have hitched a ride on 'Interstellar Overdrive''s return leg. But an easy plurality is the key to *The Piper At The Gates Of Dawn*: esoterica, science fiction, fairytale, fantasy, childhood reminiscence and, by the way, rock'n'roll, all informing an opening statement that stands proudly alongside such contemporary masterpieces as *Sergeant Pepper*, *Surrealistic Pillow*, *Are You Experienced?* and *The Doors*.

The album was released in the US in October 1967 as *Pink Floyd* on Tower Records, adding 'See Emily Play' but omitting 'Astronomy Dominé', 'Bike' and 'Flaming' (which, backed by 'The Gnome', was a non-charting US single). On release, most pressers were favourable, while *Piper*'s reputation would skyrocket in later years. Even today, a highly vocal Team Syd swears blind that Floyd couldn't better the first album and that the band were never the same after their hero departed (the latter, at least, was true). Most important of all was the conferring of the Royal Warrant: on first hearing the finished item, Paul McCartney declared *Piper* 'a knockout.'

## **'Astronomy Dominé'** 4.13 (Barrett)

Using an EMI-approved megaphone, Peter Jenner counts down astronomical coordinates from a homegrown Mission Control. Roger plucks at a high single bass note. Rick's Farfisa does a believable if nonsensical Morse Code impression. A thumping of Nick's tom-toms heralds Syd's chiming, Dick Dale-style guitar theme. With an intro so tense it might have been recorded on the brink of a black hole, Pink Floyd invent psychedelic space rock.

Docked to music never before heard from a rock'n'roll band, singers Syd and Rick evoke, in stirring close harmony, an outer space that's at once awe-inspiring, haunting, scary, enchanting and playful; in places a portentous novel by Asimov or Heinlein, in others a page from the children's astronomy book from which Jenner recited the intro. Nick once likened 'Astronomy Dominé' to the Pop Art of Roy Lichtenstein – he of the famous WHAAM! and POW! comic-strip lithographs. Nick's view is given weight by the presence of similar vocal exclamations and of Dan Dare, *The Eagle*'s Pilot of the Future, the intrepid cartoon cosmonaut darting mischievously between galactic outposts that are both celestial and Shakespearian:

Jupiter and Saturn, Oberon, Miranda and Titania
Neptune, Titan, stars can frighten
Blinding signs flap
Flicker, flicker, flicker blam. Pow, pow
Stairway scare, Dan Dare, who's there?

'Astronomy Dominé' is one of Floyd's most enduringly exciting songs; a space odyssey – even Roger concurred with that – that would be dropped from live performance in 1971 but resurrected more than 20 years later.

### **'Lucifer Sam'** 3.07 (Barrett)

In April 1967, *Melody Maker* reported on a Floyd work-in-progress tentatively entitled 'The Life Story Of Percy The Ratcatcher'. After the stillbirth of a half-hour animated film, Syd revived and renamed the rodent operative for a cracking rock'n'roll song. 'Lucifer Sam' celebrates Syd's love of cats, his girlfriend Jenny Spires – here branded a witch named Jennifer Gentle – and the acidic, left-brain-right-brain chaos of Barrett's current lifestyle.

From Syd's descending surf-guitar intro, the song carries a similar urban excitement to Neal Hefti's *Batman* theme, driven with unusual urgency by Roger and Nick, everyone scurrying madly around, things to do, people to see. Hard rock this might be, but the affair is far from straightforward; the middle break features Waters bowing his bass over a backing that seems to falter to the point of breakdown, Syd's crumpled guitar rescued by a Waters/Mason rhythm machine pumping vigour and momentum.

Punctuated throughout by whooshing SFX unlikely to have been missed by a then-infant Hawkwind, there's a club solo from Rick at 2.33 that's so 1960s it nearly trips over the go-go dancers. The great early single that never was, 'Lucifer Sam' proves Floyd could rock out as enthusiastically as anyone – but always with a twist of Barrett lemon.

### **'Matilda Mother'** 3.08 (Barrett)

'Matilda, who told lies and was burned to death' was a character from *Cautionary Tales For Children* by Hilaire Belloc, the magical realism of whose stories, like those of Lewis Carroll's, was gratefully requisitioned in so many corners of the 1967 underground. Syd originally transcribed words for 'Matilda Mother' directly from Belloc's text. However, cease-and-desist letters on behalf of the late author's estate sent Floyd back to the studio with new lyrics for a re-record.

The track intros with an eerie organ/bass theme before Rick Wright sings promisingly:

There was a king who ruled the land
His majesty was in command
With silver eyes the scarlet eagle
Showers silver on the people

At this point, Syd's lyric swerves away from the story which his mother is narrating to the thoughts of the young recipient himself, who is disappointed to have been left 'Hanging in my infant air, waiting'. Superficially the song is Syd's simple recollection of childhood and hearthside fairytales. But as he switches from a story of kings and scarlet eagles to the listener's response to its interruption, is the frustration he vents born of a wish to reside permanently in a realm of fantasy? If so, Barrett would hardly be the first or last writer to have used psychotropic drugs to escape a harsher, more prosaic reality. 'Matilda Mother', the first track Floyd recorded for the new album, has a sad and mildly unsettling air, the melancholic sentiments and the eastern-aired arrangement distancing the song from Syd's more obviously upbeat storytelling in 'The Gnome', while closing in on the wraithlike beauty of 'Chapter 24'.

## **'Flaming'** 2.46 (Barrett)

Originally called 'Snowing', *Piper*'s third track is another obvious tilt towards childhood storytelling, but lacking the previous track's postmodern element. There Syd adopted the detachment of a listener saddened that his maternal narrator left the story hanging, unresolved. In 'Flaming' he occupies the fairytale as an active participant, a spritelike flibbertigibbet frolicking from 'Lazing in the foggy dew/sitting on a unicorn' to 'Screaming through the starlit sky/travelling by telephone', all the while happily beyond the ken of the observer: 'Yippee! You can't see me/but I can you'. Needless to say, 'Flaming' is as drenched in acid as, say, John Lennon's 'Lucy In The Sky With Diamonds'. But if sensible interpretation of such internal visions is impossible, the arrangement is a joy, full of unusual SFX produced on a variety of instruments and objects: a cuckoo's call at 0.39 is probably Roger's swanee whistle; Nick's rimshots make a fine ticking clock. Meanwhile, bells, varispeeds, compression, phasing and the ubiquitous Binson Echorec all converge to create a whirring sound collage that captures the zeitgeist as effectively as any track on *Piper*.

## **'Pow R. Toc H'.** 4.26 (Barrett/Waters/Wright/Mason)

It was probably a little unfair that sensitivities as delicate as Dr Keller's should be subjected to a live onslaught of *Piper*'s oddest track. 'Pow R. Toc H'. bends so many of even 1967's pop norms that the traumatised academic must have rushed home from the QEH for cold towels and a stiff Schnapps before the upstarts could even start on 'Interstellar Overdrive.'

Arguably a natural extension of Floyd's signature track, it's likely 'Pow R. Toc H'. started life as 'Power Toc H.', named after an army signals' name for 'Talbot House', a Christian movement originally founded during World War I as an egalitarian servicemen's club. Perhaps the title of this mainly improvised instrumental is early evidence of war and the military mingling with Roger Waters' creative juices. 'Pow R. Toc H'. certainly begins in an environment not unknown for fierce Darwinian conflict. Over sparse percussion and bass, the band vocally ape the myriad species of the Amazonian rainforest with a series of rhythmic squawks, yelps and coos. Two years on, Roger will extend the conceit for his solo quarter of *Ummagumma*.

The forest having spoken, Rick takes over with delightful jazzy piano, abetted by Nick's malleted toms. At 1.45, a crashing cymbal and a thunderclap usher back the menagerie and some indistinct human voices, and the piece settles into Rick's Farfisa and a more conventionally Floydian structure. At the end, it's complete mayhem, as if the critters are chasing Mason and half-a-dozen Burundi drummers around Andy's Guitar Shop. 'Pow R. Toc H'. would be reimagined, as was Floyd's wont, as 'The Pink Jungle' and factored into their forthcoming suite *The Man/The Journey*.

## **'Take Up Thy Stethoscope And Walk'** 3.07 (Waters)

If ever Pink Floyd could have been identified as punk rockers, this track nails it. With its primitive stop-start rhythm and a crazed middle break that can't help straying into 'Interstellar' airspace, the closest relatives to 'Stethoscope' are arguably the creations of the mid-'60s proto-punks thrown up by middle America in response to the Beatles-led US beat invasion.

Within months of the Fabs taking all five top spots on the *Billboard* 100 singles chart in the same week, bands like ? and the Mysterians, Count Five, The Shadows of Knight and The Seeds had occupied their parents' garages spitting out energetic two-chord wonders on cheap Mosrite, Standell and Farfisa equipment, more than making up in brio what they lacked in musicianship. 'Stethoscope' plays to this from the intro. Nick punishes his snare drum like he's caught it trampling on his roses, then an apparently delirious and bedridden Roger presents a stream-of-consciousness laundry-list of unrelated observations:

'Doctor doctor!/I'm in bed
Achin' head/Gold is lead
Choke on bread/Underfed

Gold is lead/Jesus bled
Pain is red

... and more of the same, broken amidships by a mad instrumental bridge – an acidic chaos of Syd's scrubbed lead guitar and Rick's reedy organ apparently auditioning for Lenny Kaye's *Nuggets* compilation. 'Stethoscope' is Roger's first stab at songwriting, and it shows. But like the spirited young scamps in those midwestern lockups, there's no gainsaying the combination of sheer brass neck and snot-sneer verve.

### **'Interstellar Overdrive'** 9.42 (Barrett/Waters/Wright/Mason)

In 1965, Manfred Mann politely covered Burt Bacharach's 'My Little Red Book' for the movie *What's New Pussycat?* A year later, Love disembowelled the same staid torch song for a blistering debut single. In pre-*Forever Changes* days, Love were Stones/Byrds aspirants, a sneery gang of LA street punks with attitudes as long as Long Beach. Syd Barrett was a big fan; serious enough, with a little help from Peter Jenner's hummed, off-key *aide-memoire*, to adapt the song's descending riff for the space rock Floyd later denied they'd anything to do with.

In the 2008 documentary *A Technicolor Dream*, Waters cited live versions of 'Interstellar Overdrive' as evidence of Floyd's early garage-band leanings: '[It] was a chromatic riff played twice', Roger recounted, 'then free-form over a single minor chord for however long we wanted it to go on. Then we'd play the riff again twice and it was all over.'

Musically naïve it might have been. But Roger's reductive argument appears to forget the seismic effect of this extraordinary nine or more minutes of psychedelic experimentation when Floyd first performed it in autumn 1966. As eldritch and formless in parts as the vastnesses of space itself, with 'Interstellar Overdrive' – after a 1953 short story, 'The Ruum', by sci-fi author Arthur Porges – Pink Floyd were putting not just clear blue water but several light years of pitch-black vacuum between themselves and almost every other rock'n'roll band on Planet Earth.

As Roger intimates, it's that sprawling mid-section that allows free rein to such outlandish exploration. Once the two initial riffs are out of the way, the boosters escape Earth's gravitational pull for something the other side of unknown, as Floyd let go with squeaking Farfisa, unhinged guitar, Nick Mason's drums sounding like a pantry falling down a mineshaft and some frankly weird SFX, all roughly adding up to whatever the hell it is out there. Order breaks down the further they journey into a space that is clearly far from benign, although Floyd betray their relative infancy as sonic explorers: the effects occasionally sound like a serial killer loose in a boneyard. Finally, the descending riff, panning frantically across the speakers, crashes down through the atmosphere and everything comes to rest. But is this Earth, or another realm or dimension altogether? As 'Interstellar Overdrive' decays into the next track and its tiny virtuous twin, the effect is similar to the final parts of *2001: A Space Odyssey*. Spoiler alert: Dave Bowman, having survived his tumultuous voyage beyond Jupiter and the Star Gate, finds himself in an elegant and suspiciously Earthbound suite of rooms, there to be confronted by his older, younger and even embryonic selves. Despite Roger Waters' later stated aversion to the space rock sobriquet, perhaps the bassist wasn't far off the mark when he opined that Floyd should have scored the soundtrack for Kubrick's masterpiece.

## **'The Gnome'** 2.13 (Barrett)

With the cosy ticking of a grandfatherly clock (actually Nick Mason's cowbell), early Floyd's most kaleidoscopic recorded music segues neatly into its polar opposite. In 'The Gnome', those so disposed will surely discern a drug reference in the line 'He had a big adventure/Amidst the grass/Fresh air at last'. But Barrett's lyrics weren't always that arch; Syd had too much respect for the children's fairy tale, both as a literary form and as a key to creating a sense of wonder in young minds, to introduce such knowing and unsubtle wordplay.

That same year, Jefferson Airplane enjoyed huge success in the US by similarly referencing children's fantasy. Lewis Carroll's *Alice* tales were mobilised by the composer of 'White Rabbit', Grace Slick, to create a narrative that wore LSD like a badge of honour. Rightly or wrongly, Grace saw the stories of Carroll, Milne, Tolkien and, indeed, Grahame as natural progenitors to the acid sonnets that comprised much of Airplane's material.

Syd Barrett mines a similar seam. But instead of paraphrasing a children's classic with modern, grown-up allusion, he's written a little nursery rhyme of his own, with no side or hidden meaning. Astral travellers, of course, are free to make up their own minds as to where the song's *Magic Roundabout* sentiments might take them. But to paraphrase a modern cliché, 'The Gnome' is what it is – nothing more.

The playschool flavour is underscored by a sweetly simple arrangement featuring Rick Wright playing a celeste, a keyboard instrument that hammers chime bars suspended over resonating wooden boxes. The celeste is perhaps most immediately recognised for its dainty resonances on Tchaikovsky's 'Dance of the Sugar Plum Fairy' and, by association, music that has illuminated children's storytelling since the days of *Listen With Mother*. Injudiciously applied, the celeste can be cloying and twee; in 'The Gnome', it beautifully sets off the words and Syd's precise enunciation. Placed alongside the sound and fury of 'Interstellar Overdrive', there's no better example of the rich diversity of Pink Floyd's early music.

## **'Chapter 24'** 3.42 (Barrett)

From Nick Mason's votive cymbal crash, through Rick Wright's tinkling piano arpeggios, quietly droning harmonium and otherworldly Farfisa, 'Chapter 24', its atmosphere of delicious incorporeality creating a natural companion to 'Matilda Mother', is a perfect demonstration of how esoterica was as readily fuelling Syd Barrett's muse as fantasy.

Since the London underground's first rumblings in the early 1960s, its dwellers had rooted through comparative religions to see what Eastern delights could most happily replace the Western mainstream's stout megalith of Christianity as a metaphysical leaning post. But approaching religiosity the way a magpie plunders bottle tops risked creating hybrid belief systems confusing enough to turn the sternest adept to drink: Hinduism, Sufism and Buddhism (with or without the Zen) were among the orthodoxies cast gleefully into the hippies' doctrinal DIY melting pot, to be blended fancifully with astrology, Wicca, Theosophy, yoga, Tarot, the Golden Dawn, Thelemite workings and whatever other borderline-potty mysticism was wafting from the pages of *IT* and *Oz*.

Somewhere among this uncertain amalgam of isms was the I Ching, an ancient Chinese method of divination based on random numbers and hexagrams. Much as John Lennon had forged 'Tomorrow Never Knows' from *The Tibetan Book Of The Dead*, Syd turns to I Ching's core text, the Book Of Changes, lifting a title from the tome's 24th chapter and refloating its hauntingly enigmatic verses:

All movement is accomplished in six stages
And the seventh brings return
For seven is the number of the young light
It forms when darkness is increased by one.

On adapting the 5,000-year-old text, Syd was typically circumspect: 'There was someone around who was very into that', he said in 1974, possibly referring to one or more of the ne'er-do-wells who tarried, not always constructively, at Syd's Earlham Street apartment, where he wrote 'Chapter 24'. Another source might have been Syd's old Cambridge pal Seamus O'Connell, whose mother was interested in occult lore and whose bookshelf of arcana was a constant source of fascination for the tyro songwriter.

Meanwhile, Rick conjures the most ethereal flavours ever heard from a Farfisa, an Italian-made electric organ whose thin, reedy tones had typified 1960s pop and would return at the end of the following decade, albeit in the hands of ironists such as Elvis Costello and the B52s. In its own way, the Farfisa was like a Mellotron (also heard briefly at 3.07): just as the tape-replay keyboard is more interestingly utilised for its icily eerie native properties than for its original – failed – remit of simulating an orchestra, so can the Farfisa be morphed from a plain electric organ to something quite different. In places in 'Chapter 24', Rick sounds like a cross-legged Brahmin charming a cobra: a suitably exotic and un-Western image for Syd's, and Floyd's, most exquisitely mysterious song.

## **'Scarecrow'** 2.11 (Barrett)

A hickory-dickory-dock intro – created by Nick Mason and friends on snare-rim, cowbell and woodblock, it could almost be an early, chime-free run-through of *DSOTM*'s 'Time' – is joined by the sinuous curlicues of Rick Wright's Farfisa, followed by Barrett accompanying himself on clipped electric guitar. A tiny vignette of three brief verses, with a beautiful coda played by Rick, Syd on acoustic guitar and Roger bowing his bass, 'Scarecrow' has a melancholy, autumnal flavour. If it's a fairytale, it's probably from the macabre Brothers Grimm/Judderman end of storytelling. Syd's own Wurzel Gummidge cuts a suitably creepy figure; not as ironically malevolent as that other creature given life by children's fable, the clown, but certainly disconcerting enough to put listeners in the same mindset as the birdlife he's been erected to deter. He's lonely, but he's learned to accept a life whose only job is to frighten other lifeforms:

His head did no thinking
His arms didn't move except when the wind cut up rough
And mice ran around on the ground
He stood in a field where barley grows
The black and green scarecrow is sadder than me
But now he's resigned to his fate
'Cause life's not unkind – he doesn't mind
He stood in a field where barley grows.

It almost goes without saying that some have construed 'Scarecrow' to be another barely disguised self-portrait of Syd Barrett. This may very well be so, but equally, the reality might be more innocent. Could this be, rather, a simple portrayal wholly in keeping with the frequent rurality of Pink Floyd's music? Like 'The Gnome', perhaps 'Scarecrow' merely represents the uncomplicated storytelling instincts of a writer whose work could often be more lucid than his fabled drug consumption ought to have allowed. You choose.

## **'Bike'** 3.22 (Barrett)

In *Piper*'s final track, similar worthies have discerned solid evidence of Syd Barrett's impending breakdown. The idea seems to have been provoked by the contrast between a cheery singalong that speaks to childhood, toys, the joy of innocent creativity and, at its most profound, nascent sexuality; and a mildly disordered finale that might conveniently symbolise the chaos raging inside Syd's head. For this author, 'Bike' is far less ominous. In a charming exposition of childhood roleplay, the singer evokes a boy, perhaps eight or nine years of age, and his attempts to woo a potential lady-love of the same age: a schoolfriend, or the girl next door. From the very beginning, he's setting out his store:

I've got a bike, you can ride it if you like
It's got a basket, a bell that rings and
Things to make it look good
I'd give it to you if I could, but I borrowed it
You're the kind of girl that fits in with my world
I'll give you anything, everything if you want things.

Keen to catch his quarry's eye, the youthful would-be Casanova moves on from proudly displaying his cherished bicycle to his tatty red and black cloak, a mouse called Gerald and a clan of gingerbread men. By the last verse, the young lady, finally bewitched by the promise of a 'room full of musical tunes', follows her new beau next door to 'make it work'. The song ends with an assemblage of SFX that might have been recorded in an Edwardian toyshop; it's easy to see two kiddies gleefully up to their young necks in clockwork trains, toy-town xylophones and alphabetical building bricks. Finally, a team of rubber ducks paddles in, quacking excitedly as they loop electronically into the song's fade.

'Bike' is a sheer delight and totally guileless: there's not a single dope reference, nor can one be inferred by any but the most earnestly forensic interpreter of English psychedelia. It combines a catchy tune with a superb lyrical structure; where a lesser writer might rely on poetic licence or overworked metaphorical flourish, Syd effortlessly puts to song the nonchalance of natural conversation. Floyd's regular instrumentation is augmented with musique concrète, celeste, bells, whistles, mechanical toys and those ducks. 'Bike' is the perfect finale to a wonderful debut, an album to be doubly treasured: for in no other context will Syd Barrett's brief, incandescent genius be captured so beautifully.

## Singles #3 and #4

### **'Apples And Oranges'** 3.09 (Barrett) b/w **'Paint Box'** 3.49 (Wright)

Recorded at: Abbey Road Studios, London, 26-27 October 1967
Produced by: Norman Smith
Released: 17 November 1967
Highest UK chart position: did not chart

'Apples And Oranges' had big boots to fill. The underground kudos garnered by 'Arnold Layne' had converted to overground chart success for 'See Emily Play' with little loss of musical integrity; that difficult third single ought to have been a cakewalk. Unfortunately, Floyd were caught between a record company pressing for another hit single (the Christmas market was looming) and their own wish to focus on albums and live performance.

Such dichotomies frequently lead to uncomfortable compromise. 'Apples And Oranges' is lyrically terrific, possibly basing the narrator's object of fancy on another girlfriend, Lindsay Corner. 'Lorry driver man' Syd spots a cool, sassy lass out shopping, catches her eye and immediately begins to feel 'very pink'; a hint of the title's euphemistic not-quite-opposites, perhaps. But the interesting premise hangs on a tortuously cluttered arrangement that lacks the sublime slide-guitar-with-Zippo tricks of its predecessor. Although the record-buying public acted with their feet – the single tanked everywhere – Roger liked it, with reservations: 'A very good song, in spite of mistakes', the bassist said. ''Apples And Oranges' was destroyed by the production.'

Better news was on the flipside. Rick Wright's maiden songwriting effort lands a fish similarly out of water, and it's not half bad. More musically coherent than its A-side, 'Paint Box' slides easily into the psychedelic assumptions of the era, telling in a first-person narrative of a confused individual having difficulties with life's simple rituals. The singer sets himself apart from the crowd, solipsistically bemused by fools playing their games, striving to impress and failing miserably. But Rick gives the impression not of studied exceptionalism but of plain bewilderment; this hick from the sticks, philosophically lost among the West End trendies, even scores a date, only to dazedly squander it all by being late and not even knowing why.

A few months later, Billy Nicholls would release his criminally neglected album *Would You Believe*: as near a perfect crystallisation of English sonic psychedelia as realised by anyone other than Pink Floyd or The Beatles themselves. As 1967 closed, Billy's creative receptors must have been zeroing in on the shimmering 'Paint Box.'

### **'It Would Be So Nice'** 3.47 (Wright) b/w **'Julia Dream'** 2.35 (Waters)

Recorded at: Abbey Road Studios, London, 13 February-3 April 1968
Produced by: Norman Smith

Released: 13 April 1968
Highest UK chart position: did not chart

Blame Syd Barrett with a little help from John Lennon. Both were superlative lyricists, able to conjure Day-Glo worlds in which the everyday becomes fantastical, where polite suburban fancies – gnomes and bikes, newspapers and taxis, scarecrows and cornflakes – are celebrated, mixed, matched, juxtaposed and hooked into memorable tunes, evoking surreally English parallel worlds. By the end of 1967, however, the year-long ingestion of psychedelic whimsy was the cause of some queasiness, despite the best efforts of lesser lights such as Spencer Davis, Donovan, Nirvana and Kaleidoscope (the two latter English bands both – no relation to their US namesakes). Most pretenders not only lacked the gift for a smart couplet, but the all-important souring of ergot that made Lennon's and Barrett's most flowery writing so appetising.

Of course, vanishingly fewer were The Beatles or Pink Floyd. But with the latter's potential for hits now working to rule in solidarity with the retrenched guitarist, Floyd found themselves with a massive, Syd-shaped hole. Step forward Rick Wright, tasked with taking up the psychedelic slack and re-establishing Syd's regal lineage of commercial, crisply trippy pop singles following the failure of 'Apples And Oranges'. If the organist's vision of lysergic Albion falls some way short of Barrett's innocent and clever wordplay, however, perhaps it's apt that Floyd should be manufacturing this analgesic at the same time as the astounding mindscapes of *A Saucerful Of Secrets*.

Musical and lyrical uncertainty reigns, with too many degraded Beatle-isms for comfort. The arrangement begins with an archetypally psychedelic 'It Would Be So Nice' refrain, before the song is drowned in jaunty verses that anticipate, by almost eighteen months, Paul McCartney's vaudevillian trifle 'Maxwell's Silver Hammer'. Judged on lyrics alone, avowed Stockhausen fan Wright sounds as if he'd sooner be anywhere but here: 'Have you ever read the Daily Standard?/reading all about the plane that's landed/upside down?' he chirrups, dismembering Lennon's lyrical conceits from 'A Day In The Life'. (Unsurprisingly, the BBC objected to the original *Evening Standard* line, obliging Floyd to return studio-wards and spend £750 on a re-record). David Gilmour later adds a little wah-wah guitar figure reminiscent of those ghastly bits of business used in old comedy film soundtracks to denote wistful, pie-in-the-face resignation. 'What a waste of time', Rick sings at 2.07. For once, Pink Floyd fans and hit-parade compilers agree.

More tolerable – and certainly more Floydian – the B-side was meant to be titled after the conveniently alliterative 'Doreen'. Likely a close relative of Emily, Julia is another hippie chick to be caught dreaming in Floyd's sylvan glades, her gossamer-thin, *faux*-profound storyline concerning 'velvet brides' and 'scaly armadillos', carried by a prettily bucolic arrangement that Floyd will further explore on the *More* soundtrack the following year.

# A Saucerful Of Secrets (1968)

Personnel:
Roger Waters: bass guitar, vocals
David Gilmour: lead guitar, vocals
Rick Wright: keyboards, vibraphone, vocals
Nick Mason: drums, percussion
Syd Barrett: guitar, vocals ('Remember A Day', 'Set The Controls For The Heart Of The Sun', 'Corporal Clegg', 'Jugband Blues')
Norman Smith: drums ('Remember A Day')
Stanley Myers Orchestra: horns ('Corporal Clegg')
Salvation Army Brass Band: horns ('Jugband Blues')
Produced at: Abbey Road Studios, London, by Norman Smith
Engineers: Ken Scott, Martin Benger, Pete Bown, Michael Weighell
Released: 29 June 1968 (UK); 27 July 1968 (US)
Highest chart position: UK: 9, US: 158

The most infamous no-show in rock history occurred on 26 January 1968, when Pink Floyd 'didn't bother' picking up Syd Barrett for a gig at Southampton University. A month earlier, fearing for Syd's mental stability, Floyd had recruited to the lead guitar/vocals chair Syd's old Cambridge friend, David Gilmour. The band wanted to complement their errant frontman, not replace him. (A precedent was cited: The Beach Boys were similarly forced to sideline Brian Wilson, as the BBs' own conflicted genius grappled with drugs and creative angst). For onstage Syd was now a liability, his impetuosity forcing the cancellation of numerous gigs at home and potetial dope-fuelled embarrassments on Floyd's first US tour that autumn. On 14 November, Pink Floyd joined a UK package tour alongside The Jimi Hendrix Experience, The Move, Eire Apparent, Amen Corner and The Nice, whose talented guitarist Davy O'List was pleased to dep one night at short notice for an absent, acid-tinctured Syd.

However, Barrett's songwriting was still seen as a valuable asset. He also continued to enjoy the advocacy of managers Jenner and King. So for a handful of shows between 12 and 20 January 1968, Floyd became a five-piece, David's flair for mimicry enabling passable impressions of Syd's voice and guitar while his subject wandered around the stage, occasionally finding the impetus to play along. Following the Southampton debacle, Syd's now inevitable departure was formalised on 6 April 1968.

The previous August, days after the release of *The Piper At The Gates Of Dawn*, Floyd began work at Abbey Road on their second album, Norman Smith again at the desk. While *Ummagumma*, *Atom Heart Mother* and *The Final Cut* are targets of more derision, *A Saucerful Of Secrets* is Pink Floyd's most persistently underrated album. The roots of the reputational damage are twofold: as the first Floyd LP release following Barrett's departure, *Saucerful* would always struggle for acceptance among purists who saw a Sydless Floyd as a vacant shell that could never survive, artistically or commercially, the loss of their brilliant but wayward figurehead. Among such sceptics were – strangely, given his record with Syd – Norman Smith. Ever the professional, Norman would soldier on with the new album despite highly ambitious music in which he scarcely believed. Other naysayers resided at Blackhill Enterprises: in April 1968, displaying the genius of Decca Records when EMI's chief UK competitor declined The Beatles, Jenner and King bet the farm on Barrett as a solo, leaving Floyd in the steady managerial hands of the Bryan Morrison Agency's Steve O'Rourke. The second reason derives from the surviving Floyds themselves; despite a softening of rhetoric in recent years, the Floyd family have been, at best, ambivalent towards an album that did even more than *Piper* to stoke the band's early reputation as space rockers.

Rightly or wrongly, Floyd show that they've learned much since 'Interstellar Overdrive'. Earlier sonic adventures sometimes sounded like Wayne and Waynetta Slob's bedsprings after a rowdy Friday night in the pub; now the requisite Floydian mid-track escape feels less a happily slapdash accident, more a product of the band's diligent application. It's all still properly psychedelic; like before, lengthily eccentric instrumental passages nudge up against conventional song structures and whimsical paeans to the hippie dream. But *Piper* succeeded equally whether a song was three minutes of fairytale or three times that of science fiction. With their chief purveyor of bite-sized psychedelia gone and Roger's songwriting craft still at early doors, Floyd are now more at home with massive tone poems exploring the void than with post-flower power bagatelles. Waters' first implicit exhumation of his late father's service to King and Country is present and correct, if musically forgettable. And even after his ignominious dismissal, Syd Barrett maintains a phantom presence, the album culminating in perhaps the eeriest adieu in all of rock.

*Saucerful*'s is only the second sleeve EMI allowed an outside firm to design (the first, naturally, had been *Sergeant Pepper*). Floyd expressly asked not to be pictured but were vetoed; the compromise was a tiny shot of the quartet on the front and a monochrome montage, mainly of Mason's moustache, on the reverse. It was also Hipgnosis' first Floyd cover: a colourful potpourri of what Aubrey Powell called 'cosmic swirls': Marvel's Doctor Strange and the Living Tribunal, flying saucers, orbiting moons and astrological symbols, all of which, according to Storm Thorgerson, was meant to evoke 'three altered states of consciousness'. All good, but nothing to do with space rock, apparently.

## **'Let There Be More Light'** 5.39 (Waters)

Following a sprightly bass intro accompanied by tinkling ride cymbal, swirling Hammond organ and pattering percussion, the slowed-down main theme of 'Let There Be More Light' sounds like incidental music denoting the mystic East in an episode of *The Saint*. In fact, the song is soaked in science fiction, a favourite literary genre of Roger's, quoting from and alluding to the work of Arthur C. Clarke, A. E. van Vogt and Edgar Rice Burroughs. Cameos come both fanciful (Vogt's shapeshifting Rull and Lennon's Lucy In The Sky) and down-to-earth (Hereward the Wake and the father of Pip Carter, a Cambridge 'face' and, according to Nick, 'one of the world's most spectacularly inept roadies').

With incoming aliens apparently bearers of enlightenment (like Klaatu in *The Day The Earth Stood Still*, another reference), the song is a jolly but confused promenade around the inside of Roger's head. Astoundingly he predicts that humans will be closely encountering the third kind at nowhere other than Mildenhall, at which point the bathos falls to earth like ten tonnes of spam rations from the International Space Station. Why the exotic visitors have chosen the homely Suffolk town to make landfall is uncertain, although it's unlikely the nearby USAF base would be welcoming any Martian commies without at least a tank division in attendance.

While 'Let There Be More Light' gives little hint of the incoming excellence of Waters' songwriting, musically it's an immediate joy, sung by Roger and Rick, with a great guitar solo from David at the close and plenty of distance between the new-model Floyd and their Barrett-led predecessor. 'Let There Be More Light' was released as Floyd's fourth US single, coupled with 'Remember A Day' failing to chart.

## **'Remember A Day'** 4.33 (Wright)

Rick wrote this pretty childhood reminiscence while the band were recording *Piper*. There's talk that it was to be called 'Sunshine' and that it was an early run-through for 'Matilda Mother'. More certain is that Syd played guitar and that the drum parts were by Norman Smith. In his memoir, Mason averred that the song 'had a different drum feel to our usual pounding style', although it's hard to discern why Nick – a better percussionist than many credit – felt it beyond him. The opening, a descending note from Syd's slide guitar, sounds like Roger's extra-terrestrials on the intergalactic bus to Mildenhall, but instead we're quickly lazing with Rick in Arcadia, trying to 'catch the sun' and 'blow the years away'. Wright's lyrical tendency was to nostalgia, in stark contrast to the aural blitzkriegs he delivered to the band's more extreme instrumentals and his coming solo material. This said, 'Remember A Day' features light-touch piano tinkling around Roger's nimble bass, before Norman's drum pattern arrives enlivened by Syd's guitar. The middle eight sits more obviously with Floyd's current MO, however, as Barrett breaks out his Zippo to a gathering rhythmic storm and a variety of electronic pops and cymbal crashes.

## **'Set The Controls For The Heart Of The Sun'** 5.27 (Waters)

One of Pink Floyd's best-loved set pieces, an object lesson in how skilfully the group could create a huge amount out of very little, 'Set The Controls For The Heart Of The Sun' marks an important moment in the group's development. Among Roger Waters' earliest compositions, 'Set The Controls' is thought to be the first by the bassist to occupy what had been, until August 1967, decidedly

Syd Barrett territory. It's also the only Floyd song to feature the five-man line-up; David Gilmour's guitar parts were added in early 1968.

Lyrically the song appears to be light years from Waters' forthcoming dark dissertations on the human condition. Roger lifted some of the words from Chinese T'ang Dynasty poetry and the title from Michael Moorcock's novella, *The Fireclown*. From Eastern esoterica to Western parallel-world science fantasy, the song encompasses just about every 1967 hippie reference point. Yet explaining the storyline in an unattributed interview, Roger set down a marker for his subsequent denials that Floyd's music had anything to do with outer space:

> An unknown person who, while piloting a mighty flying saucer, is overcome with solar suicidal tendencies and sets the controls for the heart of the sun.

In other words, the song questions the cosmonaut's interior mental state, not the coordinates and physical circumstances of his demise. As his faculties fade, he's as likely to be driving an Austin Cambridge up the A10 as pointing an Apollo capsule at the stars. For not the only time on a surpassing album, this saga of one man's descent into stellar madness signposts where Waters' songwriting instincts would soon be taking him: setting the controls for the dark side of the Moon and beyond, if you will.

But if Roger's intentions for 'Set The Controls' are more prosaic than typically star-struck stoner fans might allow, there's no denying the cosmic flavour of this sonic poetry. With the literary influences washed into a hypnotic drift through the spheres, driven with gathering percussive insistence by Nick's tympani mallets on his regular kit, embellished by Rick's bubbling vibraphone and the organist's ethereal keyboard effects, the result is memorably mind-bending, tailor-made for extended live performance. Written by an avowed non-space rocker and still more definite non-doper, it's the Indian-flavoured, trance-inducing Floyd space epic that launched a thousand joints rolled on a thousand *Saucerful* sleeves.

'Set The Controls' has been covered by no fewer than 19 artists. Witness to its staying power is the fact that the song was still part of Roger's live set decades after the bassist had quit the band.

## **'Corporal Clegg'** 4.12 (Waters)

If only in the titling, there were vague military overtones to 'Pow R. Toc H.'. Now 'Corporal Clegg' develops a theme that will run through Roger's career and find its apogee in *The Final Cut* fifteen years later. But while in 1968 the world and Fat Freddie's cat have Vietnam in their sights, Waters denounces those who would prosecute an earlier war and leave behind the battle-scarred infantry once hostilities have ceased.

Roger lost his father during the Anzio landings in 1944. The death at 31 of Lt. Eric Fletcher Waters, a former pacifist and ardent anti-fascist, would haunt Roger's art for decades. For Waters would continue to berate a system he believed placed no value on its human capital once the guns were silenced; for the deaths of millions, he held the Allied military machine as culpable as the enemy.

'Corporal Clegg' is the first explicit example of this contempt, wherein Captain Clegg (a character from a 1962 horror movie, *Night Creatures*) is demoted and portrayed as a shell-shocked fantasist. While the damaged subaltern dreams of receiving a medal from the Queen, his only mementos from serving his country are his wooden leg and an alcoholic wife. Floyd begin the satire with a heavy, ponderous twin-guitar attack from Syd and David, after which the pair toggle lead vocal duties with Nick. Sadly for not the last time on the album, a kazoo leads a raucous oompah break, similar to Dylan's chaotic 'Rainy Day Women'. The song retreats on a mess of crowd noises, exploding shells, an air-raid siren and the redoubtable Norman Smith, his own sardonic contribution low in the mix: 'Get yer 'air cut!' It's all rather unappealing, a bloodied thumb on *Saucerful*'s stylish hand. But the real importance of 'Corporal Clegg' lies in the sentiments that would inform their writer's subsequent career.

**'A Saucerful Of Secrets'** 12.00 (Waters/Wright/Mason/Gilmour)

If with the elegant autocade of 'Set The Controls For The Heart Of The Sun' Floyd evoked a Steady State model of the universe, 'A Saucerful Of Secrets' is the band's own Big Bang, a devastating audial exposition of the ultimate violence of the cosmos. It's the musical equivalent of extreme spectrum shift, the galaxies hurling apart like Ronnie O'Sullivan developing reds in an exhibition match. An exemplar of Floydian dynamics, 'Saucerful' showcases the band's gift for shifting mood and pace at precisely the right moments and of understanding the elevating effect of transitioning from passages of molten sonic hell through to a finale of ambrosiac heaven.

Unable to read music, the former architecture students Roger and Nick famously charted 'Saucerful' as a series of diagrams. 'It wasn't music for beauty's sake, or for emotion's sake', David Gilmour told *MOJO* in 2001. 'It never had a story line'. But the quasi-symphonic structure, not to mention the breathtaking uplift of the final few minutes, might contradict the guitarist's reservations; perhaps he was trying too hard for objective detachment. Happily, by 2006, David – 'Saucerful' is his only credit on his first album with the group – was waxing more enthusiastic: 'Trying to organise noise into an emotive, musical experience is something I see as a very bold, good thing to attempt. I think 'A Saucerful Of Secrets' is fantastic.'

The four-part instrumental fades in with 'Something Else', featuring rumbling percussion and an organ-led mess of SFX. Comforting familiarity is already long gone; we are beyond the fields we know, headed for the outer reaches of cold alienation. But by the end of the first movement at 3.57, we're stuck in a galactic traffic jam, Rick's keys disproving the maxim that in space, no one can hear a billion airhorns. Abruptly the logjam clears for 'Syncopated Pandemonium', as Nick whirls around his kit and someone twiddles a shortwave radio dial, desperate for communication. Another lull at 7.04, then 'Storm Signal' brings Wright's gothic organ and, at the last, the Floydian solemnity that John Peel famously likened to 'a religious experience'. With the band apparently trying, and largely succeeding, to bottle entropy itself, one would fear for delicate psyches had this sci-fi odyssey not concluded with the relieving grandeur of 'Celestial Voices': an impossibly beautiful sequence of organ chords and Mellotron strings attached to an episcopal choir. It's divine deliverance from the galactic sensory overload, topping off nothing other than a Pink Floyd masterpiece.

## **'See-Saw'** 4.37 (Wright)

Following the most extreme twelve minutes of controlled tumult Pink Floyd ever recorded comes *Saucerful*'s slightest track. 'See-Saw' finds Rick Wright still channelling the gentle psychedelia which the band's better music of the period suggested he'd sooner leave far behind. But it's not all bad: often too conveniently compared with The Beach Boys, 'See-Saw' feels closer in spirit to the mid-'60s sunshine pop manufactured in the US by producer Gary Usher with groups such as Sagittarius and The Millennium. Soaked in Mellotron strings and wordless backing vocals, beneath unabashedly sentimental lyrics that again gaze winsomely back on a simpler, bucolic adolescence, 'See-Saw' offers a shimmering comedown after the sonic Armageddon-to-Paradise of 'Saucerful'. Apparently, Rick's original title was 'The Most Boring Song I've Ever Heard, Bar Two'. So what were the other two?

## **'Jugband Blues'** 3.00 (Barrett)

Anyone else would have concluded *A Saucerful Of Secrets* with the majesty of its title track. But Pink Floyd weren't anyone else. For while at the time 'Saucerful' was perfectly suited to an anthemic, lighters-in-the-air onstage climax, there could be no more poignant a closure to Floyd's first post-Barrett album than with Syd's last recorded Pink Floyd song.

The deeply unsettling 'Jugband Blues' is notable for being neither blues nor jugband – nor anything else, come to that. Sessioneers work to a similar brief as the orchestra on The Beatles' 'A Day In The Life': like Paul McCartney before him, Syd apparently wanted his hired hands to improvise, a concept entirely alien to the good dot-reading squaddies of the Sally Army. In some accounts, the musicians' puzzlement only subsided after Smith wrote out charts for the aural disarray that Syd was seeking, much as George Martin had done for the Fabs. As the horns stumble in at 1.05, following Syd's sardonic valedictions to his bandmates over acoustic guitar, dissonant recorder, castanets and that kazoo, the effect is of a tambourine-led street procession trying hard for gaiety but desultorily failing. Everything decays to a discordant chaos, brought to an abrupt halt by the briefest burst of fiercely scrubbed guitar. Then a false ending precedes Syd's return with his acoustic and a quietly ominous payoff:

And the sea isn't green/And I love the Queen
And what exactly is a dream/And what exactly is a joke.

Instead of the quasi-spiritual euphoria conjured by the finale of 'Saucerful', the listener awakening from a dream in the transept of a vast cathedral, the aftertaste of 'Jugband Blues' is ghostly and disturbing, as if the dreamer has come to outside in the graveyard, the ambience minor-key, autumnal and desolately lonely. By now, Syd was away with the fairies; as a rock'n'roll swansong, nothing else comes close.

## Associated tracks

### 'Vegetable Man' 2.24 (Barrett)

According to Nick, Syd took just a few minutes to knock out this deeply strange song. Given 'Vegetable Man' is basically the sound of a psyche falling apart, this is understandable. Syd's gush of near-automatism – a stream-of-consciousness thumbnail of himself as everyone's favourite King's Road dandy who's hating every minute of it – is testament to his ability to craft a lightning lyric. But mapped into a raggedly insistent and tuneless arrangement, this is acutely uneasy listening. Recorded four days after the release of *Piper*, 'Vegetable Man' was tabled for inclusion on the second album and as a single for release that September. Instead, Roger Waters ensured neither would happen; possibly a wise decision, since it's hard to imagine this messy motorcade of self-loathing doing anything to arrest the post-'Emily' dip in Floyd's singles fortunes. Long bootlegged, 'Vegetable Man' was remixed in 2010 and released legitimately on *The Early Years Volume 1: 1965–1967: Cambridge St/ation*.

### 'Scream Thy Last Scream' 4.31 (Barrett)

Recorded the day before 'Vegetable Man', 'Scream Thy Last Scream' is almost as difficult a proposition, but saved by an exhilaratingly violent instrumental section. Originally titled after its first line, 'Scream Thy Last Scream Old Woman With A Casket', the piece is superficially further evidence of the songwriter's mental collapse, apparently absurdist words sung by Nick Mason as a leering fairground barker against pitchbent, Pinky-&-Perky-on-helium backing vocals. After a wobbly beginning, the music pounds into a maddening middle eight of rising speed and intensity, driven hard by Nick's powerful drumming and wah-wah organ effects from Rick. Though dismissed by Roger as 'too dark', it's a great track, and probably no more nonsensical than anything then being dreamed up by fellow lysergic questers John Lennon and Captain Beefheart. Prior to Waters' veto, EMI had blocked a single release with, interestingly, 'Set The Controls For The Heart Of The Sun' as the putative A-side. 'Scream Thy Last Scream' was remixed for authorised inclusion on *The Early Years Volume 1: 1965–1967: Cambridge St/ation*.

## The final early single

**'Point Me At The Sky'** 3.40 (Waters/Gilmour) b/w **'Careful With That Axe, Eugene'** 5.46 (Waters/Wright/Mason/Gilmour)

Released: 7 December 1968

A guilty pleasure for this aircraft-fixated author, 'Point Me At The Sky' remains one of Floyd's most oft-dismissed songs, its failure to chart dissuading band, management and EMI from releasing another 45 to the UK market for eleven years. 'It was a constructed attempt and it didn't happen', offered Roger Waters. The bassist later conceded that, when it came to hit singles, 'we were just no bloody good at it.'

'Point Me At The Sky' concerns the efforts of an inventor and his co-pilot to escape the rat race in a new 'cosmic glider'. In this semi-psychedelic paean to the pleasures of flight, metaphorical or otherwise, Waters gives more early notice of the lyricist's concerns over the insanity of the 'games we've been playing for thousands of years'. With superficial optimism, David and Roger toggle vocal duties between placid verses and the more abrasive choruses before keys, FX and wah-wah/slide guitar erupt beneath the flying machine's apparent launch and final demise, the aviators crashing gaily into an unknown oblivion. A demonstration of the malleability of the Floydian middle eight can be found on a terrific version of 'Point Me At The Sky' recorded at the BBC just before the single's release, when the band threaten, entirely plausibly, to float off into 'A Saucerful Of Secrets.'

By far this 45's more important side is its 'B'. 'Careful With That Axe, Eugene' is an instrumental lumbered with so many different titles that the eponymous lumberjack's potentially homicidal instincts must be fuelled by a schizophrenic identity crisis. The piece began life in spring 1968 as 'Keep Smiling People' (partially recorded for Floyd's score for Peter Sykes' movie, *The Committee*); would morph a year later into 'Beset By Creatures Of The Deep' as part of Floyd's suite *The Man/The Journey*; did further soundtrack duties for Michelangelo Antonioni's 1970 film *Zabriskie Point* as 'Come In Number 51, Your Time Is Up'; and was variously 'Murderistic Women' and 'Murderotic Women' before Eugene was finally spotted and declared keeper of the titular chopper. The axeman is also namechecked in the intro to the A-side, where Henry McClean rhymingly advises Eugene that he's completed his 'beautiful flying machine'. Furthermore, he has nothing to do with The Nice's 'The Cry Of Eugene', an equally and mysteriously Eugenic album track that was doing the rounds at about the same time.

Of this one-chord wonder, David Gilmour was mildly dismissive: 'We were just creating textures and moods over the top', said the guitarist, declaring it 'unsubtle'. Nevertheless, 'Careful With That Axe, Eugene' remains an object lesson in musical dynamics and a stirring template for the soundscaping that now typifies Pink Floyd's direction of travel. The piece begins languidly, Roger's menacing bass notes embellished by Rick's organ and vibraphone, Nick's stickwork building the intensity, all underscored by David's spooky wordless vocal. At 1.33, Roger hisses the title and issues a sequence of primal screams so cathartic John Lennon's cold turkey must have been begging for Christmas. Following a frantic, guitar-driven crescendo, everything dies back and an uncertain peace is restored. As good as this studio original is, 'Eugene' would flourish with astounding power on stage, extended to eleven or more minutes as a regular and fearsomely exciting portion of Floyd's live show until 1973.

## Music from the Film 'More' (1969)

Personnel:
Roger Waters: bass guitar, vocals
David Gilmour: lead guitar, vocals
Rick Wright: keyboards, vibraphone, Mellotron, vocals
Nick Mason: drums, percussion
Produced at: Pye Studios, London, by Pink Floyd
Executive producer: Norman Smith
Engineer: Brian Humphreys
Released: 13 June 1969 (UK); 9 August 1969 (US)
Highest chart position: UK: 9, USA: 153 (1973 re-release)

By the beginning of 1969, Pink Floyd were the new darlings of the European avant-garde. A soundtrack commission for one of the fashionably arty auteurs was inevitable. The band briefly even pondered writing movie scores full-time.

In December 1967, Floyd put music to Mike Leonard's experimental light shows for BBC-TV's *Tomorrow's World*, a year later scoring *The Committee*. Meanwhile, John Peel, then still a committed fan, was among the pundits lamenting Floyd's absence from the music credits for *2001*. Even if Peel's view was echoed at the time by Roger Waters, Floyd's alleged wish not to be tagged as space rockers meant this was probably no help at all.

In March 1969, Floyd were commissioned by the Swiss director Barbet Schroeder to score his forthcoming debut movie, *More*. Because the instruction was private, EMI denied Floyd use of its facilities, obliging a reroute to Pye Studios at Marble Arch. Timing their contributions with a stop-watch to a rough cut brought to London by Schroeder, the band took just a fortnight to write and record the album, Floyd's first as an entirely Syd-free zone – Gilmour handled all lead vocals – and with Norman Smith pushed sideways to executive producer. So impressed was Schroeder with Floyd's speed and work ethic that he would return three years later with another commission.

Although officially billed as Floyd's third studio album, *More* feels transitionary, an uncertain waystation between 'proper' titles *A Saucerful Of Secrets* and the forthcoming *Ummagumma*. Even the band considered the part-improvised *More* a 'stop-gap'. The set's air of patchy fragmentation was common to film scores, but here the variances in flavour between tracks are further stretched due to Schroeder's insistence on diegetic 'source' music, where songs are, in effect, 'heard' by the film's characters – a radio being switched on, ambient bar or party music and so forth – rather than as a semi-detached overlay ornamenting the narrative and strengthening emotional atmosphere. Schroeder's dull, largely English-language film follows the (mis)fortunes in 1960s Ibiza of an irritating pair of hippie junkies, Stefan and Estelle, and an ex-Nazi; a full-on set of Floydian soundscapes might have lifted what proved to be a depressing viewing experience. However, there's decent music here. Some we've heard before, and will again; Floyd's unwillingness to discard unused stuff would pay dividends later.

For *More*'s sleeve, Hipgnosis solarised a still of the film's stoner duo tilting quixotically at a Balearic windmill. For the sleeve typography, although the band had officially adjusted their branding at around the same time as UFO friends/rivals (The) Soft Machine, (The) Floyd's definite article was proving difficult to shift. The album performed well in France, selling 300,000 copies and reaching number two on that country's album charts. Given the music's bitty, not-quite-Floyd nature, and the average Brit's inbuilt suspicion of European arthouse films, *More*'s performance in the UK was respectable, charting at number nine.

### **'Cirrus Minor'** 5.18 (Waters)

*More*'s most memorable tune by far. 'Cirrus Minor' could be Pink Floyd's elevator pitch, compressing into its five minutes the pastoral, the ethereal and the spookily cosmic. From the opening birdsong, acoustic guitar lingers with eerie organ as David sings Roger's words about lazing in a churchyard 'on a trip to Cirrus Minor'. As befits the movie the atmosphere is avowedly druggy, especially since Roger apparently confuses a cloud formation for a planet. Waters' lyrics show that, like any good method actor, he needs only minimal personal experience to inhabit a psychedelic theme. For the churchy organ coda, Rick switches from Farfisa to Hammond to echo the 'Celestial Voices' final movement of 'A Saucerful Of Secrets.'

### **'The Nile Song'** 3.27 (Waters)

An unsuccessful single in France, New Zealand and Japan (backed with 'Ibiza Bar'), 'The Nile Song' sees Floyd in punk-metal mode. In contrast to the preceding calm, the heavily big-muffed guitar and cluttered bass and drums hint at what might have happened had an aggressively pilled-up 1966 Floyd played at UFO without the passive lysergic explorations of Syd Barrett. Gilmour barks the words as if willing a lifetime of throat surgery, while the lyrics evoke the fall of Stefan into the arms of Estelle's heroin addiction and, eventually, his suicide. 'The Nile Song' is far from Floyd's strong suit; lumpen and untidy, it's overdriven proof that The MC5 were much better at this sort of thing.

### **'Crying Song'** 3.34 (Waters)

Lurching from one extreme to the other, 'Crying Song' starts promisingly with Rick's glistening vibraphone, but quickly descends to filler. David's lead vocal is so lazy it's still in bed, although this sits well with a scene in the movie that deals with, well, dealing, as our blissed-out protagonists share ill-tempered conversation washed down with a nice pipe of H. Within the context of the film, it's tolerable, but as a standalone, 'Crying Song' provokes only crying.

### **'Up The Khyber'** 2.13 (Mason/Wright)

The first and only Floyd piece to credit Wright and Mason as sole joint composers, 'Up The Khyber' is shown in by Nick's enthused drumming, which is quickly joined by jaggedly percussive piano; clearly Rick's in the same Cecil Taylor mood that will reach its acme in his devastating 'Sysyphus' on *Ummagumma*. Soon he's on Farfisa duetting with himself, as the whole track morphs into what could easily be the middle instrumental section of an extended Floyd freakout. In the movie, 'Up The Khyber' – the reference is the then still open hippie pot trail to India rather than the slapstick comedy – emanates from a cassette player straight after 'Crying Song', by which time the irritating smackheads onscreen are reducing the cinema audience to tears.

### **'Green Is The Colour'** 2.59 (Waters)

With its acoustic guitar, plaintive vocal and naïve penny-whistle (courtesy of Nick's wife, Lindy), this immensely pretty, carefree tune marks a point in the film where Stefan and Estelle are yet to plummet into their chasm of narcotic despond. Onstage Floyd would lengthen and intensify 'Green Is The Colour', pressing the song into service as 'The Beginning' from *The Man/The Journey*, usually as an intro to 'Careful With That Axe, Eugene' and its riotous decibel fest.

### **'Cymbaline'** 4.50 (Waters)

Floyd's live sets were also graced by 'Cymbaline', often extended to eleven or more minutes. The song with the almost-Shakespearean name would be blended into *The Man/The Journey*, enduring as a standalone for some time after Floyd had shelved the conceptual suite. It begins with an arpeggiated guitar chord and Rick's piano against Nick's quiet timekeeping on snare and conga, followed by one of David's best vocals on the album and some beautiful Farfisa meandering from Wright. 'It's groovy!' trills Estelle as she turns up the radio on an extended 'Cymbaline' and the pair settle down for a quiet toke. Yet despite observing 'It's high time, Cymbaline', Roger's lyrics are full of foreboding, equating more to a bad trip ('A butterfly with broken wings/ is falling by your side/The ravens all are closing in/There's nowhere you can hide') than a pot-fed afternoon of Parisian euphoria. This would accord with the name change 'Cymbaline' was given for *The Man/The Journey*: 'Nightmare'.

### **'Party Sequence'** 1.07 (Waters/Wright/Gilmour/Mason)

Nick (congas) and Lindy (penny-whistle) do the rhythmic honours for a slight interlude at a typically 1960s/Ibiza hippie party. Roger, David and Rick are likely helping out with various things to hit, hence the group credit.

### **'Main Theme'** 5.28 (Waters/Wright/Gilmour/Mason)

Accompanying *More*'s opening credits, this instrumental fades in with shimmering cymbals and gong before Rick arrives with a disjointed – and perfectly Floydian – exploration on his Farfisa. Nick slips into a simple bossanova-like rhythm of tom-tom and snare rimshots, and the band set the scene on a movie for which both promise and musical score far outweigh what's actually delivered. Almost a decade later, electro maven Jean-Michel Jarre's *Oxygene* will carry a tune suspiciously similar to that of 'Main Theme', which develops and threads its way through the piece alongside spacy slide-guitar effects from Gilmour.

**'Ibiza Bar'** 3.19 (Waters/Wright/Gilmour/Mason)
An almost identical riff suggests a plain reprise of 'The Nile Song', although slightly different arrangements and words tell another story. If anything, Floyd dial down on the headbanging from earlier; there's a greater sense of restraint and of dynamic light and shade, while this time Gilmour probably needn't fear for his vocal cords. This said, the guitarist gets to show off a few tasty Hendrixisms. Though the heavy-metal crunch suits the song's setting in the Balearic bar of the title, obliquely apologetic lyrics bear only the loosest relationship to the business onscreen.

**'More Blues'** 2.13 (Waters/Wright/Gilmour/Mason)
A standard-issue slow blues instrumental that by now Floyd can probably play backwards. Used in the film to accompany Stefan dealing dope from behind that Ibizan bar, 'More Blues' would pop up at later Floyd shows, often as an encore, when the band could relax after a *sturm und drang* set-ending of 'Saucerful' or 'Atom Heart Mother.'

**'Quicksilver'** 7.14 (Waters/Wright/Gilmour/Mason)
Full of Farfisa and swishing cymbal, this is an exquisitely Floydian soundscape, mood music for two scenes in which the undynamic duo get off their tits on acid and smack. The track from *More* that most closely equates to what Floyd were about as they made *A Saucerful Of Secrets* – and therefore among the album's most popular with long-term fans – 'Quicksilver' would partially be reworked by Rick Wright into 'Sysyphus'. A shorter version would also do time as 'Sleep' in *The Man/The Journey*.

**'A Spanish Piece'** 1.05 (Gilmour)
On David Gilmour's maiden solo composition for Floyd, the guitarist gets to show off a fine Flamenco technique, accompanied by his own strummed acoustic and percussive soundbox tapping. Once again briefed by Schroeder to evoke an Ibizan boozer, David goes full-on spaghetti-western bandido, with a muttered approximation of local ambient chatter, although sadly the hilarious lyric – 'Pass the tequila, Manuel/Listen, gringo, laugh at my lisp and I kill you/Ah, this Spanish music, it sets my soul on fire' – does not feature in a movie sorely in need of levity.

**'Dramatic Theme'** 2.15 (Waters/Wright/Gilmour)
Roger's intro revisits and slows his bass pattern from 'Let There Be More Light' to Nick's steady rimshots and ride cymbal and some smeary slide guitar from

David. Although used in the movie to complement Stefan's final, terminal heroin hit, the tune has a strangely 'Peter Gunn' feel: evoking the gathering suspense and anxiety that attends someone being watched or followed, or preceding a bank heist. Fading off to heavy reverb, 'Dramatic Theme' ultimately belies its title, giving the soundtrack a decidedly downbeat and wholly appropriate finale.

# Ummagumma (1969)

Personnel:
Roger Waters: bass guitar, guitar, vocals
David Gilmour: lead guitar, bass, keyboards, percussion, vocals
Rick Wright: keyboards, vibraphone, Mellotron, guitar, vocals
Nick Mason: drums, percussion
Ron Geesin: vocals (on 'Several Species…')
Lindy Mason: flute (on 'The Grand Vizier's Garden Party')
Produced at: Abbey Road Studios, London, by Pink Floyd, Norman Smith
Engineers: Peter Mew, Alan Parsons
Released: 7 November 1969 (UK); 8 November 1969 (US)
Highest chart position: UK: 5, US: 74

Three years into a promisingly stellar career seemed like the right moment to combine a live album with evidence of what each Floyd might get up to if left to his own devices. The result was much better than history has judged, although a lingering feeling remains that *Ummagumma* could have been a lot more.

An early ID for the second Pink Floyd album's title track had given its name to another memorable concert. Held at the Royal Festival Hall on 14 April 1969, *The Massed Gadgets Of Auximenes* was notable for the return of the Azimuth Co-ordinator, the surround-sound kit rebuilt after the prototype's theft two years earlier; and for the conceptual *Massed Gadgets*' two lengthy conjoined parts, *The Man* and *The Journey*, which mixed new music with retitled songs the band had either recorded already or would be soon. Despite the indulgencies of ambient/industrial FX interludes which, in places, outstayed their welcome, *The Man/The Journey* was a mainly excellent 90 or more minutes of cutting-edge rock music. The audial equivalent of a patchwork quilt, the suite's discrete song components were integrated and relatively cohesive. And although after the RFH gig Roger told *Melody Maker* he feared Floyd had been doing little more onstage than to rehearse – '[the audience] were watching a happening' – *Massed Gadgets* remained an impressive statement of Floyd's exploratory intentions, with Syd Barrett still a presence, if by now an incorporeal one.

Floyd thought well enough of the repurposed material to tour *The Man/The Journey* around more than 20 British and European cities through 1969, and *Massed Gadgets* seemed a shoo-in for the upcoming live album. (One performance, on 17 September for VPRO at Amsterdam's Concertgebouw, was widely bootlegged prior to the Dutch radio station's rebroadcast in 1997/8 and an official CD release with 2016's *Early Years* set).

With Floyd now honing their live chops to a razor's edge around the UK/European concert-hall/college/club circuit, there was an appetite among a growing audience for Floyd's obvious crowd-pleasers to be preserved in their natural habitat. For *Ummagumma*'s second disc, Norman Smith encouraged each Floyd to bring his own home-studio demo into Abbey Road to be knocked into shape. At the time, *Ummagumma*'s two live and two studio sides – released on EMI's new 'progressive' imprint, Harvest Records – were all applauded. But while the concert material today still gets the thumbs-up, the studio music is largely dismissed, the opinions of many critics apparently led by the musicians who created it. It's tempting to put more recent reproaches down to the personal structural perfectionism of some bandmembers; indeed, the five solo pieces aren't flawless, and none is likely to have received the Keller stamp of approval. But as experiments in the creative use of sound and dynamics in pursuit of that inexpressibly Floydian commodity, emotive feel, this material is rarely less than bravely exploratory, and is frequently stunning.

For *Ummagumma*'s sleeve, Hipgnosis produced a part-hall of mirrors, part-*mise en abyme* (the 'Droste' effect of a picture which repeats inside itself, theoretically to infinity). The scene is a doorway exiting to an arboretum, the band individually posed as they recede into the distance. A wall mirror shows the same scene, with the personnel subtly reordered; the equivalent mirror on that frame displays a third formation... and so on. Depicted in a final shot, the game of musical chairs completed, is the tiny sleeve image of *A Saucerful Of Secrets*. That this was all quite meaningless almost goes without saying; according to Storm Thorgerson, the imagery was aimed purely at provoking debate. On the back is a neatly arrow-headed inventory of the band's impressive onstage materiel, minded by head roadies Alan Styles and Pete Watts and shot at Biggin Hill aerodrome. In the original LP gatefold were individual mono photos of the band, Roger accompanied by his first wife, Judy Trim. Mysteriously 'Jude' was airbrushed from subsequent CD releases. As for the meaning of the word *Ummagumma*, like 'poontang' or 'rumpy pumpy' it almost certainly relates to sex; on whether provenance lies in Chaucerian Cambridge folklore or with an equally Chaucerian Floyd roadie called Emo, the jury's still out. On its release, *Ummagumma* was favourably received and sold well. In later years, however, the band would dismiss the studio sides as 'pretentious'. Many critics echoed the disdain as suddenly as the disappearance of the first Mrs Waters. Just fancy that.

## Live album

**'Astronomy Dominé'** 8.30 (Barrett)

**'Careful With That Axe, Eugene'** 8.51 (Waters/Wright/Mason/Gilmour)

**'Set The Controls For The Heart Of The Sun'** 9.12 (Waters)

**'A Saucerful Of Secrets'** 12.48 (Waters/Wright/Mason/Gilmour)

Recorded April/May 1969 at Birmingham's Mothers Club – a favourite Floyd gig – and Manchester College of Commerce, *Ummagumma*'s live section is Pink Floyd's own state-of-the-union address. On the band's most popular pieces of the time, each amply extended, Floyd are bright, loose and confident, allowing themselves the space to let go in the middle sections before returning to equilibrium at precisely the right moments. 'Astronomy Dominé' rocks out as violently as the original always promised; 'Careful With That Axe, Eugene' builds inexorably from languid beginnings to the moment Waters' teeth-grinding scream heralds mayhem; driven by Nick's circling drums and Rick's swirling, Indianate organ, 'Set The Controls For The Heart Of The Sun' remains a stately evocation of spatial dynamics; and on a relatively mild 'A Saucerful Of Secrets' (Floyd were known to extend the piece to more than 20 minutes of sustained ferocity) John Peel's religious experience of the studio original – the sanctified solemnity of the 'Celestial Voices' fourth section – is resurrected as a thrillingly bass-fuelled and rousing concert finale.

## Studio album

### **'Sysyphus'** (parts 1, 2, 3 & 4) 13.48 (Wright)

Rick Wright was keenest in the band to explore the quasi-classical possibilities of writing and performing individual tracks for the new album. Although one day he'd be his own contribution's biggest critic, it's easy to understand what had been flapping to escape from beneath the cloying 'It Would Be So Nice'. 'Sysyphus' [sic] begins panoramically with 'Exodus'-like Mellotron and tympani. After 1.09, the Children of Israel give way to Rick channelling first Béla Bartók, then Cecil Taylor, at which point a disembodying solo piano visits ten atonal plagues upon every EMI sound engineer in sight. Wright (who plays every instrument except Norman Smith's occasional percussion) continues this noisily self-destructive path for just under two minutes, backed by the sound of how the menagerie from 'Pow R. Toc H'. might have behaved with their feed spiked with DMT.

But it's the final seven minutes of cerebral meltdown that really nails 'Sysyphus'. Part 4 begins with minor-key notes from Mellotron, organ and vibraphone which, superficially gentle, hint at something a lot nastier lurking behind the mixing desk. After a tantalising pause from 3.04 to 3.14, a massive *grand guignol* organ chord slams down like a lead coffin lid. Thundering tympani announce … well, Armageddon, as it goes, as doom-laden keyboards roll in, punctuated by whirring SFX that seem to multiply exponentially, all generated by electronics and a piano Rick apparently prepared with loose change. With the effects tumbling over and across each other like reproducing cells, another dissonance is faintly detected before part 1's original Mellotron theme finally liberates itself from the enveloping bedlam, an all-powerful lifeform hatching from End-of-All-Things chaos. 'Sysyphus' features one of rock's most awe-inspiring, fear-inducing climaxes, laying to rest Floyd's most criminally underrated soundscape. More than half a century after release, its cumulative sense of aural chaos remains undiluted by any insistence, from Floyd or from fellow travellers, that 'Sysyphus' was no more than an immature experiment. Norman Smith must have loved it.

## **'Grantchester Meadows'** 7.26 (Waters)

Birdsong and a buzzing fly introduce another tranquil hayseed serenade. The mood is hazily pastoral, the accompaniment just Roger's acoustic guitars and the sweet sounds of summer (which by now are becoming a common Floyd trope, emphasising rusticity wherever needed). Everything in the garden is lovely.

Only it's not. For all its peaceful evocation of nature, 'Grantchester Meadows' has a subtly melancholic edge, an acidic tinge typical of its ever-sardonic writer. Melodically beautiful, the song is less about the careless wanderings of its author as he dozes beneath a willow, more the wistful reminiscence of one who is now far from that eponymous pasture. Waters gives the game away in the second verse:

In the lazy water meadow/I lay me down
All around me/Golden sun flakes settle on the ground
Basking in the sunshine of a bygone afternoon
Bringing sounds of yesterday into this city room.

Like several songs written, separately or together, by Pink Floyd, 'Grantchester Meadows' seems to recall a childhood untroubled by the pressures of the adult world, especially one as freighted with the expectancies of others as that of a burgeoningly successful rock musician. Waters' ability to rhythmically structure a lyric is fast coming of age, and he shows that he's learned well at the feet of Master Barrett; the words of few rock songs may be read from the page as satisfyingly as these:

Hear the lark and harken to the barking of the dog fox gone to ground
See the splashing of the kingfisher flashing to the water
And a river of green is sliding unseen beneath the trees
Laughing as it passes through the endless summer making for the sea.

At the song's end, the idyllic mood is literally swatted to a close. Guitar, dog foxes, kingfishers and birdsong retreat, leaving only the fly buzzing around and across the stereo image. Suddenly the green of the rural meadow gives best to the grey of the urban interior. Someone (Storm Thorgerson?) descends a staircase and strides purposely along a corridor and through a door. Then after a couple of missed shots, a decisive *thwack* signals that 'Grantchester Meadows' could not be further away.

## **'Several Species Of Small Furry Animals Gathered Together In A Cave And Grooving With A Pict'** 5.00 (Waters)

'Just a bit of concrete poetry', explained Roger Waters of this bizarre slab of vocal sound effects and Caledonian ranting. If 'Several Species' has precedent in Floyd's canon it is 'Pow R. Toc H.'. Yet while the animal noises from the *Piper* track merely embellished a relatively conventional musical arrangement, here no instrument is in evidence save electronic and tape effects and Roger's ever-pliable voice. 'Those were sounds that I made', he said. 'The voice and the hand slapping were all human-generated.'

After an intro of more Floyd birdsong – albeit more exotic than the usual larks and blackbirds – the several species are shepherded in by a frantic percussive tapping, followed by Waters' vocal callisthenics predating by years the popularity of Bobby McFerrin and, later, the beatboxers. Roger's sampled voice settles into a strangely breathless, repeated rhythm while the electronic effects gather pace, the whole thing sounding as if the creatures of the rainforest are being pursued by some supernatural beast defoliating everything in its path. Rushing tape effects bring in the Chipmunks, apparently speeding out of their gourds. The sounds of the forest die back, and the comical gibbering continues behind a furious Scots voice bellowing madcap poetry in the manner of Robert Burns. While he's clearly the Pict of the title, it's uncertain whether he's played by Roger's new pal Ron Geesin (a mildly eccentric Ayrshire composer, with whom the bassist would soundtrack a documentary film, *The Body*, and would be a key contributor to *Atom Heart Mother*) or Waters himself, in pursuit of a second genuinely solo piece for *Ummagumma*. In its own way it's quite funny, and all the more so with its muttered punchline, in the same heavy Alloway brogue, after Jimi Hendrix: 'And the wind cries Mary.'

## **'The Narrow Way'** (parts 1, 2 & 3) 12.30 (Gilmour)

Today David Gilmour has rum words for his 25 per cent of *Ummagumma*. He insists that it was a pretentious waste of time and, by the way, he was bullshitting. But 'The Narrow Way', if not indispensable, remains a fine period piece, an excellent example of long-form composition, dynamics and texture, bringing into play much of what would be perfected later as the lairy adolescent Floyd metamorphosed to a confident young adult.

'The Narrow Way' fades in with David seemingly conjuring a spinning-top, which intros his treble-tracked acoustic guitars busily investigating a ringing folk blues, peppered with slide effects. As the FX proliferate, the Echorec-treated slide attacks the acoustic patterns, steadily relocating the music from Mississippi Delta to Alpha Centauri, in places reaching astoundingly high pitches. At 3.04, an upward spiral on one of the acoustics just fails to chase away the blues, but this is rectified a few seconds later as a vicious glissando deals the death blow and a murderous riff announces part 2.

Gilmour deploys a similar tactic to effect change to the final section, allowing the brutal theme to flounder under an increasing weight of spacy FX. Part 3 is pure, stately, anthemic Floyd, complete with ghostly vocals and late-arriving drums, all played and sung by the guitarist. It's fair to say that Gilmour's songwriting shows his infancy in the craft; the lyrics seem to mean little, their main function being to bolster the music with suitably oblique imagery. (Lyrically blocked, David had rung Roger to ask for some words to his first extended effort, but was famously rebuffed). All told, 'The Narrow Way' is much better than its writer, doubtless armed with post-*Dark Side* hindsight, has since insisted.

### **'The Grand Vizier's Garden Party'** (part 1 'Entrance', part 2 'Entertainment', part 3 'Exit') 8.48 (Mason)

By 1969 the drum solo, once a thing of wonder, was fast becoming a thing of dread. A year earlier, Ginger Baker committed an outrageous fifteen minutes of thunderous double-bass-drum rolls and sledgehammer tom-toms to the live half of Cream's *Wheels of Fire*. Colosseum's Jon Hiseman was taking piledriving onstage solos of twice that length. Led Zeppelin's John Bonham was preparing his 45-minute extravaganzas, half of which he'd execute with his bare palms. And what of Carl Palmer and his two-ton, stainless steel kit illustrated with etchings of hunting scenes? In most cases, the drum solo was over-the-top showmanship, more about allowing the rest of the band to retreat backstage for a quiet line or two than a dynamic break or a formally arranged part of a longer piece.

Not that anyone expected Nick to be propagating another 'Toad'. Floyd's percussionist didn't have the technical chops; he was a decent drummer, and better than he allowed himself, but neither his skills nor his temperament were given to the massive ego-rush of the standard traps solo. By Nick's own admission, 'I have never been a fan of gymnastic workouts at the kit, by myself or anyone else'. Most importantly, such overblown statements of technique were inimical to Floyd's music.

So come *Ummagumma* and its four solo quarters, seasoned Floyd-watchers could rest assured that the band would not stoop to the obvious drum-solo conventions. Instead, befitting the vaguely medieval/mystic-east title, Lindy Mason intros with an atmospheric two-flute fanfare, before her husband's impressively tight snare roll makes way for what sounds like tuned percussion (such as the Rototoms Nick would famously play on 'Time' for *Dark Side Of The Moon*) but is actually a treated tympani. Nick clatters happily away with various other stuff – cymbal, cowbell, gong, triangle and so on – alongside Lindy's heavily distorted flute. Far more about moody, often spooky effects than percussive heroism, the piece flows on, a foray through a darkened, alien cavern. At 3.27, the flute and tonal drone abruptly stop and start, like a needle skipping across warped vinyl, before a backward-run cymbal and, weirdest of all, what sounds like a dentist's suction tube.

And so Nick's expanse of strange sounds stretches into a short, relatively conventional kit solo and, by association, the piece's least interesting section. Lindy then returns to pipe the happy guests from their august host's garden. Drum solo? Almost, but solely within Pink Floyd's remit, which is looking increasingly like a suite of exercises in subverting the dominant paradigm. With 'Grand Vizier', Nick Mason establishes his avant-garde bona fides as readily as Rick Wright does his with 'Sysyphus'. This is drum soloing under heavy manners.

## **Atom Heart Mother** (1970)

Personnel:
Roger Waters: bass guitar, guitar, vocals
David Gilmour: lead guitar, bass, keyboards, percussion, vocals
Rick Wright: keyboards, Moog, Mellotron, harmonium, vocals
Nick Mason: drums, percussion
Alan Styles: voice (on 'Alan's Psychedelic Breakfast')
Ron Geesin: musical direction (on 'Atom Heart Mother Suite')
John Alldis: conductor, choirmaster (on 'Atom Heart Mother Suite')
Philip Jones Brass Ensemble: horns (on 'Atom Heart Mother Suite')
Produced at: Abbey Road Studios, London, by Pink Floyd
Executive Producer: Norman Smith
Engineers: Peter Bown, Alan Parsons, Phil McDonald
Released: 2 October 1970 (UK); 10 October 1970 (US)
Highest chart position: UK:1, US: 55

Although parts of *The Man/The Journey* would linger for a while, Pink Floyd's British tour of their experimental double-suite ended on 26 June 1969 at the Royal Albert Hall. For the first time, Floyd were reinforced onstage by other musicians (a brass section seconded from the Royal Philharmonic Orchestra) and a choir (the Ealing Central Amateur Choir, conducted by Norman Smith). It was an important moment. But in labelling the evening 'The Final Lunacy', were the band unwittingly anticipating the animus they'd later harbour over the music that evolved from that show?

The use of 'straight' musicians seasoned in relatively sedate classics, jazz and MOR was obviously nothing new; pop had long relied on sessioneers of every stripe. By the mid-late 1960s, and the rise of the long-player as something more than a collection of singles, B-sides and throwaways, rock was embracing high-concept, often long-form composition, its language enhanced by horns, string quartets, choral voices and orchestras. The Beatles' use of strings and brass was a matter of renown; The Moody Blues reimagined Dvořàk on *Days Of Future Passed*; The Nice summoned classical help for their symphonic *Ars Longa Vita Brevis*; even a pre-headbanging Deep Purple fashioned their own *Concerto For Group And Orchestra*.

By 1969, Floyd's standing in a genre that might conveniently be termed 'proto-prog' was high. Somehow it was inevitable that they should deliver on the promise of *The Man/The Journey* by mobilising unusual instrumentation, arrangements, formats and textures, connecting with more earnest musical categories to create something distinct, perhaps even unique. This new seriousness, developing from what many thought of as the amateurish, suck-it-and-see clamour of UFO and the early records, even won the approval of a record company already sweetened by the chart success of *Ummagumma*.

It was a relatively buoyant four musicians, then, who in November 1969 began rehearsing the early stages of their fifth album. Floyd were not long back from Rome and an ill-starred soundtrack commission for Michelangelo Antonioni's *Zabriskie Point* (see final chapter). Although the finished cut featured only three Floyd tracks, as usual the band amassed plenty of material they could redeploy later. Floyd duly seeded these compostables into a major new work: a piece based on a vaguely 'western' tune written by David Gilmour, which the guitarist provisionally titled 'Theme From An Imaginary Western' (no relation to the Jack Bruce/Pete Brown song of the same name).

Much has already been written about the gestation of *Atom Heart Mother* and its 24-minute centrepiece: how Floyd found themselves perplexed by the unforeseen intricacies of fruiting such an epically multi-faceted work; and how they asked Ron Geesin to add a brass/choral arrangement to the early tapes before setting off on their third US tour, leaving Ron toiling in his underpants through the sweltering early summer. Prior to recording, Floyd took 'Atom Heart Mother' on the road, appearing with horns and voices at the Bath Festival on 27 June and Blackhill's free Garden Party in Hyde Park on 18 July. A lossmaking tour of Europe followed, Floyd labouring with bored sessioneers who were indifferent to the music; the hired hands were there only for payday and backstage rider, their numerous personnel changes, based on availability, making rehearsals very difficult. Back at Abbey Road, Geesin was obliged to conduct EMI-sourced brass players who, according to the arranger, proved to be 'hard, uncaring types, who weren't going to tolerate anyone green or naïve'. Ron nearly decked a particularly obtuse horn player before handing the finalities to the experienced, if more diplomatic conductor and choirmaster, John Alldis.

The album would be completed with four more tracks on the second side. Waters, Wright and Gilmour wrote one each, a la *Ummagumma*, and all were excellent. The fourth, however, was a lengthy sound collage meant to demonstrate Floyd's sense of humour, in contrast to the solemnity of side one. It didn't work, but maybe it's the way they told 'em.

'If you see an album featuring a nice picture of a cow, buy it immediately', bade John Peel of his *Top Gear* audience that September. Tired of their work being overanalysed with every passing album cover, for *Atom Heart Mother* Hipgnosis photographed one Lulubelle III, a fine Friesian spotted by Thorgerson in a Hertfordshire field. By now there was nothing Hipgnosis could do to avoid the fevered scrutiny of the over-imaginative; within days of the cover populating every record-shop window in the land, someone was likening Storm's work to Andy Warhol's soup cans. Peel's appeal to purchase was as much a public service announcement as an expression of the deejay's musical preferences of the time; although three of Lulubelle's bovine homies appeared on the back cover, the sleeve was noticeably devoid of text. Even Pink Floyd's name was absent, creating a precedent for the next few albums.

Despite the travails of its infancy, *AHM* was lauded by critics and fans, who took the album to Floyd's first number one. The band professed themselves pleased, Roger noting that the work was less experimental than *Ummagumma* and was 'much nicer to listen to. I think it's by far the best, the most human thing we've done'. Within a few years, however, Floyd's initial enthusiasm had waned – and then some.

## 'Atom Heart Mother Suite' 23.44 (Mason/Gilmour/Waters/Wright/ Ron Geesin)

Six parts: 'Father's Shout'/'Breast Milky'/'Mother Fore'/'Funky Dung'/'Mind Your Throats Please'/'Remergence'

'God, it's shit', David Gilmour advised *MOJO* in October 2001. 'Possibly our lowest point'. Asked in the 1980s if he'd revisit it in concert, Roger Waters didn't mince words: 'You must be fucking joking... a good case for being thrown into the dustbin and never listened to by anyone ever again'. In his 2004 memoir *Inside Out*, Nick Mason damned with the faint praise of a schoolmaster marking a promising student's disappointing homework: 'Good idea, could try harder.'

Awash with brass, choir and quasi-symphonic pretense, 'Atom Heart Mother Suite' is inconsistent; perhaps Nick's 'failed experiment' indictment is fair. But boiling down music to the left-brain logic of intellectual conceit or technical construct – Roger and Nick *were* architecture students, after all – risks losing something more preciously human. For as soon as emotional content is cheapened or dismissed as mass-market banality aimed at people who know no better, rock'n'roll's fate can only be a pauper's burial outside the frostbitten groves of academe, Dr Keller gleefully officiating. The best popular music is about feeling, or it's about nothing.

Given Pink Floyd's leanings towards the daunting inventions of modern classical composers and the avant-garde, the injection of concentrated emotion would seem contradictory. Yet by their fifth album, Floyd had become masters of resolving lengthy instrumental passages of effects-laden, atonal noise by adroitly returning to the melodic themes stated maybe twenty minutes earlier. With great craft, they'd develop a tantalising, almost unbearable tension, as if guiding the listener towards the edge of a chasm, judge to a nanosecond the moment to pull up just short of plunging to oblivion, releasing the compressed passion in a spine-tingling, ecstatic rush. Instinctively Floyd knew how to mitigate chaos with calm – and it could be quite enthralling.

The presence of John Alldis' choristers is the most unusual ingredient of 'The Amazing Pudding', which succeeded 'Theme From An Imaginary Western' as a working title (and would soon be adjusted yet again thanks to a headline from that gospel of hippie inspiration, *The Evening Standard*). The second component is Philip Jones' Brass Ensemble, who intro the piece, against Rick's loitering background keys, sounding deliberately distressed. It's as if they're tuning up, or maybe squaring up to Ron Geesin. The brass moulds itself into a fanfare, and they're off, Floyd and the horns introducing a main theme that couldn't be more stately if it had been scored for a royal wedding. Or, indeed, a cowboy movie, for 'Atom Heart Mother' is closer to 'How The West Was Won' than 'A Saucerful Of Secrets.'

Soon the choir takes over, colouring Rick's Hammond with wordless vocalising. Up until now, little's been heard of Nick Mason, but his toms slam in at 9.10 just as the voices are becoming progressively assertive, even vaguely warlike. They're oddly Polynesian, as if these well-bred warblers have come out in sympathy with Geesin's adversary in the horn section to perform a threatening haka. But it's actually all nonsense, as confirmed by diligent 'AHM' fans interpreting the phonetics and helpfully transposing the 'words' for internet consumption:

Ráaah. Si-kh' páaah. Míh, D'oh!
Dáki-miú. Yahh! Sasasasa sáaahh bsssh!
Rrrrrrrrrrrrrrrro'ti!
Rapatìta Bogot-há! Rapatìta Bogot-cha! Bossa! Bambi'ah.

And so on. Soon it's all change again, as choir and horns are dismissed and Pink Floyd morph briefly into Booker T. & The MGs. Now Gilmour picks off a beautifully clipped solo, an economical spit for Steve Cropper, as Wright comps on his Hammond. This wraps all too soon, however, as the counterintuitive funk is gradually incorporated into typically Floydian keyboards and more southseas gibberish from the choir. Nick's snare crashes back in at 14.32, the horns follow and the uplifting main theme is restated. It seems like the end is nigh, but at 15.28, everything is abruptly interrupted by Rick's serialist keyboards whirring through a Leslie – a combined amp and rotating speaker that would play a signal role in one of Floyd's greatest pieces – the band lifting away in a barrage of noise and clashing tapes run backward and forward. At 23.44, an officious demand for 'silence in the studio' bridges chaos with catharsis, as the main theme returns, more intoxicating than ever.

### **'If'** 4.30 (Waters)

Superficially 'If' is part two of *Ummagumma*'s lilting 'Grantchester Meadows'. Yet if the earlier song part-evokes a summer's afternoon lazing in the Cambridge greensward to the calls of dog fox and kingfisher, 'If' implies something darker, perhaps even a dash of self-loathing. 'If' speaks strongly to the doubts and fears that will haunt Roger Waters' writing as it matures over the next few years. References to madness will be common. But evoked in song, are these Roger's responses to what he perceived in Syd Barrett, and the manner of the guitarist's departure? Although Floyd carried a sense of collective guilt after January 1968's stillborn rendezvous, the casting vote on whether or not to collect Syd that day might well have fallen to Roger. If so, it's small wonder that Barrett's shade would hover over the bassist's songwriting for many moons to come. More broadly, is Roger gazing elsewhere and not liking what he sees? Although 'If' falls some way short of self-flagellation, perhaps he's attempting a small personal catharsis by setting out in words what he, a learned student of the human condition, sees as flaws in our nature, along with more immediate fears over his own native shortcomings.

His ruminations begin with obliquely poetic self-admonishments. It's as if, no matter how well-adjusted he might appear to others, his own truth tells otherwise. He counters every positive with a negative: 'If I were a swan, I'd be gone/If I were a train, I'd be late'. More conditionals follow, descending from contemplative melancholy to evocation of a distressing internal darkness:

If I were to sleep, I could dream/If I were afraid, I could hide
If I go insane, please don't put your wires in my brain
If I were the moon, I'd be cool/If I were a rule, I would bend
If I were a good man, I'd understand the spaces between friends.

The sense of despair is heightened by the arrangement. The merest smattering of Moog synthesiser at 1.12, followed by Gilmour's plangently bent guitar lines against Wright's Hammond chording and piano lend an unsettling air that perfectly complements the song's overall introspection. Like 'Corporal Clegg' from *Saucerful*, 'If' is a harbinger of a career.

## **'Summer '68'** 5.28 (Wright)

'It Would Be So Nice' deserved all the opprobrium it got. 'Summer '68', however, is an unalloyed joy, one of the keyboardist's finest moments. *AHM*'s only track never to be played by Floyd live, its name revised from the too-obvious 'One Night Stand', 'Summer '68' recalls a fleeting hotel-room liaison during that eponymous season. Over the post-coital cigarette, Rick tries to discern more in the relationship than there actually is, repeating: 'And I would like to know/how do you feel?/how do you feel?' With no answer forthcoming, Rick alludes to the perfunctory nature of the transaction, before acknowledging his own position as an equal partner in rock's on-the-road sexual ritual:

Not a single word was said/The night still hid our fears
Occasionally you showed a smile, but what was the need?
I felt the cold far too soon – in a room of ninety-five
My friends are lying in the sun, I wish that I was there
Tomorrow brings another town, another girl like you
Have you time before you leave to greet another man?

The payoff is ambiguous: 'Goodbye to you/Charlotte Pringle's due'. Charlotte's identity is unknown; is she a 'proper' girlfriend, or just the next camp follower waiting on Rick's attentions? The idea of Floyd's diffident keysman as a Barry White-alike pleasured in turn by a queue of insatiable courtesans is a strange one, but not impossible. Going by the song's last words – 'I've had enough for one day' – perhaps Wright sees all the squelchy stuff on tour as part of the rock'n'roll furniture. It's a dull job, but someone's got to do it.

The arrangement is a killer: a clean, creative assembly of Beatles/Beach Boys conceits, delicious vocal harmonies (Rick's, behind his own lead), excellent piano and several perfectly judged instrumental hooks. 'Summer '68' is most memorable for the gorgeous trumpet break at 1.42, a rousing motif that more than bears repeating twice more before the song's end. In each case, the instrumentation is progressively plumped out with voluptuous keys and brass, the latter possibly courtesy of Philip Jones.

'Summer '68' was released as a single in Japan in 1971. Though Rick's instrumental contributions to Pink Floyd's music would remain crucial for several albums, he'd never write a better, purer pop song.

## **'Fat Old Sun'** 5.22 (Gilmour)

In the early days of The Rolling Stones, it's said that manager/hustler Andrew Loog Oldham, aware of The Beatles consistently hitting pay-dirt with self-penned material, locked Mick Jagger and Keith Richards in his kitchen, the pair on jankers rations until they could whistle up an original tune. The result was astounding: 'The Last Time', one of the truly great Stones singles. According to Nick Mason, in 1970 David Gilmour, whose instrumental prowess was cutting through Floyd's music like a flamelance but who was yet largely untested as a solo composer (although everyone conveniently forgets the unfairly monstered 'The Narrow Way') faced a similar lock-in at Abbey Road. The threat would realise the splendid 'Fat Old Sun.'

David supposedly wrote the song as a sequel to Roger's 'Grantchester Meadows', and it shows. A distant peal of parish church bells announces the singer lost in a bucolic haze, laid-back and lazier than a Cambridgeshire cuckoo. Peering back at a less-complicated past, David lilts wistfully about the summer evening, newly-mown grass and the sound of music in his ears. But he also knows that all things must pass, that the fat old sun is setting on that uncluttered lifestyle of his youth. As if in sympathy with the resigned air, at 3.20 the leisurely strumming (Gilmour accompanies himself with melodic bass, drums and a sweetly-sliding Stratocaster) is suddenly pounded by heavy block chords which, in live performance, would become the perfect excuse to stretch the tune out to a big, fat, Floydian fifteen minutes or more.

David's qualities as a lyricist have frequently been questioned, not least by himself. Yet if the danger of studio imprisonment doesn't necessarily release his inner Dylan, 'Fat Old Sun' nonetheless evinces a more than capable wordsmith. True, David lifts 'summer Sunday and a year' from The Doors' 'Love Street', mainly because of its poetic fit rather than anything it adds to the narrative, but that's fine; Jim Morrison probably wrote the original in the same spirit. Gilmour's singing is excellent, too, taken at a higher pitch than his usual growl and perfectly in tune with the mainly pastoral flavour.

**'Alan's Psychedelic Breakfast'** 13.00 (Waters/Mason/Gilmour/Wright)

I neither condone nor encourage the use of illegal Class 'A' drugs. But a sizeable hit of Owsley's finest might be the only way to get through this lengthy account of Alan Styles preparing for another hard day at the rock'n'roll coalface. The roadie's not alone; his employers pitch in with some gentle, fairly aimless noodling. As Alan potters in the kitchen, his ambiently frying bacon and eggs are seasoned with snatches of breakfasty conversation, predating the soundbites that will appear, more thoughtfully, on *Dark Side Of The Moon*. Similar to parts of *The Man/The Journey* but unhappily much longer, Alan's breakfast, excitingly psychedelic though it may have been, is caught for posterity over thirteen minutes you'll never get back.

## **Meddle** (1971)

Personnel:
Roger Waters: bass guitar, VCS3 synthesiser, vocals
David Gilmour: lead guitar, bass, pedal steel, vocals
Rick Wright: keyboards, vibraphone, Moog, Mellotron, harmonium, vocals
Nick Mason: drums, percussion
Liverpool FC Kop: chanting (on 'Fearless')
Seamus: barking (on 'Seamus')
Produced at: Abbey Road Studios, London; AIR Studios, London; Morgan Studios, London by Pink Floyd
Engineers: Peter Bown, Alan Parsons, Phil McDonald, John Leckie
Released: 31 October 1971 (US); 13 November 1970 (UK)
Highest chart position: UK: 3, US: 70

With album sales and touring receipts consistently in the black, Pink Floyd were now wealthy rock stars. Yet before 1970 was out, the band were running on fumes. The theft of $40,000 worth of gear on the first of two big tours of the US didn't help, although a chance encounter with a federal agent's daughter saw the equipment returned.

Despite the world-weariness, prodded mainly by Roger, Floyd still had enough in the tank to build something solid from apparently unpromising raw materials. Some they took into Abbey Road Studios in January 1971, although the band, keen to trial a sixteen-track desk, swiftly relocated to George Martin's swish new AIR Studios. The first ideas were for an album tentatively entitled *Household Objects*, which comprised exactly that: the random noises of the everyday, shaped, mainly at Nick's behest, into ambient bangs, drones and musique concrète. Although within a week the concept was dumped, Floyd pressed a number of more conventionally musical odds'n'sods into the service of one of their finest pieces, destined to become the focal point of an album that would ring positive changes for a supposedly burned-out band.

If the Barrett years were all mischievous infancy and the next three an unruly, hormonal adolescence, the sixth album saw Floyd's energies coalescing with the confidence of a band nearing the top of their game. *Meddle* has a definitive air of solidity, even respectability, as if the group have acknowledged that the daring experimentalism of their formative records, vital though its part in their upbringing has been, must now accede to a poised maturity and sense of purpose. A corporate decision has been made: it's time to act our age.

Yet suppressing that unruly adolescent brought other issues. This was an era in which mainstream British pop radio was fixated on harmlessly anodyne soft-rock, the hourly inevitability of troubadours as estate agents – Hamilton, Joe Frank & Reynolds, England Dan & John Ford Coley, Seals & Crofts and so on – making tough going of any working day theoretically lightened by Radio One or Capital Radio. Weren't Pink Floyd supposed to insulate us from this fluff?

But as Floyd grew up, a creeping lethargy threatened, the band apparently tempting a senescence more suited to established artists enjoying well-earned dotages after years of devoted service. So eager were Floyd to cleanse themselves of 'amateurism' and the lingering taint of space rock, they risked overcompensation. For resetting themselves as an East Anglian CSNY was not a good look. Following *Meddle*'s electrifying opener, the rest of side one never picks up the pace, stalling amid listless acoustic guitars, soporific vocals and derivative folk-rock dreariness. Only Roger Waters' increasingly assertive lyricism rescues the more pedestrian arrangements and lack-lustre vocals, although even he can't mitigate the singing dog.

Happily there's enough nourishment on *Meddle* to prove Pink Floyd won't be needing the elastic waistbands just yet. The album's finest moments demonstrate that Floyd are now harnessing and controlling the considerable resources at their disposal – from progressively sophisticated technical hardware to the mental-emotional software of instinctive audial questioning – rather than the other way round. The successes are qualified by managing simultaneously to be classically Floydian studies in spatial feel, dynamics and emotional release – half the record comprises a 23-minute masterclass in just that – and a mainstream rock album that you can play to your mum. The accomplishment will be cemented still more firmly two years later: as David Gilmour will tell *MOJO* in 1994, 'This album was a clear forerunner for *Dark Side Of The Moon*, the point when we first got our focus.'

*Meddle*'s sleeve is often derided as Hipgnosis' first dud, at least for Pink Floyd (alongside Roger Dean, Floyd's old muckers from Cambridge were now the go-to designers for rock album art). It's a case study in how even the best photographers value at least some direction from their clients. Responding to a garbled brief phoned in by Floyd while on tour in Japan, Bob Dowling shot a submerged human ear, so close-up the image became, if not psychedelic, messily abstract (Floyd dodged a bullet; Storm Thorgerson originally proposed a baboon's backside). Meanwhile, gazing glumly from the gatefold centre-spread are a lank-haired, granddad-shirted Floyd, looking for all the world like a road crew who'd just lost $40,000 worth of gear.

## **'One Of These Days'** 5.59 (Mason/Gilmour/Waters/Wright)

Another example of two core Floyd specialities: to magick something special from relative simplicity, and to so ratchet up musical tension that when release comes, the response is both cerebral and inescapably physical. With stabbing, treated keyboard, a one-note bass figure is blown powerfully in on a menacing wind. Two basses, in fact, one for each channel and respectively played, with help from the faithful Binson Echorec, by David and Roger. It's said that if the latter's instrument, heard in the right-hand channel, sounds 'worn', it was exactly that; if only the underling dispatched to buy replacement strings hadn't bunked off to see his girlfriend, an important nuance of 'One Of These Days' might have been lost. As it is, it's terrific; arguably Pink Floyd's first big shootout rocker, a visible signpost to their direction of travel and a gripping onstage opener and staple.

Let off the leash following his brilliant, if contained, contributions to his previous four Floyd albums, Gilmour is everywhere. At 2.08, announced by menacing thumping from Mason and doubled with his own slide, David's guitar arrives, as fuzzed up and muscular as the grid on the Daytona 500. The rhythm thunders relentlessly on to a bridge comprising Gilmour's heavily-treated bass solo against the apparent clanking of a steelyard. Like a Dalek with a sore throat, at 3.38 Nick croaks the song's only lyric: 'One of these days I'm going to cut you into little pieces', which could be a lost line from 'Careful With That Axe, Eugene' (although it's said that Roger once jokingly threatened the disc jockey and serial Floyd critic, Jimmy Young, with the same fate). Then it all goes off: driven by David's massively fuzzed and sliding leads, the band at full throttle, it's easy to imagine a theatre – or, later, enormodomes across North America – crammed with longhairs, all headbanging in unison. An absolutely thrilling start, yes, but one whose promise won't be fulfilled until side two.

'One Of These Days' was released as a non-UK single, coupled with (according to territory) 'Fearless' or 'Seamus.'

### **'A Pillow Of Winds'** 5.11 (Gilmour/Waters)

A calm, mainly acoustic respite from the relentless power drive of its predecessor, 'A Pillow Of Winds' tries too hard to channel some of the flimsier products of the otherwise excellent Crosby, Stills, Nash & Young and The Byrds. The feel suggests a parallel-world Pink Floyd, bearing the same relationship to CSNY as the influential quartet's drippy soundalikes, America. With a dreamlike atmosphere recalling earlier pastorals such as 'See-Saw', the song is so laid back and lacking in dynamics it's almost comatose, playing straight into the hands of those critics who feel Floyd's compositional talents and creative juices had been keelhauled along with Syd. David sings Roger's woozy words, which are as pretty and as insubstantial as the arrangement. The song's title comes from Mah-jong, the Chinese board game then popular with the band.

### **'Fearless'** 6.09 (Gilmour/Waters)

Although the song was liked at the time, 'Fearless' feels like two steps forward, one step back after 'Pillow'. Again there's little energy and not a lot of interest, apart from the sampled sounds of a football crowd creating a slight, pleasing dissonance. If there is substance, it is in Waters' lyrics, however, as Gilmour delivers a confident and hopeful message about being allowed to overcome life's challenges fearlessly and in one's own sweet way.

Although some of the words, notably 'Fearlessly the idiot faced the crowd', suggest a lurking Barrett, the carry-on-regardless theme aligns well with the Anfield Kop chant. Emissaries of a city historically famed for toughness and fortitude, the Liverpool FC spectators are singing the club's anthem: Gerry Marsden's (after Rogers & Hammerstein) 'You'll Never Walk Alone', whose rousing, call-to-arms potentiality chimes perfectly with a track that remains uncompromised by Roger's own football allegiances. He is, after all, an Arsenal fan. (Floyd's working title for 'Fearless' was 'Bill', presumably after Liverpool's legendary manager Bill Shankly).

## **'San Tropez'** 3.44 (Gilmour/Waters)

A jaunty trifle about lazing around the Mediterranean fleshpot necking champers. Mixing jazzy, supper-club piano licks with strangely incongruous Hawaiian guitar, 'San Tropez' is nicely played, pleasantly sung, and an excellent reason to avoid the eponymous sunspot if this is the best that comes out of it.

## **'Seamus'** 2.17 (Waters)

Howlin' Dog, anyone? Things have to get worse before getting better (and they will). Steve Marriott's mutt, Seamus, minded by David while Humble Pie's mainman was on tour, hollers backup to Gilmour's lead vocal on a lazy, throwaway blues. For all his talents for accompanying a blues harp – Seamus had been trained to by his master – the blueswailin' border collie was probably pining for an open field and a herd of sheep. Move along now, nothing to hear.

## **'Echoes'** 23.31 (Mason/Gilmour/Waters/Wright)

Finally. The centrepiece of a sixth album that's so far proven unremarkable but for one track is, thankfully, one of Pink Floyd's greatest achievements. Had they made 'Echoes' in 1968, the song would have arrived replete with semi-disciplined, 'Saucerful'-style sonic wig-outs and dissonances. That 'Echoes' plots a more settled and nuanced course accords with the band's newfound sense of restraint. While the music retains a distinct forward progression, with plenty of delicious Floydian avant-soundscaping, the band have learned to control and temper their more extreme instincts. The result is a long-form work that obeys Floyd's own experimental conventions while squaring the circle of accessibility; anyone who might have felt alienated by early Floyd now receives a warm welcome.

'Echoes' was created from a series of apparently random musical sketches entitled 'Nothing 1-24'. After much refinement, Floyd wove the 24 disparate moods into the 20-minute 'Return Of The Son Of Nothing' and took it on the road. Despite its length and substance, a chance encounter with a single, tempered note would give the piece its enduring identity, as well as inspiring a better title. After Roger asked Rick to put his piano through a rotating Leslie speaker, the result was the startling 'sonar' sound, topping and tailing this grand expanse of Pink Floyd at their most majestic.

'Echoes' begins with Floyd in typically impressionist mood, the sonar dying away to spookily treated keyboards and Gilmour's guitar, until Nick comes in and David's upper-register vocals follow. After two verses, the main

**Above:** Culture wars, 1967. Dr Keller (left): 'Why does it got to be so loud?' Roger Waters (right, with Syd Barrett): 'That's the way we like it.'

**Below:** Earnest jamming among the UFO heads. Left to right Syd Barrett, Nick Mason, Roger Waters (1967).

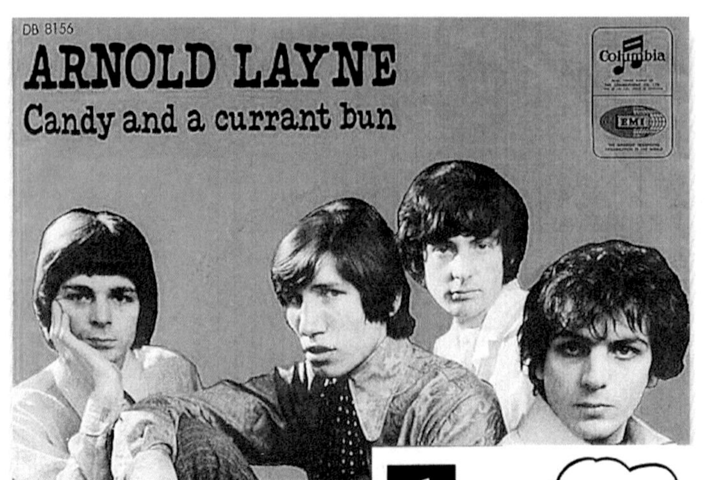


**Left:** The picture sleeve to the debut single, 'Arnold Layne'. (*EMI / Columbia*)

**Right:** The picture sleeve to the second single, 'See Emily Play'. (*EMI / Columbia*)

**Left:** Carnaby Street kaleidoscope hid a stunning debut: *The Piper At The Gates Of Dawn* (1967). (*Pink Floyd Music Ltd*)

**Right:** The picture sleeve for the third single 'Apples and Oranges'. (*EMI / Columbia*)

**Left:** The picture sleeve for the fourth single 'It Would Be So Nice'. (*EMI / Columbia*)

**Right:** *A Saucerful Of Secrets* (1968): Floyd set the controls for the heart of East Anglia. Space-rock, or not? (*Pink Floyd Music Ltd*)

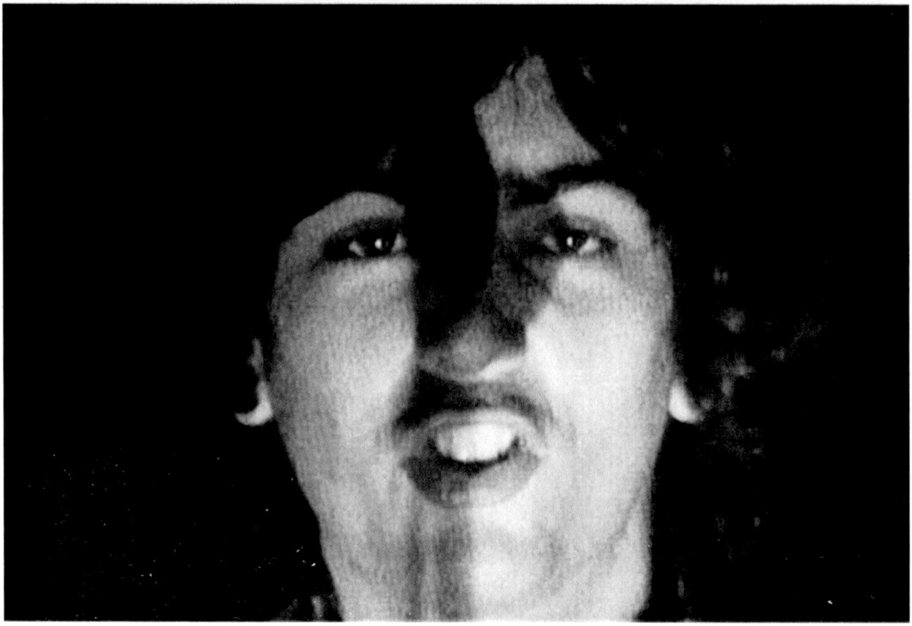

**Above:** 'A guttering malevolence suggestive of a devilish candlelit ritual': Syd on *Look Of The Week* (1967).

**Left:** Bargain-hunting in London in 1967. left to right, Nick, Rick, Syd, Roger.

**Oppostite page, top:** 14-hour Technicolour Dream, Alexandra Palace: Syd was on 'something darker than travel fatigue' (1967).

**Right:** The short-lived 5-piece Floyd (1968): l to r Syd, Roger, David Gilmour, Rick, Nick.

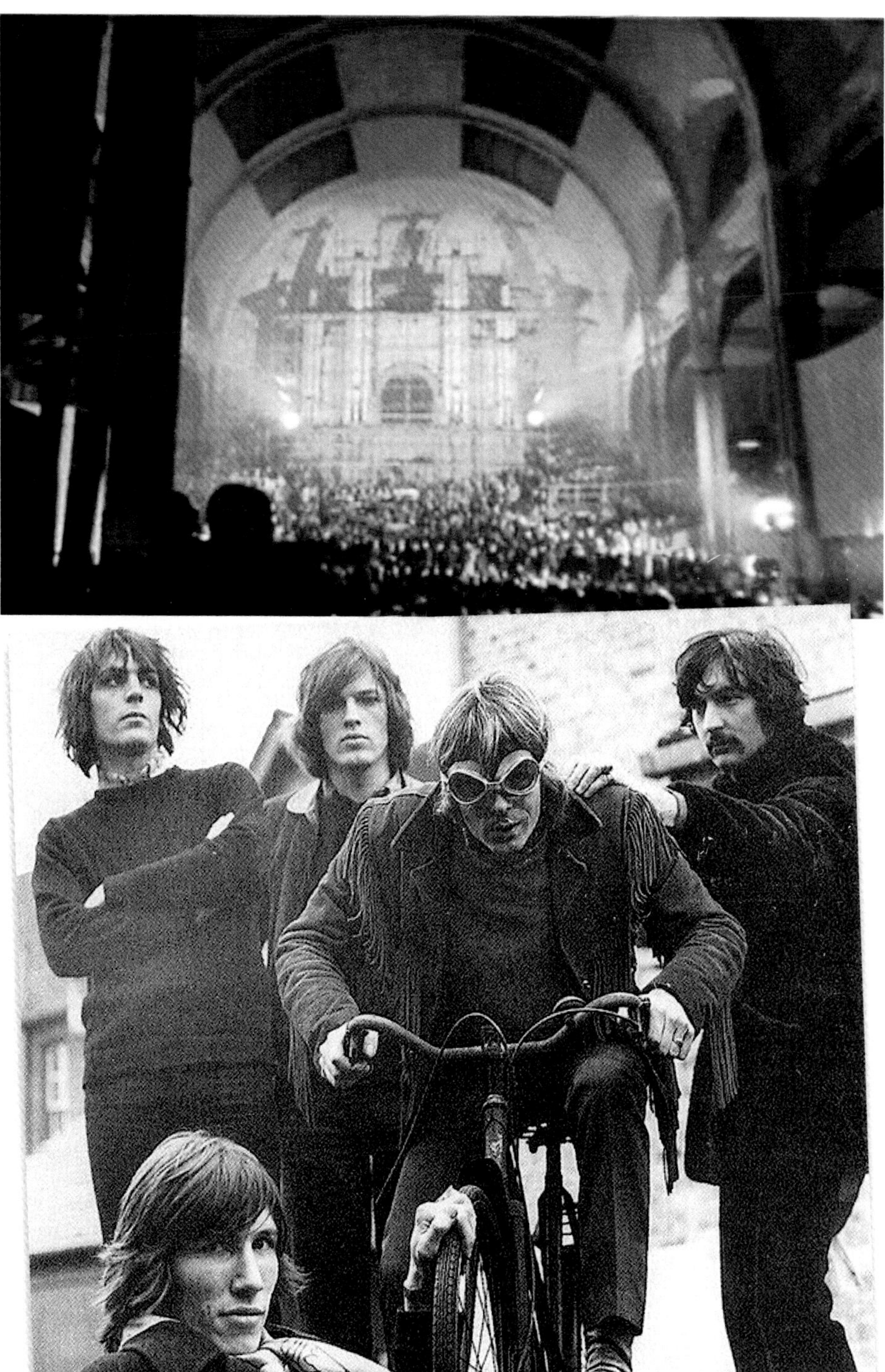

**Left:** The soundtrack to Barbet Schroeder's *More* (1969) signalled Pink Floyd's arrival among the Euro arthouse crowd. (*Pink Floyd Music Ltd*)

**Right:** *Ummagumma* (1969). It's dismissed by Floyd today, but the double album featured some stupendous music. (*Pink Floyd Music Ltd*)

**Left:** *Ummagumma*. Roadies Alan Styles and Pete Watts mind their bosses' gear at Biggin Hill and pray for a pilots' strike. (*Pink Floyd Music Ltd*)

**Right:** *Atom Heart Mother* (1970). Lulubelle III's opinion was probably higher than Roger's. (*Pink Floyd Music Ltd*)

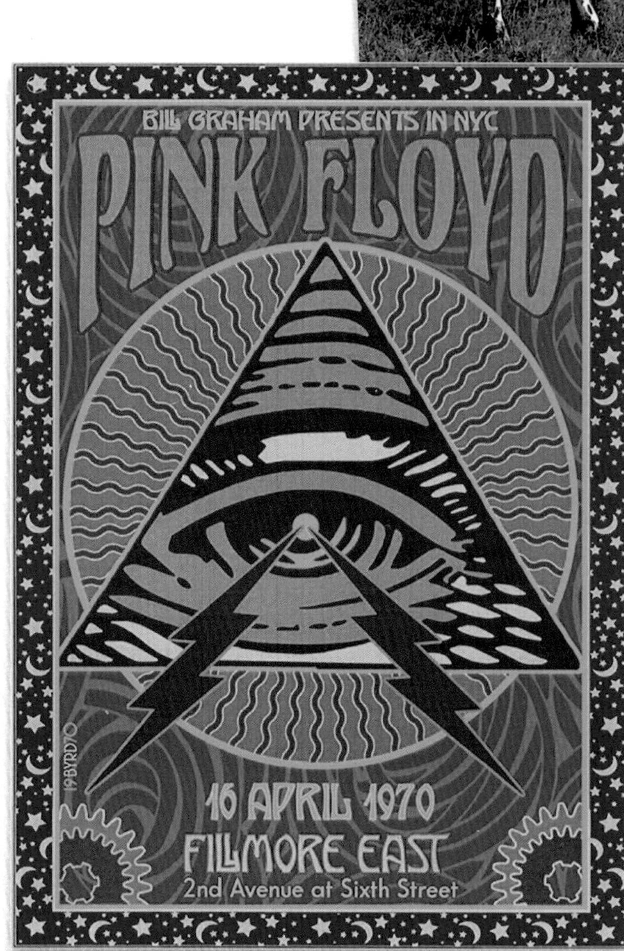


**Left:** Poster boys for Bill Graham's Fillmore, which was Floyd's third US tour.

**Above:** David at Pompeii, October 1971. A volcanic concert behind closed Ionic capitals, immortalised on film by Adrian Maben.

**Below:** Rick at Pompeii.

**Above:** Nick at Pompeii.

**Below:** Roger at Pompeii.

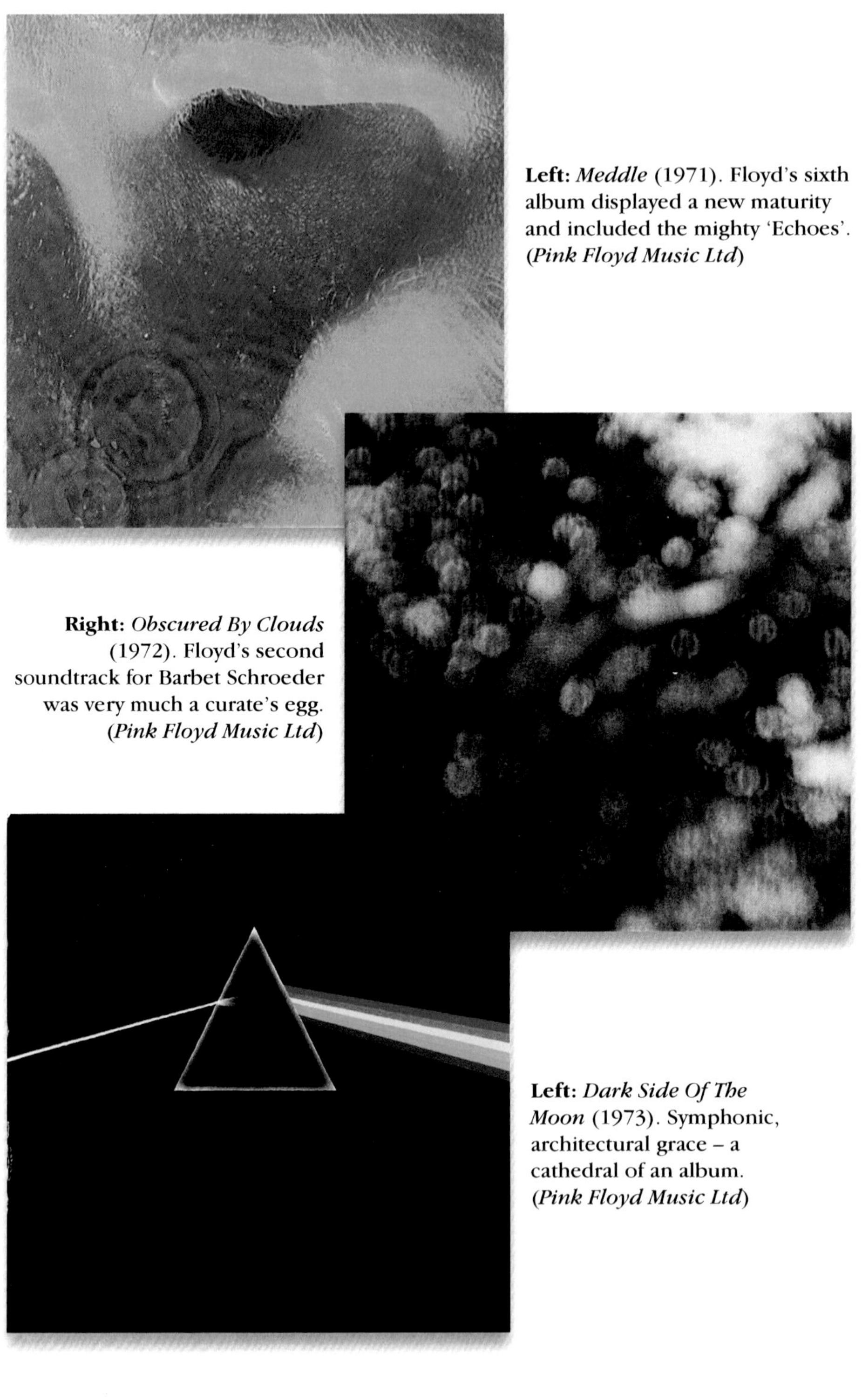

**Left:** *Meddle* (1971). Floyd's sixth album displayed a new maturity and included the mighty 'Echoes'. (*Pink Floyd Music Ltd*)

**Right:** *Obscured By Clouds* (1972). Floyd's second soundtrack for Barbet Schroeder was very much a curate's egg. (*Pink Floyd Music Ltd*)

**Left:** *Dark Side Of The Moon* (1973). Symphonic, architectural grace – a cathedral of an album. (*Pink Floyd Music Ltd*)

**Above:** Pink Floyd on the Dark Side of the Moon tour

**Left:** Dick Parry (left, with Roger) added superlative sax to *Dark Side*, *Wish You Were Here* and *The Division Bell*.

Pink Floyd on stage in France in 1974.

**Left and below:** *Wish You Were Here* (1975). Haunted by Syd Barrett, Floyd's ninth album revealed its treasures slowly. (*Pink Floyd Music Ltd*)

**Left:** *Animals* (1977): a flying pig watches over Floyd's darkest album to date. (*Pink Floyd Music Ltd*)

**Right:** *Animals*' Algy before he flew away to Kent.

**Left:** *The Wall* (1979). As far from a group effort as Floyd had yet travelled, and evidence of Roger's growing supremacy. (*Pink Floyd Music Ltd*)

**Right:** *The Wall*'s jackbooting hammers by Gerald Scarfe. The coming totalitarianism, or Pink's delusion?

**Left:** *The Wall* live: some of the most extravagant live rock shows ever mounted.

**Right:** *The Final Cut* (1983). The woefully underrated final studio collaboration between Roger, David and Nick. (*Pink Floyd Music Ltd*)

**Left:** *A Momentary Lapse Of Reason* (1987). A dehydrated Floyd embrace the 1980s and make it work. (*Pink Floyd Music Ltd*)

**Right:** *Delicate Sound Of Thunder* (1988). It was the first rock album to be played in space – so there's an irony. (*Pink Floyd Music Ltd*)

**Left:** *The Division Bell* (1994). Theoretically, Floyd's heroic last shout – but there was more to come. (*Pink Floyd Music Ltd*)

**Right:** *The Endless River* (2014). An ambient, mostly instrumental final farewell to Rick. (*Pink Floyd Music Ltd*)

**Above:** Pink Floyd reconfigured in 2022 for 'Hey Hey, Rise Up', a single for Ukraine. Left to right: Nitin Sawhney, David Gilmour, Nick Mason, Guy Pratt.

**Left:** Floyd's Ukraine partner Andriy Khlyvnyuk in Kyiv, 2022.

guitar theme roars up and down like a roller coaster and the piece gains shape and intensity. At 7.00, the escalation suddenly halts for four minutes of magnificently relaxed jamming, similar to the 'Funky Dung' portion of 'Atom Heart Mother'. As the band work their way into an interlude just made for extended onstage improv, guitar and keyboard effects never contemplated by Steve Cropper and Booker T. Jones creep in and subsume the funk until there is only abstraction. But with the atmospheres now evoking the depths of the ocean rather than the heart of the sun, the sonar chimes again, a glimmer of sentient life straining to communicate through the green submarine murk. A beautiful passage of Floydian ambience – it'll become midwife to any number of Tangerine Dream albums – slowly coalesces into organ chording and rapid strumming by Roger, high up on his bass. With percussive punctuation from Nick, the anticipation builds; after several spine-tingling minutes, we feel we know what's coming, but nothing really prepares us. And when at 18.13 the false climax finally hits, it's with the velocity of a nuclear torpedo, David's searing, double-tracked guitar delivering perhaps Floyd's consummate and most intoxicating knock-out blow.

As the band fledge, so do Roger's lyrical ambitions:

Overhead the albatross hangs motionless upon the air
And deep beneath the rolling waves in labyrinths of coral caves
The echo of a distant time comes willowing across the sand
And everything is green and submarine.

According to Roger, the song hinges on 'the potential that human beings have for recognising each other's humanity and responding to it with empathy rather than antipathy'. No more clunky trips to Mildenhall, then. Set beside his similarly thoughtful words to 'Fearless', 'Echoes' displays a distinct poetic sensitivity: a concept with which the writer himself, so abrasive and prosaically direct when puncturing the pomposity of others, might even agree.

# **Obscured By Clouds** (1972)

Personnel:
Roger Waters: bass guitar, VCS3, vocals
David Gilmour: lead guitar, VCS3, bass, pedal steel, vocals
Rick Wright: keyboards, VCS3, vibraphone, Mellotron, harmonium, vocals
Nick Mason: drums, percussion
Produced at: Strawberry Studios, Château d'Hérouville, Val-d'Oise, France; Morgan Studios, London by Pink Floyd
Engineers: Peter Watts, Dominique Blanc-Francard, Andy Scott
Released: 2 June 1972 (UK); 15 June 1972 (US)
Highest chart position: UK: 6, US: 46

On 20 January 1972 at the Brighton Dome, Pink Floyd tentatively unveiled an early version of a major new work. Electrical problems obliged an early bath, but better news would come over the next few weeks and a short British tour, including four successful nights at London's Rainbow Theatre. Thus the world was introduced to *Dark Side Of The Moon: A Piece For Assorted Lunatics*.

If it was yet a titular mouthful, on-the-road adjustments at least rendered the live work fit for purpose. However, Floyd would spread the studio refinements and recording over a year sprinkled with other diversions. Besides touring, the band were pencilled for shows with Roland Petit's Ballet de Marseille and with putting the finishing touches to their own movie, *Live At Pompeii*. Then Barbet Schroeder came to call.

Between 23 and 29 February, Floyd moved to Château d'Hérouville, outside Paris, to begin composing and recording their soundtrack for Schroeder's new movie, *La Vallée*. One month later, after a short tour of Japan, they returned for another five days. Following three days in April of final mixing at Morgan Studios, they were done.

The movie saw Schroeder once again busying himself with freewheeling, self-absorbed Westerners finding and/or losing themselves on an exotic island, this time New Guinea, herbal remedies rarely far away. The little posse seeks the eponymous *Vallée*, an undiscovered tract of rainforest apparently under permanent cloud cover and said by some to be Paradise. 'We must destroy time to become one with it', drones Gaetan, leader of the questers, adding ominously that only tribal sorcery might reveal the correct path. By now, serious alarm bells should have been ringing for the film's central character, Viviane, a spoilt young French diplomat's wife and sometime dealer in tribal curios. But this is the early 1970s: plenty of the planet is still open to independent travellers, cultural colonisation is the unspoken norm and youthful credulousness virtually an article of faith. Give or take a few leeches and the occasional New Guinea death adder, there's little to deter any seeker after Truth, or simply hornbill feathers for the Paris Flea Market, from patronising the locals then returning to Europe with the souvenir masks and a severe itch. But the narrative – the attempted absorption of materialistic

West into purportedly 'spiritual' East, en route to a Holy Grail-like revelation – proves impossibly naïve; a fact recognised alone among the impressionable troupe by Viviane's muse, Olivier. As demonstrated by Gaetan and Hermine, daubed in body paint and ululating self-importantly among their Mapuga hosts, the stylistic mix is there, but not necessarily the match.

The same might be said of the soundtrack. Floyd embrace genres as alien to the band as the tribe's ritual slaughter of fatted swine is to our virtue-signalling tourists. The results are variable. Once more the director rarely takes full advantage of the Floyd we know and love; over the opening credits and a scene-setting aerial sequence, the music fits beautifully, but this is an exception. Floyd's contributions are again deployed by Schroeder as source music trickling tinnily from transistor radios or car stereos. This is hardly the best use of the band's talents, but it might explain Floyd deviating from archetypal soundscaping in favour of shortish, conventionally-structured and occasionally insipid songcraft, of the sort first exercised on side one of *Meddle*. Despite their budding adulthood, Pink Floyd channelling *Music From Big Pink* is no more convincing than if The Band were to close their live sets with 'A Saucerful Of Secrets'. As fragmentary as its filmic predecessor, *More*, much of the music means relatively little once it's divorced from the cinematography it serves.

That said, *Obscured by Clouds* boosted still more Floyd's reputation in France and was generally well received, although not always sensibly explained. In the States, *Crawdaddy* praised Floyd's newfound sense of direction, but added curiously, 'If they can follow this up it may lead them back to their position as the premier space rock band'. The observation must have had Roger Waters spitting hornbill feathers. Floyd themselves categorised the album as less a proper PF record, more 'just a collection of songs.'

The album's sleeve design came about while Thorgerson and Powell were poring over a 35mm slideshow of movie stills. At one point the projector jammed, delivering a wildly out-of-focus image of one of the film's trippy travellers sitting in a tree. Intrigued, the Hipgnosis duo proposed the resultant mess as the album's sleeve image. An accident, then, but not necessarily a happy one. To Thorgerson's chagrin, Schroeder later accused Floyd of deliberately choosing a mediocre cover design to avoid competing with their own forthcoming *Dark Side Of The Moon*.

Like *More* and the band's few final inclusions on *Zabriskie Point*, *Obscured by Clouds* is really Floyd marking time between two far more substantial pieces of work. If they really were keen to pare back their music to strumalong, semi-acoustic basics, the notion proved thankfully transitory. And it's surely a blessing that they sidelined such a counter-intuitive impulse, even as they were preparing for world domination in 1973.

### **'Obscured By Clouds'** 3.05 (Waters/Gilmour)

The album's title track starts portentously, an incoming Cessna generated by VCS3 synthesiser over a steady 4/4 beat. Gilmour's guitars arrive, heavily fuzzed and sustained, for an archetypal film theme, used by Schroeder to aerially set the scene. In that context, accompanying a light plane flying over the New Guinea rainforest, 'Obscured By Clouds' works wonderfully. Isolated from the visuals, however, this is standard Floyd fare, adding little to what we know they can already do.

### **'When You're In'** 2.31 (Waters/Wright)

Simplistic hard-rock mood music, with an insistent riff reminiscent of Pete Townshend's 'Overture' from *Tommy*. Though structured as a natural follow-on to the title track, the instrumental was left out of the film.

### **'Burning Bridges'** 3.30 (Waters/Wright)

In the movie's context, this plodding and mournful ballad portends the fate awaiting the trekkers well before they depart on their quest; an implicit warning to the idealistic that, as 'Ancient bonds are breaking/Moving on and changing sides', there may be no coming back.

### **'The Gold It's In The…'** 3.08 (Waters/Gilmour)

David Gilmour, ever the great guitar mimic, does a convincing impression of Stephen Stills on an amiable road-trip rocker. It might be an outtake from a Manassas session, perhaps accompanying a pair of hipsters crossing Death Valley on Harley-Davidsons. Certainly, the mood is more Southern California than South-East Asia; Gaetan's observation that other fated investigators into the valley 'have no choice but to stay' anticipates The Eagles' 'You can check out, but you can never leave' idea from 'Hotel California'. Three years ahead of that allegorical epic, bizarrely (for Floyd), the music is entirely appropriate.

### **'Wot's… Uh The Deal'** 5.09 (Waters/Gilmour)

A shard of melancholy runs through 'Wot's… Uh The Deal', distancing it from the margarita mushiness of certain laid-back soft-rockers of the time, superficially echoed here. Complementing a love scene, once again a song featured early in the movie seems too soon to be sounding a caveat over what lies ahead for the adventurers. Viviane and Olivier might be slithering in ecstatic embrace, but this is transitory; the promised land is not necessarily an impossible dream, but 'grabbed with both hands' it'll come at an alienating cost. Not unpleasant, then – and it is an abundantly pretty tune – but Pink Floyd it ain't. And wot's the deal with the title? Even if 'Wot's… Uh The Deal' does appear in the lyric, Floyd's habit of appending a temporary name to a new song seems to be stuck at first base.

### **'Mudmen'** 4.18 (Wright/Gilmour)

On this slow instrumental, over Rick's Hammond and VCS3, David's feel-o-meter goes into overdrive, the guitarist squeezing from his instrument the tear-inducing emotion that was already defining Pink Floyd. Like some other mid-period Floyd tunes, 'Mudmen' sounds like it's been bodily hoisted from the middle break of a longer song. Lacking the top and tail of verses and choruses, it's a little insubstantial – again, perhaps a typical movie tune – yet Gilmour's two stunning solos keep it real.

### **'Childhood's End'** 4.34 (Gilmour)

If the title track echoes Floyd of yore, 'Childhood's End' looks forward to all manner of business to come. Nick's throbbing percussion at 1.00 will be similarly heard on 'Time', as will the style of David's opening vocal, springing assertively from Rick's Hammond chords over funky guitar. The last lyric Gilmour will write for Pink Floyd before Waters' exit is difficult to put into context, though; heard only faintly in the chums' Land Rover, Paradise still a long way off, its sense of finality is premature as Schroeder squanders a good song. A brief addition to Floyd's live show later in the year, 'Childhood's End' feels like the album's most fully-formed track.

### **'Free Four'** 4.17 (Waters)

'Free Four' is a characteristically downbeat and, by now, fairly unmistakeable slab of Roger Waters fatalism. Far from our happy wanderers horse-trading with gimlet-eyed Aussie smallholders in New Guinea – the moment in *La Vallée* the song accompanies – the sentiments seem to be targeted more on business closer to home; a theme to which Roger would return:

> Life is a short warm moment/And death is a long cold rest
> You get your chance to try/In the twinkling of an eye
> Eighty years, with luck, or even less
> So all aboard for the American tour/And maybe you'll make it to the top
> But mind how you go/I can tell you, 'cause I know
> You may find it hard to get off.

After the band count it in ('one, two, free, four') Rick's big VCS3 chord, similar to that of the title track and perhaps the only element to provide synergy with the rest of the soundtrack, runs atypically beneath jaunty strumming and handclaps. SingalongaFloyd might feel out of kilter with the gloomy lyric, but deliberate contrasts can be effective; think of how Rene Magritte's trick of floating boulders in mid-air added to their sense of weight and mass. Yet again filtered from the car's stereo, the song corresponds little with the onscreen action.

At 3.00, there's a terrific guitar break; this also feels out of place, but it lifts the song demonstrably and could be the album's best moment. 'Free Four' was released as a non-UK single, backed by 'Stay' in America, by 'Absolutely Curtains' in Japan and by 'The Gold It's In The...' in West Germany, Denmark, Italy and New Zealand.

**'Stay'** 4.08 (Wright/Waters)

Schroeder left 'Stay' out of the film, which was ironic given that the song's content – a passionate night with a passing stranger (possibly a groupie) and its ruminative aftermath – is closer in spirit to the movie than many of the tracks that did make the cut. Again unFloydian – nearer to early Steely Dan, but without the ultracool detachment – the lyric is sung by Rick Wright as a natural companion to the organist's magnificent 'Summer '68.'

**'Absolutely Curtains'** 5.51 (Mason/Gilmour/Waters/Wright)

In 1983, Tangerine Dream's 'Logos', as used in the Berlin soundsmiths' score for Michael Mann's *The Keep*, would be hugely influenced by the moody organ opening to this instrumental, which provides a suitably evocative musical finale to the travellers' quest. 'Absolutely Curtains' also brings World Music into Pink Floyd's orbit, as tribal chanting seamlessly takes over from Rick's organ and Mellotron and Nick's percussion, a nice touch of the orient meeting the occident more happily than for the doomed seekers.

It's a fitting end to a Floyd album that's something of a curate's egg. Unquestionably there's good music here, and it improves with repeated play; but its overall indeterminacy, and wilful departure from what the band do best, leaves *Obscured By Clouds* a largely inessential part of Floyd's canon.

## Dark Side Of The Moon (1973)

Personnel:
Roger Waters: bass guitar, VCS3, vocals
David Gilmour: lead guitar, VCS3, EMS Synthi AKS, bass, pedal steel, vocals
Rick Wright: keyboards, VCS3, EMS Synthi AKS, vibraphone, Mellotron, Minimoog, vocals
Nick Mason: drums, percussion
Dick Parry: tenor saxophone (on 'Money')
Clare Torry: vocals (on 'The Great Gig In The Sky')
Doris Troy, Lesley Duncan, Liza Strike, Barry St John: backing vocals
Chris Adamson, Gerry O'Driscoll, Peter Watts, Patricia Watts, Henry McCullough, Roger 'The Hat' Manifold: voices
Produced at: Abbey Road Studios, London by Pink Floyd
Engineers: Alan Parsons, Chris Thomas, Peter James
Released: 1 March 1973 (US); 16 March 1973 (UK)
Highest chart position:UK: 2, US: 1

Concept album or rock opera? Ignoring the latter expression's awfulness – as if only snootily attaching the 'superior' art form will rescue parvenu little rock'n'roll from populist moshpit to High Table approval – both apply to *Dark Side Of The Moon*. As a thematically-linked suite of songs, with its recurring musical motifs and consistency of vision, this cathedral of an album clearly obeys the conventions of the former. Yet there's record-wide narrative structure here, too. Nick Mason later recorded how, before Floyd's December 1971 tour of Britain, Japan and the US, the band sat in the drummer's Camden kitchen and kicked around the ideas about mental instability that Roger Waters was then incubating. To prepare something shipshape and ready to tour, the group woodshedded a thematic sequence of human circumstances that might, particularly in the pressure-cooker of the music business, trigger madness: the stress of working, endless deadlines, travelling and the enticement of money, all leading inexorably to ageing, mental issues and death. Rather than examine how such conditions might play out over the life of a fictitious archetype (*pace* The Pretty Things' *S. F. Sorrow* or The Who's *Tommy*), Waters created a nameless Everyman: the You or Me as conduit and receptacle for the highs, plateaus and lows of existence itself. While these are universal themes, Roger based them empirically on his own experiences, those of Pink Floyd and – relating particularly to mental illness – of Syd Barrett. Above all, the piece would be about empathy; as Roger would tell Karl Dallas in a 1987 interview:

> The line 'I'll see you on the Dark Side Of The Moon' is me speaking to the listener, saying, I know you have these bad feelings and impulses, because I do too, and one of the ways I can make contact with you is to share the fact that I feel bad sometimes. We all fight small battles between the positive and the negative in our everyday lives, and I'm obsessed with truth and how

> the futile scramble for material things obscures our path to a more fulfilling existence. That's what *Dark Side Of The Moon* is about. And despite the rather depressing ending with 'Brain Damage' and 'Eclipse', there is an allowance that all things are possible, that the potential is in our hands.

In articulating these lofty matters, Roger was keen to avoid 'psychedelic patter and strange and mysterious warblings' in favour of writing the new album 'absolutely straight, clear and direct'. Musically the album would deliver on the maturity promised by *Meddle*, but without downsizing to the pretty but undistinguished folk rock to which Pink Floyd had recently proven themselves ill-suited.

This wasn't the first time Floyd had explored an extended narrative. *The Man/The Journey*, with its theme of one man's working day and its routines, was as much a testbed for *Dark Side* as it had been for 'Atom Heart Mother'. But the self-conscious onstage joinery and housekeeping were gone, while roaming around the cosmos like a deviant comet was now largely grounded. Instead, thanks mainly to Gilmour and Rick Wright, what David characterised as 'that psychedelic noodling stuff' would be transplanted with formal structures which nonetheless retained a melodic, memorable, ineffably Floydian celebration of mood and aesthetics, pushing beautifully on towards a climax as anthemic and liberating as anything the band had yet achieved, or would again.

After early demos created by Roger in his Islington home studio, Floyd began rehearsals early in 1972 at a Bermondsey warehouse owned by The Rolling Stones. More sessions followed at the Rainbow Theatre, after which the Brighton Dome hosted the first aborted public performance of what was then alternately titled *Eclipse* or *Dark Side Of The Moon: A Piece For Assorted Lunatics*. The press corps were formally alerted to the new music at the Rainbow on 17 February. Although yet to be set to master tape, exhaustive test piloting before audiences in Britain, Japan, Europe and North America enabled Floyd to sculpt the new work into studio readiness by the end of May, when the band entered Abbey Road for the first of many sessions between then and January 1973.

Manning EMI's shiny new 24-track desk was the golden-eared staff engineer Alan Parsons. Later Alan would rise again with his own rock act, The Alan Parsons Project. Although Parsons' contributions were crucial, he was later replaced by Chris Thomas after the band decided the final mix needed 'a fresh pair of ears'. Less officially, Thomas was tasked with healing early fractures between Waters and Gilmour. This said, the pair seemed umbilically tied during most of the *Dark Side* sessions; so relaxed, according to Parsons, they effectively 'produced each other'. Meanwhile, all four Floyds were driven by rekindled enthusiasm, a unity of intent and the dawning confidence that they were creating something momentous.

Everyone was keen to exploit the newest technology. In one of several *DSOTM*-related sequences in the film *Live At Pompeii*, Roger is seen at Abbey

Road tinkering with a VCS3. The 'suitcase' synthesiser, invented in a garden shed by a BBC Radiophonic Workshop techie called Peter Zinovieff, was first used by Floyd on *Obscured By Clouds*. It would play a key role in creating *Dark Side*'s many unusual textures and effects (as well as becoming the economy synth option for dozens of artists deterred by the cost and size of Robert Moog's telephone-exchange original). Floyd also became adept at extracting outlandish noises from the primitively makeshift; Parsons recalls producing delays and echoes by spooling long ribbons of recording tape around mic-stands.

On learning that an album called *Dark Side Of The Moon* had been released by Medicine Head, Floyd reluctantly renamed the new suite *Eclipse*. They circled back on discovering that the folk-pop band's LP had tanked into obscurity. The title was far from a retreat to space rock, although many fans were fooled; *Dark Side Of The Moon* was a reference to lunacy, based on an occult term for the subconscious.

For *DSOTM*'s cover, Thorgerson presented several options. Floyd 'took three seconds' to unanimously choose a strikingly minimalist illustration by George Hardie. It would become one of rock's most iconic images. Against a plain black ground, Hipgnosis' ace illustrator airbrushed a simple pyramid/prism converting a thin stream of white light to the colours of the visible spectrum (artistic licence permitting an erroneous purple). The rainbow hues were carried through the gatefold into an ECG pulse – a visual representation of the heartbeat that bookends the music – while the entire cover was created as a repeatable mandala that nobody passing a record shop window after 1 March 1973 could possibly miss, still less confuse with *Obscured By Clouds*.

In splendidly punkish fashion, everyone but Rick boycotted EMI's PR launch due to the inexcusable absence of a quadraphonic playback system. The event was held at the London Planetarium, proving that the band's disdain for space rock, not to mention *Dark Side*'s broader meaning, was yet to filter through to the record company's marketing department. With his album *Billion Dollar Babies*, Alice Cooper unwittingly prevented the original edition of a work of genius from climbing to no further than number two on the UK charts (reprising Engelbert Humperdinck, whose gruesome 1967 ballad 'Please Release Me' infamously kept 'Strawberry Fields Forever' from reaching number one). Although at first the album topped out in the US for just one week, *Dark Side* went on to spend 960 weeks on the American chart, selling more than 45 million copies and receiving worldwide critical acclaim.

50-plus years after its release, the album remains an Ur-text of modern popular music. *Dark Side* has weathered tribal musical fashions to win pan-generational, prog-not-prog appeal, proving that smart, exquisitely conceived, played, arranged and produced rock music need be neither bland brain-candy, nor dustbins-of-your-mind pretentiousness, nor synapse-shattering technoflash. And it has *tunes* in abundance. On the Waters-Gilmour axis – the yin-yang, architect-musician relationship so critical to *Dark Side*'s success, later so sadly fractured – sound engineer Nick Griffiths nailed it: 'Dave made people enjoy it, Roger made them think'. Gilmour was happy to take that. 'It's a great combination', the guitarist said, 'if you can please both minds and hearts'. But be it concept album or rock opera, this rich, nourishing banquet for all the senses has become the template for every themed narrative work to be produced on rock'n'roll's watch.

## **'Speak To Me'/'Breathe'** 4.01 (Mason/Waters/Gilmour/Wright)

'I've been mad for fucking years, absolutely years, been over the edge for yonks…' So advises Floyd roadie Chris Adamson, echoed in similarly resigned tones by Abbey Road doorman Gerry O'Driscoll, over a solemn heartbeat and the ticking of a watch. The pair are among a number of individuals there present invited by Roger Waters to record spontaneous answers to 15 questions, relating mainly to violence, madness and death, which the bassist had written out on cue cards. With the results salted judiciously throughout the album, the concept was one of Roger's masterstrokes, adding another dimension to a work already brimming with ideas. Not every contributor's response was as spontaneous; one Paul McCartney (then in Studio 2 touching up Wings' *Red Rose Speedway*) couldn't resist a few knowing Macca-isms; incompatible with Waters' vision, these were left off the record. But other participants gladly entered into the spirit, including Wings' guitarist Henry McCullough, Floyd crewmen Roger 'The Hat' Manifold, Liverpool Bobby and Pete Watts and Pete's wife, Patricia.

Credited to Nick Mason, 'Speak To Me' is really just a 1.17 sound collage of Messrs Adamson and O'Driscoll, a VCS3-generated helicopter, Pete Watts' manic laughter, the cash-register effects later heard on 'Money' and a dash of Clare Torry's extraordinary vocal from 'The Great Gig In The Sky'. 'Speak To Me' (so named after Alan Parsons' standard test for voice levels) settles into 'Breathe', whose roots lay in a similar song worked up by Waters and Ron Geesin for the soundtrack of *The Body*. Roger, ever his own sternest critic, would later decry his words as 'lower sixth stuff', but they work beautifully, obeying the writer's original stricture that the album's storyline should be expressed as unequivocally as possible. The gorgeous piano chording, which Rick Wright borrowed from Miles Davis' *Kind of Blue*, are coloured winsomely by David impersonating a lap-steel guitar on his open-tuned Strat. As Roger told *MOJO*, 'Breathe' is:

> An exhortation directed mainly at myself but also at anybody else who cares to listen. It's about trying to be true to one's path.

## **'On The Run'** 3.33 (Gilmour/Waters)

In Adrian Maben's film *Live At Pompeii*, Pink Floyd are seen at Abbey Road working on early parts for *Dark Side Of The Moon*. Earnestly Roger ferrets around in a brown briefcase. Doomy electronic noises promptly issue from the machine within, a VCS3 synthesiser. 'Can I put this down?' the bemused bassist calls up to someone in the control room, as he shapes the abstract sonic emissions into *Dark Side*'s instantly familiar 'Travel Sequence', AKA 'On The Run'. Other accounts have asserted that David Gilmour created the effect by keying eight notes into an EMS-1 Synthi AKS sequencer and increasing the tempo. But whoever got there first, this short instrumental, built mainly on electronics, reimagined from its earliest version as an onstage guitar jam, radiates movement and energy.

With its tannoy announcer, a tone generator filling in for a hi-hat, vehicle noises, Roger Manifold's laughing 'Live for today, gone tomorrow, that's me' vox-pop and a final plane crash, 'On The Run' effortlessly conveys the anxious, time-waits-for-no-one pressures of a busy airport, or anywhere else grimly familiar to every successful rock band. As noted by Rick, who hated flying, the pressures of travel could often provoke fears of death: an appropriate sentiment since, more broadly, Roger saw paranoia as a theme of the piece.

### **'Time'** 7.06 (Mason/Waters/Wright/Gilmour)

As if startling the listener out of a bad dream, a clock alarm interrupts the air disaster, quickly accompanied by – literally, thanks to Alan Parsons – a roomful of clocks ringing, ticking and chiming the hour. 'I recorded them in a watchmaker's shop for a quadraphonic sound demonstration record', the engineer explained, subsequently inviting Floyd to use them as extra effects. The sampling couldn't have been more suitable. As the clocks fade, Waters produces a rapid, metronomic pulse on his muted Fender P-bass, followed by huge Gilmour guitar chords soaked in Echorec and Mason on a pattern of what sounds like electronic percussion. In fact, Nick had unearthed a studio set of Rototoms: shallow, die-cast frames housing drumheads of various sizes, individually tuned by hand rotation. Welcome then, my friends, to one of the most famous intros in all rock music.

Nick steps away from the Rototoms and thumps at his kit as David's assertive vocal (assumed by Rick on the song's two bridges) delivers Roger's ruminative words about how one's life is shaped by the passage of time. The bassist told *MOJO* in 1998:

> I had the strangest feeling growing up that childhood and adolescence and one's early adult life are preparing for something that's going to happen later. I suddenly thought, at 29, hang on, it's happening, it has been right from the beginning, and there isn't suddenly a line where the training stops and life starts. 'No-one told you when to run/You missed the starting gun'. The idea in 'Time' is a similar exhortation to 'Breathe'. To be here now, this is it. Make the most of it.

> And you run and you run to catch up with the sun but it's sinking
> Racing around to come up behind you again

The sun is the same in a relative way, but you're older
Shorter of breath and one day closer to death
Every year is getting shorter, never seem to find the time
Plans that either come to naught or half a page of scribbled lines
Hanging on in quiet desperation is the English way
The time is gone, the song is over, thought I'd something more to say.

Another major feature of 'Time' is its stunning guitar solo. With generous helpings of the whammy bar he was virtually patenting and more bent notes than a mobster's lockup, David teases out an emotive statement that would influence legions of wannabe axemen. The Floyd of five years before would surely have run a mile from backing vocalists; here the wordless, soulful colourations of Doris Troy, Lesley Duncan, Liza Strike and Barry St John, peerless professionals all, are crucial, particularly at 6.10, where 'Time' gives way to a reprise of 'Breathe'. Funkier than the earlier iteration, the piece showcases David's rhythmic picking over Rick comping at an electric piano, as Roger's words reflect on the undemanding comforts of hearthside and religion's weekly support network:

Home, home again/I like to be here when I can
When I come home cold and tired
It's good to warm my bones beside the fire
Far away, across the field/The tolling of the iron bell
Calls the faithful to their knees/To hear the softly spoken magic spell.

Not only was 'Time' the album's only track written by all four Floyds, but it was the last to be credited to the group until the big split of 1985. For many years, the song remained in the band's concert repertoire and those of both Gilmour and Waters as solo artists.

## **'The Great Gig In The Sky'** 4.44 (Wright/Torry)

A frequent accompaniment to 1970s Amsterdam sex shows and still a sonic Viagra perfect for lovemaking – not bad for a metaphor for death – 'The Great Gig In The Sky' is measurably pepped-up by the contribution, following a suggestion by Alan Parsons, of a little-known EMI staff songwriter and session singer named Clare Torry. Effectively an afterthought added at mixdown stage to Rick Wright's beautifully chorded instrumental, Clare's wordless, improvised, positively ecstatic vocal has become justly renowned, even though it took a 2004 lawsuit to get her name on the credits (and a belated royalty boost to her original session fee of £30). The singer, whose soaring expressions of emotive rapture could give Lorraine Ellison a run for her money, arrives alongside Nick's drums. The arrangement moves from Rick's slow, regal piano chords and David's slide guitar to a full-on, impassioned and almost unbearably moving Floyd anthem. It's perfectly positioned within *Dark Side*'s sequencing as the breathless final track on the original vinyl's side one. Late to the party or not, no vocal could have fitted better.

The earliest live versions of 'The Great Gig In The Sky' were called, variously, 'The Mortality Sequence' and 'Religious Theme'. Seeded in were readings from Ecclesiastes and a sampled rant by the broadcaster and Mary Whitehouse disciple Malcolm Muggeridge. Happily for Whitehouse and her reactionary Divine Light Mission, Floyd decided to drop the religious satire, fearing reprisals from American evangelicals. And so the saintly moral voice of witch-trial Britain was spared the spiritual turmoil of sharing songspace with a young, unmarried woman apparently engaged in sexual congress. Voices other than Torry's that did make the cut were Gerry O'Driscoll and Patricia Watts, from Roger's vox-pop questionnaires.

## **'Money'** 6.32 (Waters)

The unmistakable 20-foot tape loops of cash registers and loose change (actually tearing paper and bags of coins tossed into a bowl) introduce the most famous 7/4 time signature in pop singles history. Along with Abba's 'Money Money Money' and Barrett Strong's 'Money (That's What I Want)', side two's opening track has become every film director's lazy audial shorthand for documentaries about city traders, budget reports, super-yachts and Kim Kardashian. Which is effectively what Roger Waters is talking about as he gleefully slams consumerism, avarice, ownership of football teams and Lear Jets, the power of filthy lucre and pretty much the entire capitalist shebang.

Notwithstanding the band's early 1970s transformations, 'Money' is a very different Floyd track. Just as changes were rung elsewhere on *DSOTM* with backing vocalists and a generally more mature approach to music-making, the eminently funky and – whisper it softly – danceable 'Money' features a saxophone solo for the first time in a Floyd mix. David's old Cambridge compadre Dick Parry blows a soulfully oily tenor just before a stunning change – Gilmour later wryly apologised to Parry for having him play over the notoriously tricky 7/4 – at which point a 4/4 signature kicks up for a frantic, get-on-down middle boogie and some savagely lyrical soloing from the guitarist. 'Money' ends with Rick comping at electric piano and more vox-pops, notably Henry McCullough helpfully repeating, 'I don't know, I was really drunk at the time.'

Naturally Floyd, and especially Roger Waters as credited songwriter, made a huge amount of money from 'Money'. This arguably places its sentiments alongside those of John Lennon's 'Imagine' ('imagine no possessions', fretted one of the world's wealthiest songwriters and property owners). But Waters was as aware as Lennon of the inherent ironies. As Roger told *Melody Maker*'s Michael Watts in 1970:

> It's all very tricky. We have great arguments in the band about [money] because I proclaim vaguely socialist principles, and I sit there spouting a lot of crap about how having a lot of bread worries me – and we are earning a lot of bread now.

In an interview 20 years after *Dark Side*'s release, he conceded:

> I remember thinking, well, this is it and I have to decide whether I'm really a socialist or not. I'm still keen on a general welfare society, but I became a capitalist. You have to accept it.

Something else Floyd were forced to accept was the not-so-subtle change in fans' perceptions and what they expected of the band, particularly in the US. Suddenly the once hushed, quasi-religious gravitas of a Pink Floyd recital had become a frenzy of screaming and stomping, as if the holy spirit had descended and gotten the faithful speaking in tongues. It was the antithesis of what the band wanted, sowing the seeds of Roger's barely suppressed contempt for 1970s Floyd audiences and, by association, germinating the ideas that would underpin *The Wall*. As Gilmour remarked to *Rolling Stone*'s David Fricke in 1982:

> We were used to all these reverent fans who'd come in and you could hear a pin drop. We'd try to get really quiet, especially at the beginning of 'Echoes'… trying to create a beautiful atmosphere, and all these kids would be there shouting for 'Money.'

Released as a non-UK single (with the 'bullshit' lyric excised) and backed with 'Any Colour You Like', 'Money' was Floyd's induction into the US Cash Box and *Billboard* singles charts, making number 10 and number 13, respectively. With and without Waters, Floyd would perform no song more often, while both Roger and David (who took the lead vocal on the original) retained 'Money' on their respective solo setlists. The die was cast; Pink Floyd would never be the same again.

## **'Us And Them'** 7.41 (Waters/Wright)

The lovely piano motif of 'Us And Them' was birthed in Rick Wright's 'The Violent Sequence' from *Zabriskie Point*. The movie's director, Michelangelo Antonioni, had ditched the piece from his soundtrack, along with a number of other Floyd contributions, because it was 'beautiful, but too sad' and it reminded him of church. ('He was obviously waiting to be reborn', Gilmour drily remarked on the director's endless stonewalling). Oddly, given Antonioni's fussiness, early run-throughs for 'Us And Them' were briefly deemed by Floyd's record company 'too depressing'. The loss to both a dull film and an even duller EMI executive's ego proved brilliant for *Dark Side*, however, as once more Wright – the organist would rarely again be so consistently inspired – weighs in with one of the album's most memorable tracks.

With Waters' words sung by Gilmour, backing vocals from Strike, Duncan, St John and Troy and some magnificent tenor soloing from Parry (recorded during the same session as Dick's 'Money' monologue, yet very different in structure – clearly the saxist was on song that day), 'Us And Them' is another big, portentous production. Roger rationalised the song as broadly about 'those fundamental issues of whether or not the human race is capable of being humane'. Using simple opposites – us and them, officers and grunts, rich and poor – along with vox-popped pearls of wisdom from Floyd roadie Roger The Hat ('I only hit him once. It's only the difference between right and wrong, innit?') Waters illustrates how conflict and indifference towards the plight of others are born of human beings not talking to, or understanding each other:

> Us and them/And after all we're only ordinary men
> Me and you/God only knows it's not what we would choose to do.
> Forward he cried from the rear/And the front rank died
> The general sat/And the lines on the map
> Moved from side to side.

As verses break into the thick, roiling choruses, the sax, BVs and guitar/keyboard chording create towering walls of sound almost Spectorish in their sheer mass, volume and, well, *thickness*. Climactic in effect, yet only pointing towards still more stirring themes and dynamics to come, the longest track on *Dark Side* is among its most uplifting.

Backed by 'Time', 'Us and Them' was *DSOTM*'s second US single, reaching an absurdly modest number72 on the Cash Box chart in March 1974.

### **'Any Colour You Like'** 3.26 (Gilmour/Mason/Wright)

Wright's VCS3 meets Gilmour's treated Stratocaster (inspired, according to David, by Eric Clapton's Leslie-generated effect on Cream's 'Badge'), this affable instrumental is a perfect example of Floydian dynamics in action, serving as a buffer and relief between 'Us And Them' and the equally massive 'Brain Damage'. 'Any Colour You Like' was named after roadie Chris Adamson's standard line whenever requested a guitar: 'Any colour you like, as long as it's blue'. Deliberate or not, Adamson was paraphrasing Henry Ford's famous aphorism relating to the industrialist's always-black Model-T. No doubt for this reason, the tune has been interpreted as a critique of capitalism; the 'choices' offered in society to the proletariat masses by the elite few amounting to no real choices at all. Others posit that, with mental illness looming large in *Dark Side*'s narrative, the psychedelic flavouring points directly at Syd Barrett. But Roger's claim that the piece was really no more than a 'little instrumental fill' would seem to be the most adhesive.

### **'Brain Damage'** 3.51 (Waters)
### **'Eclipse'** 2.04 (Waters)

Every preceding moment has been targeted at the final double-whammy: two songs that display perfect synergy in style and substance, crying out to be considered as one. The arrangement breaks from the tour of David Gilmour's guitar cabinet (double-tracked arpeggiated Stratocaster, with dog whistle flourishes from a higher-pitched Bill Lewis) into a rousing chorus swirling with Rick Wright's Hammond and the soulful cooing of the backing vocalists. Here, as everywhere else, Alan Parsons' attentions at the desk are vital. The segue is as natural as day, Rick's brief Minimoog solo and Pete Watts' vox-pop leading into what is effectively a coda to 'Brain Damage' – and indeed, the album.

For Roger Waters, 'Brain Damage' is about 'defending the notion of being different' and references the mental deterioration of Syd Barrett, long held to be the human face of *Dark Side*'s inquiries into the dark side. As he toyed with early versions during the *Meddle* sessions, Roger had originally called the song itself 'Dark Side Of The Moon'; it's fair, therefore, to consider 'Brain Damage' as the source text for the entire album.

The open spaces behind King's College, Cambridge inspired the opening verse:

> The lunatic is on the grass/The lunatic is on the grass
> Remembering games, and daisy chains and laughs
> Got to keep the loonies on the path.

Lead vocalist Roger plays up his satire: the idea that 'loonies' – and everyone else, except for the powers-that-be – must be marshalled into mechanistic regiments of the socially uniform; that any grown adult apparently obsessed with memories of childhood is clearly mad and must therefore be knocked into shape for the greater good. This, of course, fits Syd to a tee, and dovetails nicely with another Waters bogeyman, the crushing of identity by a warmongering military machine. Roger later elaborated to *Uncut*:

> There's a tendency within most societies to try and force everyone into a particular regimen… to stop people walking on the grass. It's the idea of the desire being [considered] wrong, or mad.

Ken Kesey's 1962 novel *One Flew Over the Cuckoo's Nest* explored similar themes. The book and the 1975 film demonstrated how the lines between madness and sanity become institutionally blurred, the 'mad' central character, McMurphy, sentenced to irrevocable brain surgery for the crime of individuality. In the third verse of 'Brain Damage', Roger suggests that solutions as extreme as pre-frontal lobotomy are sometimes no more than savagely lazy cop-outs for an establishment that craves conformity:

> You raise the blade, you make the change
> You re-arrange me till I'm sane
> You lock the door, and throw away the key
> There's someone in my head but it's not me.

The line 'And if the band you're in starts playing different tunes', is a bleak reminder of Barrett's later tendency, acid gnawing hungrily at his psyche, to plough his own musical furrow even when onstage with his bandmates. Then 'I'll see you on the dark side of the Moon' signals Roger's kinship with Syd – and, implicitly, the listener – and that such is the latency of madness in the human condition that the writer could just as readily have fallen to the same imbalance as his errant colleague. This denotes the empathy, the 'writing about others', which conceptually underpins 'Brain Damage' and its parent album, and would most of Waters' work to come. As Roger observed for the 'Classic Albums' documentary *The Making of The Dark Side Of The Moon*:

> We all make mistakes, we're all human, and you can't expect to behave perfectly. But if, through your own internal efforts, you can give the empathetic side of your nature a better chance in its battle against the devil within you, that is a struggle we can all engage in every day of our lives.

'Eclipse' completes the circle. The lyrics 'All that you touch/and all that you see/all that you taste/all you feel' return to the ideas first expressed in 'Breathe'. Behind Rick's Hammond, furiously climaxing band and the almost painfully impassioned vocalists, Roger lists the different facets of thought, sense and deed that inform a lifetime; how 'all you touch and all you see/is all your life will ever be'. And although the last line, 'everything under the sun is in tune/but the sun is eclipsed by the moon' is pessimistic, suggesting that life is essentially futile and everyone is doomed to dwell on the dark side no matter what, a phenomenally emotive climax delivers on Waters' promise that, reductively, we're all in it together, and that by understanding and empathising with each other, we can survive. In Karl Dallas' book *Pink Floyd: Bricks In The Wall*, Roger said:

> The album uses the sun and the moon as symbols. The light and the dark; the good and the bad; the life force as opposed to the death force ... all the good things life can offer are there for us to grasp, but the influence of some dark force in our natures prevents us from seizing them. The song addresses the listener and says that if you are affected by that force, and if that force is a worry to you, well, I feel exactly the same too.

The album ends almost where it came in, on a heartbeat, with a final slab of Gerry O'Driscoll wisdom: 'There is no dark side of the moon. Matter of fact, it's all dark'. This arguably leaves a still more downbeat and sombre taste than Roger's lyrics. But overall, the cathartic effect of an album that cannot help but slake every appetite – emotional, intellectual, cerebral, visceral, musical – is transcendent.

## Wish You Were Here (1975)

Personnel:
Roger Waters: bass guitar, guitar, VCS3, glass harmonica, tape effects, vocals
David Gilmour: lead & rhythm guitars, VCS3, EMS Synthi AKS, bass, pedal steel, glass harmonica, tape effects, vocals
Rick Wright: organs, pianos, VCS3, ARP String Ensemble, EMS Synthi AKS, clavinet, Minimoog, glass harmonica, tape effects, vocals
Nick Mason: drums, percussion
Dick Parry: baritone & tenor saxophones (on 'Shine On You Crazy Diamond')
Roy Harper: lead vocals (on 'Have A Cigar')
Venetta Fields, Carlena Williams: backing vocals (on 'Shine On You Crazy Diamond')
Produced at: Abbey Road Studios, London by Pink Floyd
Engineers: Brian Humphries, Peter James
Released: 12 September 1975
Highest chart positions: UK, US, France, Netherlands: 1

'After the success of *Dark Side Of The Moon,* we were brought back down to earth when we had to start tackling yet another album', wrote Nick Mason in his autobiography. '*Dark Side* actually added to the burden since we were particularly anxious to avoid accusations of cashing in'. As *Dark Side* set about rearranging the rock'n'roll furniture, David Gilmour questioned whether it was time to take stock: 'You hit that strange impasse where you're really not certain of anything anymore … what on earth do we do now?'

What they did in autumn 1973, other than to kick back and enjoy their bank balances, was return to Abbey Road. Grown-ups they might have been, but the experimental instincts that drove *Games For May* and *The Man/The Journey* still lurked behind the now palatial portico. Those same impulses triggered the revival from 1971 of *Household Objects*, an exercise more thought-experiment than music-making. Nick wryly noted that two months' studio fiddling saved them having to deliver anything more formal. 'We could busy ourselves with the mechanics of the sounds rather than the creation of the music', Nick wrote, adding that to his knowledge, Floyd made no recordings of *Household Objects* (although two pieces, 'Wine Glasses' and 'The Hard Way', turned up on the 2011 'Immersion' remix of *Wish You Were Here*).

Sounds of the suburban kitchen aside, the interregnum saw Floydian spirits once again low. Individually the band devised diversion therapies: vacations, Ferraris, mansions, domesticity, producing Unicorn and Robert Wyatt, discovering Kate Bush, etc. But it took an excoriating concert review in *NME* by avowed Syd Barrett fan Nick Kent to prod the band back towards Abbey Road in January 1975.

The lethargy still took a while to shift; the band spent the first few weeks drinking and playing darts. But at least they could now draw upon three promising works-in-progress: 'Shine On You Crazy Diamond' (the album's centrepiece, already road-tested over the previous year as 'Shine On'); and 'Got

To Be Crazy' and 'Raving And Drooling' (which would be temporarily shelved, respectively to be fleshed out as 'Dogs' and 'Sheep' for 1977's *Animals*).

It's one of rock's rich ironies that Floyd's prevailing disaffection would be almost the *raison d'etre* of the new record, as Waters discerned in the band's subdued demeanour the seeds of the all-important concept. 'At times, the group was there only physically', Roger commented. 'Our minds and feelings [were] somewhere else'. Cue operatic musings on alienation, pressures of the music business and Syd Barrett: implicitly the subject of 'Shine On You Crazy Diamond' and, possibly, the rest of the album. Roger insisted only the one song was about Syd, the balance more a 'universal expression of my feelings about absence. We were very absent'. But Waters' relentless conceptualising, now life's blood to the thoughtful bassist, was taking its toll on his colleagues, as Gilmour and Wright made clear. In a later interview, Roger observed:

> [They] don't think that the subject matter or theme and the ideas developed are as important as I think they are. They're more interested in music as abstract form as much as anything else.

The impending schism would eventually destroy Pink Floyd as we had come to know them. Appropriately, *Wish You Were Here* is about estrangement – the clue's in the title. But Waters' howl of alienation is far from an academic exercise in abstract pop psychology. Fleetwood Mac and Abba would soon unblushingly be airing their respective dirty washing in their records. Yet neither group seemed interested in transposing their marital enmities into wider commentaries on the world outside. Pink Floyd were doing something a lot more subtle. As the band interrogated the broader human condition, individual foibles and shortcomings began to surface, as if conclusively to prove the points they were making even as they made them. The message was steadily becoming a self-fulfilling prophesy. Perhaps without Floyd realising it at the time, Roger's lyrics and overall vision, locked into David's and Rick's icily beautiful musical settings, were worrying away at a rift which, ten years later, would see the band lose a founding member for a second time.

Time and peer-group pressure do strange things. On the release of Pink Floyd's ninth album, critical response was mixed, muted, negative even. To be sure, following *Dark Side* was a tough call, like driving a 2CV after riding around all year in an Aston Martin. The inevitable disappointment wasn't assuaged by the slower, steadier progressions of *Wish You Were Here*. *Rolling Stone* seemed to think Floyd still dabbled in space rock, pronouncing the band bereft of 'the sincere passion for their art' that such extravagance clearly demands. *Melody Maker* called the album 'unconvincing in its ponderous sincerity'. Your servant, as avid a Floyd fan then as now, shared an overall feeling of deflation. Every artist reaches a pinnacle; had Floyd pedalled beyond top dead centre, with a prospect only of winding down the other side, fractured and potentially dissolute?

Nearly half a century on, how things have changed. 'I, for one, would have to say that it is my favourite album', enthused David. 'The end result of [recording problems] definitely left me an album I can live with very very happily'. Rick was just as keen: 'It's an album I can listen to for pleasure, and there aren't many Floyd albums that I can'. As if by magic, legions of critics and fellow travellers agreed. Though largely supportive, Roger has alluded to the 'nightmare' of the record's preparation, due partially to incipient disagreements with Gilmour. 'I knew we were over as a band-of-brothers notion of a pop group was concerned', Roger said. 'I was mourning that loss as well as that of Syd'. Problems were also encountered at the desk, particularly after engineer Brian Humphries accidentally ruined the early backing tracks for 'Shine On You Crazy Diamond', and with them, hours of work by Nick and Roger.

It's fair to say that *Wish You Were Here* reveals its treasures slowly, as soberly as the intro to 'Shine On'. Overall the album's feel is glacial and slightly remote, lacking the warmth of its predecessor despite the soulful attentions once more of saxophone and backing vocalists. In places it's as if Floyd are paying their own feedback-looped tribute to the early 1970s' German electronicists who'd been so in thrall to *A Saucerful Of Secrets*. Like the latter, *Wish You Were Here* features much impressionist soundscaping; unlike 'Saucerful', the atmospheres are frigid and sparsely vegetated, more icy northern European tundra than the chaotic white heat of interstellar re-entry. In 'Welcome To The Machine', Floyd cordon off a climate-controlled clean room of pulsating, softly whirring hi-tech, betraying more than a hint of Kraftwerk. 'Have A Cigar' snipes caustically at the recording industry via a stand-in vocalist, the maverick troubadour Roy Harper. 'Wish You Were Here' proves Floyd can write a song that's every bit as powerful accompanied by a simple acoustic guitar as by the band's massed gadgets of Stratocaster, Hammond and VCS3.

If the album was imbued with the spirit of Syd Barrett, his phantom materialised as if by dark sorcery on 5 June 1974, when Floyd's original dissident was sighted in Studio 3 at Abbey Road. 1966's bright-eyed psychedelic adventurer, now overweight, shaven of head and eyebrows, in a scruffy mac and carrying a shopping bag, slouched at the back of the studio as the band worked through 'Shine On'. Syd made gnomic small talk with a thoroughly discombobulated Floyd before vanishing once more into the St John's Wood traffic. No one in Floyd had seen Syd for seven years; none would see him again. For all concerned, it was a spooky, profoundly depressing experience.

If *Wish You Were Here* hadn't proved to be such a damn good album, Barrett's ghostly manifestation might have been put down to supernatural intervention, a portent of some nameless doom. But then again, with the new record tacitly referencing, in real-time, the opening of the Waters-Floyd chasm, maybe omen is exactly what it was.

For the sleeve, Hipgnosis ran with the idea of absence and emotional detachment by producing a cover hidden by opaque black plastic. The only visible imagery is a hard-edged George Hardie illustration of a cosmic handshake, perhaps between two of the cyborg inhabitants of 'Welcome To The Machine' and – Floyd presumably bowing to record company pressure – band and album names. For the inside, Storm Thorgerson produced a series of laterally-thought, magic-real photos and illustrations: the burning man (as in getting burned in business); a man swimming through desert sand; an 'empty suit' brandishing a 12-in silver disc (an obvious allusion to the recording industry); and the beautifully composed 'diver without a splash'. Unsurprisingly in the wake of its preceding megalith, *Wish You Were Here* struck number one in Britain, US, France and The Netherlands.

### **'Shine On You Crazy Diamond'** (parts 1-5) 12.23 (Gilmour/ Waters/Wright)

One of Pink Floyd's most celebrated set-pieces, 'Shine On You Crazy Diamond' is Floyd's ultimate paean to Syd Barrett. David Gilmour's sorrowfully transcendent theme ('it just fell out of my guitar in the rehearsal studio') inspired Roger Waters to write another song about Floyd's fallen comrade.

By now, Syd is no stranger to Floydian tribute. But for 'Shine On', Roger draws deeply upon his most carefully judged and affectionate thoughts, honouring his old friend within a musical setting as elevating and elegiac as Floyd could produce. So too does David Gilmour; yet again, the guitarist proves how, like great Italian cuisine, little is needed to create something incredibly tasty. Essentially a slow blues with some very smart, unobtrusive changes, 'Shine On You Crazy Diamond' features one of Floyd's longest intros – a single minor chord lasting almost four minutes, played by Rick on synthesisers and Hammond organ, with solos on Minimoog and guitar. This passage is notable for the resurrection of part of *Household Objects*: the time-honoured trick of creating a musical tone by running a finger around the rim of a wine glass. As is Floyd's wont, the band embellish the basic idea with an arsenal of studio widgetry, making varispeed tapes at different pitches and then combining them on Abbey Road's 24-track desk. The results are then cast into Rick's synths ahead of the main theme.

David later wondered if the most famous four notes in Pink Floyd's history had arrived by accident while he was idling one day with an A-minor chord. Serendipitous or not, if the tinglingly melancholic motif isn't enough to confer upon Gilmour the lifelong Johnny B. Goode award, the guitarist then conjures several minutes of the most sonorously bell-like and beautiful soloing of his career.

A full 8mins 40secs passes before the vocals arrive. Backed by Venetta Fields and Carlena Williams, Roger delivers his own lyrics, as elegant as the theme that inspired them. Brilliantly the writer conveys his regard for Syd; avoiding excess sentimentality and without glossing over his old friend's flaws, he alludes to simpler childhood days in Cambridge, and how a darkness – in the shape of drugs, or the music industry, or both – descended upon Syd and all but snuffed out the inner light:

> Remember when you were young, you shone like the sun
> Shine on you crazy diamond
> Now there's a look in your eyes, like black holes in the sky
> Shine on you crazy diamond
> You were caught in the crossfire of childhood and stardom, blown on the steel breeze
> Come on you target for faraway laughter, come on, you stranger, you legend, you martyr, and shine!

When Floyd hired Dick Parry for *DSOTM*, David referred the saxophonist to the playing of the legendary cool-jazz pioneer Gerry Mulligan on *Gandharva*, a 1971 album by Moog specialists Beaver & Krause. Entering 'Shine On' as soon as the second chorus is done at 11.09, Dick takes the advice to heart. The Mulligan effect is intensified through Parry's stylish soloing on baritone sax, the instrument for which Gerry was most revered. Shortly Dick exchanges the big horn for tenor, as seamless key and tempo changes quicken the song to the conclusion of its first part of the album.

That final moment, of course, should have been the halfway mark; rightly or wrongly, Floyd save the concluding parts 6-9 for the album's last cut. There's fun to be had reprogramming *WYWH* to enable consumption of the full 25 minutes as one big, rich cake; yet oddly, the split works, the top and tail corralling the album's three shorter tracks to create a satisfyingly contained package.

## **'Welcome To The Machine'** 7.27 (Waters)

The first of two contemptuous broadsides fired by Roger Waters across the bows of the music business. Roger has insisted that only 'Shine On' related to Barrett, but it's possible that Syd loitered long enough in the songwriter's head to occupy all three of the songs that follow.

For one of the album's most fascinating tracks, Roger adopts the 'voice' of the eponymous device, not so much welcoming the wide-eyed tyro pop star as eyeing him up for oblivion, much as a tiger shark would an unwary lobster. This machinery assumes less a physical form than a disembodied and wholly malevolent presence. And despite the references in the lyrics, the recording industry is perhaps just part of a broader vision of social disruption.

Rick's crystalline synths brilliantly evoke a warded, antiseptic world in which everything serves the overwhelming efficiency of an impassive superbrain. The idea of 'the machine' as the intangible representation of a dystopian, manipulative and surveilling establishment – a sort of Fat Controller on magnetic tape – was a bit hackneyed even as long ago as 1975. But sometimes a cliché is a cliché because nothing else does as good a job of distilling a big idea into a bite-sized nugget. 'Welcome To The Machine' is so effective, so chilling a slice of rock as future-shock, that Waters can be forgiven an occasional drift towards the obvious.

After the listener is buzzed in, the piece opens with a bulkhead or a security door sliding shut. There is a sense of numerical control, of contained, digitised madness. Immediately we're sucked into an alien space resounding with white noise, the oscillations of electromagnetic waves, a terrifying electronic pulse. Whatever sentient life is present is signalled by the unexpected arrival of an arpeggiated acoustic guitar chord, counter-intuitive against the high-voltage, Kraftwerk-like drones. Waters' dismembered voice lays out the red carpet, the second line emphasising the machine's godlike omniscience:

> Welcome my son, welcome to the machine
> Where have you been? It's alright we know where you've been.
> You've been in the pipeline, filling in time,
> provided with toys and Scouting for Boys
> You bought a guitar to punish your ma
> And you didn't like school, and you know you're nobody's fool,
> So welcome to the machine.

Speaking specifically to the music business, the song suggests would-be rock stars naively signing away their lives for promised yet undelivered glory. As with the hooded inhabitants of M. C. Escher's unhinged lithographs, where visual trickery permits the simultaneous rising and falling of a staircase or a waterway to nowhere, there is no escape; once you're in, you're in, and life hereafter is as aimless as it is for Escher's cowled figures. Wright layers synth upon synth, the cold algorithms crushing the beleaguered individual (embodied in the strummed acoustic guitar) and bending the listener/visitor/victim to the will of the invisible mechanical deity. One of Floyd's scariest tracks, 'Welcome To The Machine' ends abruptly, the electro-industrial facility apparently in lockdown, the synths chased away by a final air-raid siren.

### **'Have A Cigar'** 5.08 (Waters)

That the music business endures much biting of the hand that feeds is hardly surprising. Be it misappropriated royalty payments or Christmas-cracker Svengalis misguiding youthful careers, the people most likely to be affected by industry malfeasance are the feisty young musicians themselves. Weathering the skulduggery first-hand affords disenchanted singers, songwriters and instrumentalists many opportunities to rage, in song, against the music machine. Taking pot-shots at the industry and its moguls has informed the work of The Beatles, Frank Zappa, Joni Mitchell, The Clash, Prince, The Byrds, Tom Petty and many others. Plenty find their target; sadly, this example by Pink Floyd does not.

By the time Floyd came to record 'Have A Cigar', too many takes of 'Shine On' had lacerated Roger's vocal cords. Unconvinced that David could conquer the high notes of the album's second assault on the Biz (although it's also said that Gilmour, though invited, found the song's politicking too cynical), Waters drafted in old friend and Blackhill co-veteran, the singer-songwriter Roy Harper. Busy in the studio next door with his album *HQ*, the Mancunian was known for impeccable anti-establishment credentials and the abrasive delivery of his inquisitorial protest songs. Roy undoubtedly shared Roger's low opinions of the record industry; if anyone could summon the requisite vitriol it would be him.

Roy's delivery of Roger's words turned out so Floydlike that, years later, long-term fans who didn't read record sleeves were surprised to discover the vocalist was neither Waters nor Gilmour. Unlike the icy maleficence of 'Machine', 'Have A Cigar' reveals little more than a miffed commentator trotting out a few ironic, anti-showbiz platitudes. In the guise of the Havana-chomping impresario, Harper sings 'Oh by the way, which one's Pink?': an enquiry genuinely made of Floyd on more than one occasion.

An overall feeling of having been here too often is not helped by one of the less interesting arrangements in Floyd's catalogue. The hard, moody riff has a stop-start, bump'n'grind feel; it doesn't really take off, despite the best efforts of Rick's electric piano, synthesiser and clavinet and David's tightly-wound, admittedly excellent guitar solo. At the end, the solo abruptly expires and the track's levels are equalised to mimic a transistor radio – the ultimate medium for any pop manager's charges, whether they wish it or not.

Backed with 'Welcome To The Machine', 'Have A Cigar' was a non-UK single. Other than soldiering to number 15 in France, it failed to trouble the charts.

### **'Wish You Were Here'** 5.40 (Waters/Gilmour)

The third relatively compact piece sandwiched between the Gog and Magog giants of 'Shine On' is far from filler. For the second time on the album, Gilmour happens upon a winning tune by accident, as he told the documentary *The Story of Wish You Were Here*:

> In the control room in Studio 3 at Abbey Road. It's something I'd been strumming at home, and Roger said 'what's that?' and we had to immediately work it up.

The guitarist is assisted by the deftest touches of piano and Minimoog, laying his own pedal steel over his ringing acoustic. He invited the violinist Stephane Grappelli, who was recording at Abbey Road, to play on the coda; the legendary jazzman is so deeply embedded in the mix that it's difficult to hear where he earned his £300 session fee. Lyrically Roger returns to alienation, dealing with the idea of absence perhaps more obliquely, though no less powerfully, than other songs on this fine set. With Roger's marriage in trouble, the record was made at a time of turmoil for the writer. 'It's about the sensations that accompany the state of not being there', Roger told Floyd biographer Mark Blake. 'To be with people whom you know aren't there anymore'. Other 'absences' are suggested: the music industry and – despite Waters' ambiguities on the subject – Syd Barrett:

> So, so you think you can tell Heaven from Hell, blue skies from pain
> Can you tell a green field from a cold steel rail? A smile from a veil?
> Do you think you can tell?
> Did they get you to trade your heroes for ghosts? Hot ashes for trees?
> Hot air for a cool breeze? Cold comfort for change?
> Did you exchange a walk-on part in the war for a lead role in a cage?
> How I wish, how I wish you were here
> We're just two lost souls swimming in a fish bowl, year after year
> Running over the same old ground. What have we found? The same old fears
> Wish you were here.

Gilmour, his own hardest taskmaster, remains happy with a song that has quietly become a Floyd anthem without the usual Big Floyd trimmings:

> There's hundreds of different ways you can do something. Some work, and some have a little bit of magic to them. The ones that do, it's obvious there's an emotional pull.

A genuine collaboration between Roger and David, 'Wish You Were Here' is one of the few Floyd songs of which the band could get away with playing an 'unplugged' version. In fact, the album's title track, its gorgeous tune wrapped up throughout in David's warm 12-string, has been a regular acoustic feature of both Gilmour's and Waters' live shows.

SingalongaFloyd might never have been Roger's intention, but 'Wish You Were Here', especially the joyous restatement at 3.16 of the main refrain, simply begs audience participation, maybe even a stadium full of waving scarves and lighters. Also telling are the many online discussion groups for whose contributors the song evokes tearful memories of departed loved ones. Populist or not, Roger can surely wish for no more poignant an accolade to one of his finest songs.

## **'Shine On You Crazy Diamond'** (parts 6-9) 12.23 (Gilmour/ Waters/Wright)

A 'One Of These Days'-style VCS3 wind segues 'Wish You Were Here' to the final piece, which chugs away from the off with Minimoog and guitar following two basses – another nod to the earlier piece. At 2.25, the band hit a bluesy swagger, Gilmour spreading his lines over the 12-bar groove like melted butter before the band return to the main vocal theme.

At first, the balance of the album's centrepiece feels like a step too far. With the exception of the main theme's reprise and a final sung verse, the album's close lopes along as a slow, meandering instrumental coda, not a million miles from the impromptu blues with which Floyd sometimes concluded live sets. It's by no means unpleasant, and perfect for the afterglow of a strenuous session of ummagumma accompanied by 'The Great Gig In The Sky'. The worst that can be said is that it's slightly directionless and anticlimactic, as if the band have twelve minutes going spare they're unsure what else to do with.

But listen again: the song's final four parts comprise a more satisfying musical journey than a cursory first hearing suggests, the changes in signature and texture so clever and subtle they go almost unnoticed. Following the final vocal chorus, Floyd slip into another lazy groove, as Rick comps jazzily on electric piano and, on clavinet, suggests The Commodores. As David picks funkily, Wright swoops down with several bars of an ethereal Minimoog, the band circle back to a stateliness more closely aligned with the main theme, then fade to black.

Opinion is as split as the song over why Floyd, or more pertinently Roger Waters, chose to carve 'Shine On' effectively into two parts divided by three shorter tracks. I couldn't possibly comment on the cynics' reminder of the doubled royalty payments; apparently the symmetry of bookending the album with two sections of the same song appealed to Roger's desire for a running theme (although none of the others liked the idea). Another view is that pre-CD listeners were encouraged to complete the entire album experience, instead of being tiresomely obliged to lift and replace a stylus. In later live performances, Floyd limited the song to Parts 1 to 5. Presumably they were unwilling to dive into a set starter of 25 minutes, even as they accepted the effect of that astounding four-note signature chiming around a packed, darkened auditorium.

## **Animals** (1977)

Personnel:
Roger Waters: bass guitar, rhythm guitar, acoustic guitar, VCS3, tape effects, vocals
David Gilmour: lead & rhythm guitars, vocals, VCS3, bass, pedal steel, tape effects
Rick Wright: organs, pianos, VCS3, clavinet, Minimoog, tape effects, vocals
Nick Mason: drums, percussion
Produced at: Britannia Row Studios, London by Pink Floyd
Engineers: Brian Humphries, Nick Griffiths
Released: 21 January 1977
Highest chart positions: France, Germany, Netherlands, Switzerland, Spain, Portugal:1, UK: 2, US: 3

Brooding in the shadows between *Wish You Were Here* and *The Wall*, *Animals* was Pink Floyd's darkest album to date. Recorded at Floyd's own new studios at Britannia Row in north London, *Animals* is a vitriolic exposition of Roger Waters' sometime-Marxist proclivities, the songs as lengthy as a Soviet bread queue, sentiments as toxic as a poison-tipped umbrella.

In a mid-1970s Britain betrayed by both left and right, rage was in the air. The rose-tinted optimism of the previous decade had collapsed into a damp midden of inflation, industrial unrest, rising unemployment, race riots and a sense of almost irretrievable social decay. Pub-rock bands Dr Feelgood, Ducks Deluxe and Kursaal Flyers were already pushing playfully retro, back-to-basics rock based on short, high-octane songs and good-time R'n'B. But by 1976 the enemy was at the gates, as the DMs and bike chains of punk began administering a sound kicking to the perceived excesses of prog.

Naturally Pink Floyd were seen by the seditionaries as part of the problem: a dining club of middle-class millionaires, their gift to society nothing more than cod-classical grandiloquence, their pomposity completely out of touch with the streets. Now the UK's national decline, combined with the personal affront of being a target for the punks' artillery, galvanised Waters into making his angriest statements yet. For without pandering to the fashion for musical arrangements as stripped-down as a ripped t-shirt (noting how other 'progressive' musicians were steadily cutting both their hair and the length of their songs), Roger decided to join up and fight the power.

It's tempting, but inaccurate, to read into *Animals* an adaptation of George Orwell's *Animal Farm*. While the novelist famously satirised the Soviet Union and Stalinism, Roger used his and Floyd's lyrical and musical eloquence mercilessly to skewer the forces of British conservatism: from corporate city-slicker rapaciousness (the 'Dogs', representing the corrupt boss class); through Mary Whitehouse's censoriousness and the right-wing authoritarianism, dressed in libertarian clothes, of Margaret Thatcher (the dogs' political masters, the equally ruthless, aspirational 'Pigs'); to the poor bloody infantry at the bottom obliged mindlessly to grin and bear the resulting damage, yet who finally rise up and wrest power from the dogs (the proletariat 'Sheep').

Roger's dystopian fury is reflected in the music. Dispatched to the outer reaches along with space rock are the early psychedelic whimsy, the experimental soundscapes, the folk-rock dalliances, the quasi-symphonic, conceptual stateliness of *Dark Side Of The Moon*, the cold grace of *Wish You Were Here*. On the coattails of punk is felt a raw, abrasive fury. The new music is not exactly pared-back – Floyd weren't about to reduce everything to inchoate, three-minute bellowing – but put in rock'n'roll terms, if *The Piper At The Gates Of Dawn* had been the optimistic spring meadow of acid and grass, *Animals* is the blocked and wintry nihilism of barbiturates and opiates. It's a downer album for a grim era.

The gloomy tenor of the times was, in turn, mirrored uncannily by the mood and makeup of the band, as Waters steadily assumed leadership. Not only did he provide *Animals*' conceptual propulsion, but he wrote every word and took sole composer's plaudits for four of the album's five tracks ('Dogs' alone being credited to Waters/Gilmour). He sang lead vocals on everything except one song he shared with David. He even claimed ownership of the famous 'flying pig' sleeve design (to the annoyance of Storm Thorgerson, who would produce no more Floyd covers during Roger's tenure). But while Gilmour's lead guitar went from strength to savage strength, Rick Wright felt marginalised. By his own admission, the keyboardist, distracted by marital problems, had nothing compositionally new to add. In truth, Rick was given less to do than usual, although his colourations and flourishes were still crucial. Rick had also tired of the bassist's confrontational manner, concerned that Floyd were becoming little more than Roger Waters and a backing band. (It was another rich Floydian irony that Roger should, allegedly, have behaved so autocratically, even as he created a concept album that hinted at a coming UK dictatorship). Neither did Nick Mason's contributions extend beyond the drum stool, although he remained, as ever, the cheerful, honest broker between Floyd's malcontents.

Among much else, and as time would prove, the brittleness of Roger's and David's relationship was informed by who did what on *Animals*. Despite the credits, Gilmour insisted to *MOJO* that he was 'the prime musical force' and that 'Roger was the motivator and lyric writer'. When Roger decided the album would be topped and tailed with two halves of a short acoustic song he'd written about his second wife, coincidentally doubling his royalties, David observed that the bassist would earn at least three times as much for a three-minute ditty broken into two as the guitarist would for a 17-minute, single-part epic.

Another blockbuster was the tale of the sleeve image. Roger briefed Hipgnosis to photograph the 'four phallic towers' of London's Battersea Power Station as 'symbols of domination'. During WWII, the imposing edifice was a handy navigational aid for Luftwaffe bombers, which would have encountered defensive barrage balloons (none shaped like a pig, presumably) positioned above such a strategic target. The bassist visualised the giant porker in the sky as 'a symbol of hope', which is surprising, given that everywhere else on *Animals* the poor creature suggests anything but.

With Roger refusing to countenance retouching, a Belgian firm was commissioned to fabricate a huge, pig-shaped helium balloon to be photographed as it floated above south London on the end of a guy rope. With bad weather forcing a two-day shoot, the porcine blimp – whom Roger dubbed Algy – slipped his moorings on the second day, drifted off into commercial and RAF flightpaths and fetched up in a cow field owned by a Kentish farmer. The aerial display – usefully, in terms of album publicity – made the national news. Despite Roger's aversion to studio tinkering, the image he finally approved was a composite of shots taken over the two sessions, the magnificent power station apparently sunlit beneath black, doom-laden stormclouds, Algy hovering hopefully. Algy, or one of his cousins, would soon be doing sterling service as a feature of Floyd's stage show.

Later, David conceded the album's lack of 'sweet, sing-along stuff', explaining that *Animals*' demographic was narrower than that of the two previous albums. 'But I think it's just as good, the quality is just as high'. Critical response for *Animals* was as mixed as for *WYWH*. *Rolling Stone* finally admitted that Floyd were no longer a space rock band; agonised Frank Rose, 'In 1968 Floyd was chanting lines like: 'Why can't we reach the sun?/ Why can't we throw the years away?' The 1977 Floyd has turned bitter and morose'. *NME* couldn't resist a trifling slice of Floyd/*Dark Side* wordplay: *Animals* was 'one of the most extreme, relentless, harrowing, downright iconoclastic hunks of music this side of the sun'. Over at *Melody Maker*, Karl Dallas took up the theme: 'Perhaps they should rename themselves Punk Floyd'. The pun was awful, but he had a point.

## **'Pigs On The Wing'** (part 1) 1.25 (Waters)

Bisecting 'Shine On You Crazy Diamond' for *Wish You Were Here* clearly gave Roger a taste for tidy bookending. 'Pigs On The Wing' could scarcely be further removed from its predecessor, though, being both 22 minutes shorter and emitting a squillion watts less electricity. While Waters wrote the song some months ahead of *Animals*' first sessions, only towards the end did he decide on its inclusion, perhaps because he felt an album full of wrathful anthropomorphs could benefit from some downhome humanity.

That's not to belittle the song's relevance to *Animals*' theme, though; 'Pigs On The Wing' (which Roger later acknowledged saved the album from ending up as 'just a kind of scream of rage') is a touching panegyric to his new wife Carolyne, without whom he dreads spending a lonely life merely waiting for something good to happen. This aligns with his assertion that on the titular airborne porkers hangs a glimmer of hope. This said, 'Pigs On The Wing' is also fighter-pilot argot for incoming bandits – surely the very antithesis of hopefulness.

Notwithstanding this typical opacity, as Roger sweetly accompanies himself on acoustic guitar, his simple serenade gives little hint of the Orwellian nightmares to come.

## **'Dogs'** 17.04 (Waters/Gilmour)

The pillow talk safely out of the way, Floyd can crack on with breakfast in the ruins. 'Got To Be Crazy', on ice since the *WYWH* sessions, is now reworded to fit Roger's *Animals* concept and extended to Floyd length, the band's flair for dynamics, not to mention some sublimely nasty David Gilmour fretwork, ensuring 'Dogs' feels much shorter than its ostensibly gargantuan 17 minutes.

'Dogs', along with much of the album, has been compared with heavy metal and with punk. This is wrong on both counts, although the latter is nearer the mark. With exceptions, metal uses volume, power, distortion and speed to make its creator's point; the medium is the only message, all else subsumed by extended guitar shredding, simple, bass-heavy four-to-the-floor rhythms and busy, jackhammer percussion. But while the punks were no shrinking violets when it came to rowdiness, there was no mistaking the concise way in which they expressed their angst. Waters may have needed more than three minutes to make his case, but his righteous fury is plain. And even if some felt Roger's principles to be compromised by his wealth and his comfortable corner of the dinosaur park, the new insurrectionists would surely have approved of his targeting.

'Dogs' begins with David's strummed acoustic guitar and Rick's Hammond, the thin, ominous swelling suggesting the ethereal, Farfisa-derived tones of the band's early records. Quickly Gilmour's lead vocal (he toggles the singing with Roger) arrives with Waters' lyrics, astringent enough to strip the paint from the Stock Exchange door. The point of 'Dogs', the grim flavour of the entire album, glares up at the listener immediately; Roger evokes the cynical predator in his club tie, with his arsenal of spreadsheets and market forecasts, conditioned to hunt and kill as efficiently as a feral mastiff:

> You got to be crazy, gotta have a real need
> Gotta sleep on your toes, and when you're on the street
> You got to be able to pick out the easy meat with your eyes closed
> And then moving in silently, down wind and out of sight
> You got to strike when the moment is right without thinking.

A portrait emerges of a ruthless, alpha backstabber, at first high on his own genius for corporate piracy, later uncertain of his continued ascendancy in this cutthroat world. Like an ageing gunslinger faced with younger, hungrier rivals, who'll have his legs as readily as he'd had others', he finds himself with 'one eye looking over your shoulder/You know it's going to get harder, and harder, and harder as you get older'. Ultimately this once inviolable privateer is all alone, down south, dying of cancer, his survival instincts no longer able to prevent being 'dragged down by the stone.'

It's hard not to share Waters' vindictive glee as he proposes a dark fate, one that thrusting young *Apprentice* competitors might be wise to heed. Roger may be Floyd's resident conscience, but David seems to share his lyricist's ire, slicing into 'Dogs' with three solos of varying degrees of acuity. Is the intensity of his playing due to the nascent hostility between guitarist and bassist? Was he making a point, even subconsciously? If so, it spans the album. Gilmour was less a political animal than Waters; perhaps this was just superb method acting, the guitarist demonstrating an uncanny ability to precisely temper an attack; if he's not as affronted as Roger by the running dogs of capitalism, we'd never know it.

The unusual tone of the first solo derives from Leslie-style rotating Yamaha speakers; later, David duets with himself, the song slowing to acoustic guitar, electric piano and SFX of dogs barking distantly in a post-industrial wasteland (partially decommissioned in 1975, Battersea Power Station once generated 509Mw of electricity and had been a major south London employer; the area is also famous for its dogs' home). In his third solo, the song's subject on the cusp of losing control, Gilmour is suddenly Norman Bates in the motel shower, slashing out coldly and apparently uncontrollably, in reality absolutely on top of his game.

At the end, we can hear Waters shaking with a cold fury as he peels off a list of where his subject has gone awry. Oddly, Roger sings of how his protagonist 'was trained not to spit in the fan'. That he'll soon be doing something similar, as Floyd tour *Animals* in Canada, is surely pure coincidence.

## **'Pigs (Three Different Ones)'** 11.22 (Waters)

Porcine grumbling greets a hurdy-gurdy figure from Rick's Hammond and a melodic bassline, pierced by David's stabbing guitar. A crash from Nick, and we're off into another Waters polemic against society's elders but not necessarily betters.

Spitting invective and sparing none his fury, Roger (taking lead vocals throughout) assigns a verse each to the three pigs. The first is an archetypal fat cat (bad pun intended), 'head down in the pig bin' and with the 'pig stain on your fat chin'. The second is a 'fucked up old hag', allegedly representing the then Leader of H. M. Opposition, who was awaiting democratic elevation to Prime Minister. To many disaffected voters after she became Tory leader in 1975, Margaret Thatcher felt like a breath of fresh air; only astute political observers, of whom Roger was one, had any inkling of the social devastation to come. The third pig is obvious from the line 'Hey you Whitehouse/Ha ha, charade you are' – the Mary of that name, the veteran campaigner for national moral rectitude, for whom read intolerant, buttoned-up, right-wing busybody.

Although in Waters' world the dogs and pigs represent two discrete societal strata, events and social adjustments since would imply there's really little distinction between them. The 'well-heeled big wheel' of the first verse may as easily be one of the corporate marauders from 'Dogs'. On Thatcher's watch, the patrician, one-nation brand of Conservatism was seized by sharp-suited professionals, monetarist ideologues and unscrupulous city-slickers, the modest social backgrounds of the 'estate agent class' mirroring that of the Iron

Lady herself. Here again, dogs and pigs feel effectively like the same animal, with neither owning superiority over, nor responsibility for, the other. Mother Thatcher may be the despised target of 'Pigs', but her bastard children are all over 'Dogs'.

'Pigs (Three Different Ones)' is almost relentlessly violent, but never wanting for judicious shafts of light where needed. At 1.50 and various points thereafter, Nick offers a cowbell – yes, a cowbell – which metronomic thunking carries under the first verse and on into David's switchblade guitar. There are more piggy grunts, growing in anguish. The band pick up on the discord, marching stolidly for the second stanza, the pigsty now so tormented you start wondering if an abattoir's opened next door. Before the third verse, with Rick's smooth Hammond underlay and all hell breaking loose above it, there's a classic Floydian false climax; for at 7.10, we're back where we started, with the melodic solo bassline and David's perforating guitar. By the time Roger is done deflating puritan arrogance, it's as if everyone's had enough, Gilmour's stunning, screaming lead ushering to the fade. It's shattering stuff – but the best is still to come.

## **'Sheep'** 10.24 (Waters)

If Mary Whitehouse wasn't bruised enough from the assault and battery of 'Pigs', the champion of Old Testament values would surely have been calling down the Tribulation on 'Sheep' like a vengeful witchfinder. Waters takes his irreverent sledgehammer to the 23rd Psalm, its spoken recitation so heavily treated (by a Vocoder or similar talkbox) it's as if a Sunday sermon is being given by a Klingon high priest. It's also very funny and worth reproducing here:

> The Lord is my shepherd, I shall not want/He makes me down to lie
> Through pastures green he leadeth me the silent waters by
> With bright knives he releaseth my soul
> He maketh me to hang on hooks in high places
> He converteth me to lamb cutlets
> For lo, he hath great power and great hunger
> When cometh the day we lowly ones
> Through quiet reflection and great dedication/Master the art of karate
> Lo, we shall rise up/And then we'll make the bugger's eyes water.

Despite the impiety of this mid-section, Roger is not tilting at religion per se. It's just that its certainties get in the way – not to mention its supply of a few convenient sheep references – as he gleefully tells of how the ovine ones rise up to take the repressive dogs by the canines and assume control of this broken society.

'Sheep' (formerly 'Raving And Drooling') begins with a doleful portrayal of the herd harmlessly passing its time in the grassland, 'only dimly aware of a certain unease in the air'. That disquiet, of course, is caused by the lurking pack of hounds, the sheep their sitting targets, evisceration their sole reason for being. Yet the natural order is about to be upset, as the Lord our Shepherd releases the sheep from their servitude and the herd falls mercilessly upon the pack.

Roger told *Melody Maker* of his sense that something bad was about to happen in England:

> [as] it did with the riots in Brixton and Toxteth… and it will happen again. There are too many of us in the world and we treat each other badly. There aren't enough things, products, to go round. If we're persuaded it's important to have them, that we're nothing without them, the people without them are going to get angry.

The pitchfork-wielding proletariat might elicit more sympathy than the doomed boss class. But with no hint of what might replace the current tyranny apart from anarchic chaos or the rise of a single, all-powerful dictator, there's no happy ending to this scenario.

The music matches the bloodthirsty sentiments perfectly. Following the intro's soft SFX bleating beneath Rick's beautiful, jazzy electric piano and Roger's insistent bassline, Nick gives a little roll on his snare and the band kick up in earnest. The song rips along like a rabid pit-bull loose among a herd of Merinos, pulsing its way through swirling Hammond organ and Gilmour's scalpel-sharp guitar. After the middle eight and the parodic Gospel according to St Drogo, the mad sugar-rush of conquest emboldens Floyd, like the sheep themselves, to still more ferocity. 'Sheep' finally expires with the album's most liberating moment: at 8.12, David Gilmour tears unstoppably through the dying embers of the song with a devastating descending motif. It's a flash of classic Pink Floyd release.

'The creatures outside looked from pig to man, and from man to pig, and from pig to man again', wrote George Orwell at the end of *Animal Farm*, 'but already it was impossible to say which was which'. With some adjustment for species, Pink Floyd are bang on the money.

## **'Pigs On The Wing'** (part 2) 1.25 (Waters)

The second part of Roger's paean to his wife finds the writer happily ensconced with Carolyne and, cheekily, 'somewhere safe to bury my bone'. As he enjoys the comfort of family, here the pigs represent only a threat from which to shelter. But as with his previous authorly contradictions, such as the mixed, light/shade messages of *Dark Side Of The Moon*, perhaps Roger is happy to allow baked-in ambiguities to convey dual meanings – a classic case of a writer asking listeners to make of it all what they will. But if this tranquil ending to Pink Floyd's most brutal album yet suggests Roger has laid his personal demons, the next record will prove otherwise.

# The Wall (1979)

Personnel:
Roger Waters: bass guitar, rhythm guitar, acoustic guitar, synthesisers, vocals
David Gilmour: lead guitar, rhythm guitar, vocals, synthesisers, bass
Rick Wright: organs, pianos, synthesisers, Wurlitzer, vocals
Nick Mason: drums, percussion
Fred Mandel: Hammond organ (on 'In The Flesh')
Jeff Porcaro: drums (on 'Mother', 'Bring The Boys Back Home')
Bob Ezrin: keyboards (on 'Mother', 'One of my Turns', 'Nobody Home', 'The Show Must Go On', 'Waiting for the Worms', 'The Trial')
Lee Ritenour: guitar (on 'One of my Turns', 'Comfortably Numb')
Joe DiBlasi: classical guitar (on 'Is There Anybody Out There?')
Bobbye Hall: percussion (on 'Run Like Hell')
Frank Marocco: concertina (on 'Outside The Wall')
Trevor Veitch: mandolin (on 'Outside The Wall')
Larry Williams: clarinet (on 'Outside The Wall')
Bruce Johnston, Toni Tennille, Joe Chemay, Stan Farber, Jim Haas, Jon Joyce: backing vocals (on 'The Show Must Go On', 'In The Flesh', 'Waiting For The Worms')
Islington Green School students: vocals (on 'Another Brick In The Wall, Part 2')
Michael Kamen/New York Symphony Orchestra (on 'Nobody Home', 'Vera', 'Bring The Boys Back Home', 'Comfortably Numb', 'Stop', 'The Trial')
New York City Opera: vocals (on 'Bring The Boys Back Home')
Produced at: Britannia Row Studios, London; Superbear, France; Studio Miraval, France; CBS, New York; The Producers' Workshop, Los Angeles; Cherokee, Los Angeles by Bob Ezrin, Roger Waters, David Gilmour, James Guthrie
Engineers: Brian Humphries, Nick Griffiths, Patrice Quef, Brian Christian, Rick Hart, John McClure
Released: 30 November 1979
Highest chart positions: France, US, Canada, W Germany, Netherlands, Sweden, Norway: 1, UK: 3

By 1979, bankruptcy was looming over the planet's biggest rock group. Pink Floyd should have seen it coming; a firm of accountants – its directors could have been prototypes for 'Dogs' – had invested much of the band's hard-earned in ventures doomed to fail, from skateboards to pizza parlours to a chequebook printing scheme. The firm, Norton Warburg, was eventually found to have trousered a chunk of change for themselves from Floyd's missing £2.5 million. Already in hock to the Inland Revenue at a time when the UK government was levying supertax at a pipsqueaking 83 per cent, Floyd were advised they should keep their heads down and come up with a new album forthwith.

A record had been in the wind since July 1977, following a mid-performance incident at Montreal's Olympic Stadium on the final date of the In The Flesh tour. His patience sapped by an 80,000-strong crowd becoming rowdier by the minute, Roger Waters spat at an obnoxious fan. Though he was later contrite, this was a prime example of the bassist's disaffection with mega-shows and the now irrevocable loss, as he put it, 'of intimacy of connection between the audience and the band.' Added to issues surrounding society, war, lunacy, his late father, Syd Barrett and the recording industry, the gulf Roger now perceived between the thinking man's rock group and fans for whom Pink Floyd were merely a soundtrack to stadium-sized aerobics classes would fuel a concept piece of epic proportions.

On the arrival of an idea, Roger's first call would normally have been to his Floyd brethren. But now he felt no one in the band could muster sufficient empathy. 'Dave's just not interested', said Roger. 'Rick was pretty closed down at that point, and Nick would be happy to listen, but he's still more interested in his racing cars'. Enter Bob Ezrin, suggested by Carolyne (a former employee of the New York-based Canadian) and highly rated for his production work with Peter Gabriel, Alice Cooper and Lou Reed. Hooking up during the *In The Flesh* tour, Roger told Bob of his abiding worries of alienation and an inescapable wish to erect a wall between band and fans; indeed, of his worries about the barriers that potentially exist within and between us all. 'I recall saying flippantly, well, why don't you?' Ezrin noted. 'Eighteen months later, I got a call asking me to come to [Waters'] home to talk about working together on this project called *The Wall*'. After hearing Roger's primitive first stab of 90-odd minutes, Bob agreed to co-produce and, in due course, reorder the bassist's early, somewhat chaotic thoughts into a 40-page script.

Floyd were now brought aboard to consider two infant Waters pieces. The first was a lengthy demo, which the band declined as 'too personal' and would become Roger's first solo album proper, *The Pros And Cons Of Hitch Hiking*. The second was the monumental *Bricks In The Wall*: the working title for a concept album to be structured, this time just like *S. F. Sorrow* and *Tommy*, as a personal narrative arc. The story concerns Pink, a jaded composite of Syd Barrett and Roger himself, who feels abandoned after the wartime death of his father. A rebelliousness instilled by vindictive authority, embodied by his over-protective mother and his tyrannical schoolmasters, leads Pink to become a rock star. But with success and adulation come the inevitable infidelity and drug abuse, while Pink's compounding delusions of grandeur are eventually crystallised as he heads a fascist dictatorship far worse than the repression he originally rebelled against. Symbolising isolation and abandonment, the titular wall is a protective metaphor with which Pink mentally surrounds himself, its bricks the events which inform his life and his madness. The idea grew on David Gilmour, who said for the release in 2000 of *Is There Anybody Out There?*, a live version of *The Wall*:

> Building a wall between ourselves and the audience was a striking metaphor for the intimacy we had lost as a stadium band. And though I believe that we were still delivering to the majority of fans – despite the noise and conditions

> – the loss of control over our environment definitely troubled me. It obviously got to Roger a lot more.

From April 1979, Floyd decamped to Superbear (the studio in France where Gilmour and Wright had both made solo albums), to CBS in New York and The Producers' Workshop in Los Angeles. Stints at their own Britannia Row facility were left undeclared lest the taxman came to call. Infamously the sessions were potholed with numerous Floyd-shaped problems, as early tensions arose between all concerned: Ezrin was persistently late to the studio due to the producer's wish to avoid Roger, who he was now finding brittle and punctilious; James Guthrie was hired to complement Ezrin at the desk, whereupon Roger neglected to advise either man that he wouldn't be the album's sole producer; Nick Mason put down his drum parts in early sessions in order to bounce from Superbear and spend more time with his Ferrari. Most ominously, Roger's already shaky relationship with Rick Wright now hit the skids, mainly over Rick's overall listlessness and Ezrin's production credits; the keyboardist believed that these should have been his, even though his input was negligible. The rift went nuclear; on pain of scrapping the entire album – and with it any foreseeable escape from a baying Revenue – Waters obtained Gilmour's and Mason's sanction to dismiss Wright from Pink Floyd. Roger later re-hired Rick for live shows, for which the now-salaried sideman ironically earned more than his production-stretched employers.

With Floyd in disarray during the making of the biggest project of their careers, it was unsurprising that Waters should summon help. Hired guns included orchestral conductor Michael Kamen, Toto's serial sessioneer Jeff Porcaro (depping for Nick in places where Floyd's drummer feared to tread), guitarist Lee Ritenour and singers Toni Tennille and sometime-Beach Boy Bruce Johnston. The Beach Boys themselves were pencilled, but nothing came of it. (Toni, velvet-voiced frontperson with the relentlessly MOR The Captain & Tennille, was pleasantly surprised when Floyd proved urbane and civilised employers – far from the brain-fracked English stoners the Alabaman half-expected).

The arrival of heavy friends suggested the new album was as far from a group effort as Floyd had yet travelled. And Gilmour's relatively modest input while Mason and Wright were missing in (in)action is telling. Those whose tastes run to 1930s Berlin decadence might disagree, but *The Wall* contains relatively few archetypally Floydian showstoppers, although there is still much superb music. *Dark Side Of The Moon* was the result of four musicians pulling genuinely together; to remove any one of the core quartet would have fatally compromised Floyd's most coherent work. *Wish You Were Here* and *Animals*, conceptually Roger's, profited massively from David's musicianly instincts for the emotionally liberating, writ plain on songs such as 'Shine On You Crazy Diamond' and 'Sheep'. But more than any Floyd album to this point, *The Wall* is the creature of Roger Waters: a brilliant artist, writer and conceptual helm, but no match for Gilmour as an arranger and instrumentalist. Nick does his usual diligent job, while Rick is almost invisible, the organist's fears that Floyd might become Roger's backing band apparently realised. Gilmour is the lone impediment to the bassist's dominion, his principal contribution to *The Wall*, 'Comfortably Numb', standing proudly with any big Floyd set-piece.

*The Wall* is undoubtedly Floyd's most exhaustingly dense and complex construction. Conversely, its sleeve is the least cluttered. Hipgnosis, with whom Roger had fallen out over the credits to *Animals*, were sidelined for Gerald Scarfe. The edgy illustrator created a stark, white wall, the artists' and album titles written inside by Scarfe in his trademark inky scrawl and scenes from the story depicted as bricks in the gatefold. Nick and Rick suffered the indignity of having their names left off the original credits, although both were restored in time.

*The Wall* is Floyd's eleventh album and second most successful, its sales of more than 30 million only outdone by *Dark Side Of The Moon*. Some offcuts would rise again in 1983 for Floyd's next album (and last with Waters) *The Final Cut*. Like *Wish You Were Here*, *The Wall* has gained plaudits with age; even *Rolling Stone* deigned to honour it in consecutive lists of all-time greatest albums. The elaborate stage setups devised to promote the record in concert became the stuff of rock legend, while in 1982, *The Wall* was adapted for a partially-animated feature film (starring Bob Geldof as Pink) by director Alan Parker and the perennially-involved Waters. And as if Roger needed to remind anyone whence it all came, from 2010 to 2013, his own tour of *The Wall* raked in more than any other show by a solo musician.

The album realised three singles: 'Another Brick In The Wall, part 2' c/w 'One Of My Turns' (which topped the UK and US charts and, straddling Christmas 1979 and New Year 1980, famously was number one in two decades at once), 'Run Like Hell' c/w 'Don't Leave Me Now' and 'Comfortably Numb' c/w 'Hey You'. While Floyd would spend a small fortune on the stage sets, it's safe to say that *The Wall* and its ancillary offerings went a long way to re-upping the band's coffers.

Nb: the details below refer to the original album tracks. Changes made for the subsequent movie script – such as 'When The Tigers Broke Free' (the first song in the film, held over from the album but included on *The Final Cut*) – are not referred to except where clarification is necessary.

## **'In The Flesh?'** 3.16 (Waters)

Following a brief snatch of a melody mournfully redolent of soldiers returning from the front – its apparently unfinished nature is resolved at the end of the album – crashing block chords open *The Wall* on a song whose title Roger lifted from the 1977 tour that sparked the whole idea. 'In The Flesh?' is actually a flashback. The band take no prisoners as the bombastic theme gives way to Pink, a successful though troubled rock star, advising his fans that 'the warm thrill of confusion/that space cadet glow' hides something darker. At the song's end, the big-production rock show's ritualistic pyrotechnics, overlaid with the sounds of military ordnance and the terrifying siren of a Stuka dive-bomber, cause Pink/Roger to recall the death of his father at Anzio in 1944.

*The Wall*'s stage shows would be opened by a 'surrogate' Floyd. In 1980 the temporary replacements, who performed 'In The Flesh?', 'Goodbye Blue Sky' and part of 'Run Like Hell', comprised Snowy White (guitar), Andy Bown (bass), Peter Wood (keys) and Willie Wilson (drums), each wearing a latex 'lifemask' to represent his equivalent Floyd. Qualifying the first song's querying title, Roger asserted that whoever were onstage was immaterial as long as they delivered the goods for the baying arena audiences (who were usually too far from their heroes to permit accurate identification anyway).

### **'The Thin Ice'** 2.27 (Waters)

A baby's cry and a mother's slightly soured lullaby, sung by David, precede Pink's ruminations on his birth and early childhood. 'The Thin Ice' is what lies ahead; there but for the grace of God go we, as we're obliged to navigate unknown terrors from which only the most tenuous circumstances may protect us. Following the warnings, delivered by Roger's plaintive vocal against Rick's insistent piano, the band crash back in, as heavy, ponderous and immovable as an iced-in armoured division.

### **'Another Brick In The Wall, part 1'** 3.11 (Waters)

To the familiar tune, slowed for maximum menace, punctuated by Roger's throbbing bass and David's skittering guitar, Pink explicitly references his father flying fatefully away to war and wonders: 'Daddy what d'ya leave behind for me?' It's here that Pink begins mentally to shut himself off behind a metaphorical wall, its first brick the doleful news of his father's death.

### **'The Happiest Days Of Our Lives'** 1.46 (Waters)

Now at school, Pink is bullied by sadistic masters, as Roger's teacherly, *faux*-Scottish admonishments scream in, accompanied by the ominous sound of a helicopter: an aircraft freighted with more Orwellian malice than any other. The title is, of course, hugely ironic; the term is an ancient shibboleth, almost certainly concocted by adults, to convince children that they'll never again enjoy a world so free of care. With the cementing of the next brick, the reality for Pink is very different – as it is for so many damaged adults once forced to tolerate the hair-shirts, cold showers and beatings inherent to an obsolete English schools' system. This short track merges perfectly into 'Another Brick… pt2'; many radio presenters would play it as an intro to the big hit as a matter of course.

### **'Another Brick In The Wall, part 2'** 3.59 (Waters)

Pink Floyd go disco! 'It wasn't my idea', David assured *MOJO*, 'It was Bob's'. Back in New York, Ezrin had worked next door to Nile Rodgers and Bernie Edwards, whose characteristic disco-drums-and-hi-hat rhythms were propelling monster floor-fillers by Chic, Sister Sledge, Sheila & B. Devotion and, later, David Bowie. The insistent sonics fired the future Floyd producer's imagination. 'When I got to England and I started listening to 'Another Brick' that beat kept playing in my head', Bob said. With his certainty that Floyd had a serious hit on their hands gently rebuffed by the band ('we don't do singles, so fuck you'), the producer toyed with the tapes in Floyd's absence and hired 23 kids from Islington Green school, close to Britannia Row, to add the famous vocal flourishes. On hearing the results, the band were won over: 'It was great', Roger said, 'exactly what I expected', while David confirmed, 'it doesn't in the end not sound like Pink Floyd'. And so the band who didn't do singles released a single; the rest, as they say, is economics.

'The education I went through in boys' grammar school in the '50s was very controlling and demanded rebellion', Roger said in 2009. 'The teachers were weak and therefore easy targets. 'Another Brick' is meant to be a rebellion against errant government, against people who have power over you, who are wrong'. Pink's (or Roger's) memories of lifetime milestones, among them teacher cruelty and the disciplinary torments of schooldays, are some of the metaphorical bricks of which the wall is built.

Naturally, the Whitehouses of Britain had a collective fit of the vapours over the song's apparent knock at education. Equally naturally they got it wrong. Far from criticising the idea of learning and intellectual training, Waters attacks the 'thought control' and 'dark sarcasm' that have permeated the classroom, and the begowned, bullying martinets charged with keeping young minds and bodies in check: ideas that readily extrapolate to a critique of broader societal repression.

For the teacher's bellowed rebukes, Roger whistles up another dubious Scots brogue. The song's assault is pressed home by Scarfe's animated promo video, in which the teacher feeds kids into a meat grinder (producing worms, which appear in frightening strength later in the album) before shape-shifting into a malevolent hammer. The same implement eventually takes a still more worrying turn as it represents the jackbooted march of fascism. All these dark conceits are papered over, perhaps for the sake of hit potential and jiveability, by an irresistible dance beat and some funky picking from David, who spoons out a glorious solo at 2.10 that's pure liquid honey.

## **'Mother'** 5.32 (Waters)

Roger was at pains to insist that he was not here questioning his own mother, a CND activist and, interestingly, a teacher. In fact, this deceptively gentle song interrogates the broader idea that excessively maternal instincts can inhibit a young person's development. Now an adult, Pink trowels a third brick into the wall to dwell on repressive matronly overprotection. But he gains no coherent answers to his most pressing enquiries:

> Mother, do you think they'll drop the bomb?
> Mother, do you think they'll like this song?

Mother, do you think they'll try to break my balls?
Ooh, aah, mother, should I build the wall?
Mother, should I run for president?
Mother, should I trust the government?
Mother, will they put me in the firing line?
Ooh, aah, is it just a waste of time?

Instead, she seeks to shield her son from the world's ills with a portcullis of safeguards whose levers she alone controls. Stifled by the pseudo-kindness – the best that can be said is that she is naïve and that she means well, the worst is that she employs her cloying benevolence only to feel better about herself – Pink is starved of the motivation to build resistance by acting off his own bat. The lyric hints at Pink seeking motherly approval for a partner, before we discover that 'Mama's gonna check out all your girlfriends for you/Mama won't let anyone dirty get through'. Roger's vocal, accompanied by David's excellent lead guitar, Jeff Porcaro's drums and Ezrin's piano and ethereal organ, is heartbreaking.

### **'Goodbye Blue Sky'** 2.45 (Waters)

'Look mummy, there's an aeroplane up in the sky', exclaims a young voice – actually Roger's son, Harry – as pastoral birdsong is obliterated by an approaching flight of Heinkel IIIs. 'Goodbye Blue Sky' captures perfectly a childhood blackened by the London Blitz, the carefree 'blue sky' to which every youngster is entitled here destroyed by human hand. Sung by David, the song begins the original vinyl's second side. 'Goodbye Blue Sky' reminds us of the fears and tribulations of Pink's upbringing: 'The flames are all long gone/But the pain lingers on'. The intro is passive/aggressive menace itself: the chirping blackbird, the incoming bombers, David's gentle acoustic guitar and a frightening synthesiser theme courtesy of Roger or Rick.

### **'Empty Spaces'** 2.10 (Waters)

For such a short, transitional song – albeit one stuffed full of instrumental threat – 'Empty Spaces' has provoked inordinate speculation over its meaning. This is mainly because of the lyrics: 'Congratulations, you have just discovered the secret message. Send your answer to Ol' Pink, care of the Funny Farm, Chalfont…'; and, shortly after, 'Roger, Carolyne's on the phone'. Both replay backwards on the record – thus requiring all manner of stylus-threatening stratagems to decode – and were impishly included by Roger as a joke aimed at those listeners who revel in seeking significance where none exists. This said, whatever's conveyed by the words that *are* intelligible is teasingly ambiguous, suggesting that Pink is preparing to complete the wall but is yet uncertain with what. The song was originally meant to have been followed by the similar 'What Shall We Do Now' – replacing 'Empty Spaces' in the film – clarifying the vacuum, otherwise occupied by meaningless consumerism, now sucking the normalcy from Pink's confused mind. (So late was the excision of 'What Shall We Do Now' that its lyrics were still included on the early sleeves).

## **'Young Lust'** 3.25 (Waters/Gilmour)

Pink is now grown, married and a rock star. On tour in the US, he seeks to temper the tedium of life on the road by playing away with 'a dirty woman'. He's not alone in his betrayal: back home the wife has similarly strayed. The song's impudent rock'n'roll strut is interrupted when Pink discovers spousal disloyalty by way of a phone call. This is answered by an unknown male voice, and given added Zappa-esque *verité* via the sampling of a genuine US telephone exchange operator. (Whether the functionary ever learned of her important contribution and sought royalties isn't known). 'Young Lust' is rockaboogie Floyd, sung by Gilmour in the tradition of *More*'s 'The Nile Song', with a suitably solid, powerhouse rhythm, confidently heavy drumming from Mason and a diamond-cutting lead solo from the guitarist. Roger later explained that the song was 'meant to be a pastiche of any young rock and roll band out on the road.'

## **'One of My Turns'** 3.41 (Waters)

More Zappa-style vox-pops accompany Pink's return to his apartment, a groupie in tow. His guest gets little action – at least of the sort she seeks – as the star collapses in front of the TV to watch *The Dambusters*. For by now, even sexual release fails to arrest the torment of Pink's boredom, and the feeling that his life has become meaningless:

> Day after day, love turns grey, like the skin of a dying man
> Night after night, we pretend it's all right
> But I have grown older and you have grown colder
> And nothing is very much fun any more
> And I can feel one of my turns coming on
> I feel cold as a razor blade, tight as a tourniquet
> Dry as a funeral drum.

As Pink finally cracks and trashes the hotel room, we hear the crashing evidence of the damage that attends one of his 'bad days'. But this is more sinister than casual, by-rote violence, or Keith Moon's cheeky, cherry-bombs-behind-the-telly rockist excess; Pink's belligerence is an expression of unformed nihilism, damning evidence of his ongoing mental collapse. His raging fit scares his friend from the room, while the music ups the ante from a solemn, synthesiser-driven vehicle for Pink's fatalistic, up-close-to-the-mic musings to another blazing hard-rock attack. Choice of *The Dambusters* was probably not accidental; Group Captain Leonard Cheshire led the dambusting 617 Squadron (although he did not fly on the Ruhr dams sortie) and founded the charity for which Roger would perform *The Wall* in Berlin in

1990. The connection between a dam and a wall is also unlikely to have been by chance.

### **'Don't Leave Me Now'** 4.08 (Waters)

'Don't Leave Me Now' is either the craven blubbering of a privileged, self-pitying pop star, or a plea for understanding from a damaged man who is genuinely hurting. The cleverness of the song is that it is both. Pink's words smack of self-serving insincerity:

> Don't say it's the end of the road/Remember the flowers I sent
> I need you babe
> To put through the shredder/In front of my friends
> Ooh babe, don't leave me now
> How could you go, when you know how I need you?
> To beat to a pulp on a Saturday night.

Trapped in his room, Pink's concern is not for the relationship with his wife, still less for her happiness. It's all about him and how things might look to his fans and peers. The pathos is bogus, evidence of little more than entitled narcissism, as if a floral tribute compensates for the beatings, betrayals and macho ill-treatment. Yet it's impossible to hear Roger's vocal without the slightest feelings of sympathy, even if they're cut with an icy sense of *schadenfreude*; it's too easy to judge from a distance others' misfortune, self-inflicted or not.

At the beginning, Roger is accompanied only by synth, bass and mournfully low piano notes. But at 3.06, the band play the song out on a stately coda that could have come from *Animals*. 'Don't Leave Me Now' is an affecting *crie de coeur*, almost a primal scream, revealing a sorrowful desolation that might be as heartrendingly biographical as anything on the album.

### **'Another Brick In The Wall, part 3'** 1.18 (Waters)

His protective wall almost completed, Pink's sense of rejection and borderline schizophrenia reach a new pitch. He craves solitude, eliminating from his thoughts his mother, his wife, the rock-star acolytes, maybe even the 'drugs to calm me'. Increasingly solipsistic, he's 'seen the writing on the wall' and needs nothing, contemptuously dismissing everything in his past, good and bad, as mere bricks in the wall. As Roger said in 1979, Pink is 'convincing himself really that his isolation is a desirable thing. That's the moment of catharsis'. The band retread the familiar 'Another Brick' theme, but in a downbeat and more subdued manner than on Part 2.

### **'Goodbye Cruel World'** 1.16 (Waters)

The wall now complete, Pink isolates himself from all human intercourse. Featuring only Roger's eyewateringly plaintive vocal, his bass and Rick's synthesiser, 'Goodbye Cruel World' would have been a natural end to the album, leaving the suspicion that Pink was literally about to check out, and at his own hand. But Roger has a lot more to say.

### **'Hey You'** 4.40 (Waters)

Roger had wanted 'Is There Anybody Out There' as *The Wall*'s first track but was vetoed by Ezrin; the producer felt the saga would no longer make sense within four sides of vinyl, obliging some late track-shuffling. This confusion over where 'Hey You' should be placed prised an interesting admission from Waters: 'I thought about it and in a couple of minutes I realised that 'Hey You' could conceptually go anywhere.'

On the understanding that a flashback, or even a flash-forward, could theoretically appear at any point in a narrative, this would be a fair comment. As it is, 'Hey You' couldn't be more appropriately sited, as a remorseful Pink, his wall now complete, starts to question his reasons for building it in the first place. 'Be careful what you wish for' is the (albeit reductive) message, for Pink's self-imposed confinement has only compounded his feelings of alienation. Desperately he calls out to the world, but so high has he built the wall that his pleas cannot be heard. 'At the end of 'Hey You' he makes this cry for help', Roger said, 'but it's too late.'

'Hey You' begins quietly, as Pink enjoins anyone who can hear to give him a pass. With the apparently optimistic 'Hey, you!/Would you help me to carry the stone?/Open your heart, I'm coming home', the melody line from 'Another Brick' comes in hard and heavy, markedly slower than the original, with Gilmour's dog-whistle soloing over the top. The song is a tour de force for the guitarist; arranged to take full dynamic advantage of light and shade, perfectly complementing Waters' superb lyrics, 'Hey You' would be among the few songs from *The Wall* to remain on Floyd's setlist following Waters' departure.

Now a third-party observer takes up Pink's plight:

> But it was only fantasy.
> The wall was too high as you can see.
> No matter how he tried he could not break free.
> And the worms ate into his brain.

Other than Scarfe's visuals for 'Another Brick... Part 2', this is *The Wall*'s first reference to the worms, for which read decay, the putrefaction of a soul. Roger told *MOJO* the song was about the dissolution of his first marriage. 'All that misery and pain... It's a complete disaster, especially if you're someone like I was ... Hopeless, really, I could do nothing but go foetal and weep.'

### **'Is There Anybody Out There?'** 2.44 (Waters)

Alone in his hotel room watching *Gunsmoke* on TV, Pink is increasingly desperate to be heard. Musically the main interest lies in the classical guitar part from 1.24, following Roger's plea 'Is there anybody out there?' – he repeats it four times, sounding at once aggressive and resigned – along with subtle, 10cc-ish synths. Apparently, Gilmour created the dismembered seagulls, redolent of 'Echoes', on his Stratocaster with the wah-wah pedal connections reversed. The Spanish guitar is performed by Joe DiBlasi; David admitted that, though able to play the piece using a leather pick, he was unhappy with the fingerstyling thought more appropriate. This exquisite, Michael Kamen-supervised melody, in its setting of delicate synths and violin, provides the perfect dynamic counterpoint to Pink's agonising appeals.

### **'Nobody Home'** 3.26 (Waters)

Now thoroughly depressed, Pink wallows in self-pity, turning for phoney comfort to onanism and inanimate, soulless ephemera:

> I've got a little black book with my poems in
> I've got a bag with a toothbrush and a comb in
> When I'm a good dog they sometimes throw me a bone in
> I got elastic bands keeping my shoes on
> Got those swollen hand blues.
> I got thirteen channels of shit on the TV to choose from.

There's even a fleeting glimpse of Syd Barrett, as Waters unhappily sings of 'the obligatory Hendrix perm' and the 'favourite satin shirt'. Few in 1979, and certainly not Pink Floyd, were still swanning around in silks and mock 'fros, but the styles were everywhere back in '67, the same year in which a satin-clad, bepermed Syd was fronting Floyd even as he steadily decoupled from reality. Beyond Barrett, 'Nobody Home' is a portrait of the archetypal pop-culture burnout, similarly essayed by everyone from Tom Petty to Neil Young to Lou Reed; indeed, an overall sense of Broadway-ish drama recalls Lou's 1973 post-Velvets concept album *Berlin*, as well as Alice Cooper's *Billion Dollar Babies* (both produced, as it goes, by Bob Ezrin).

For the first time on *The Wall* we hear the strings and brass of the New York Symphony Orchestra: a placemarker for where startlingly new musical textures are introduced; perhaps to heighten Pink's dramatic decline, maybe even to signal a slow departure from the rock'n'roll by which the star has plied his trade and been brought to his current impasse.

### **'Vera'** 1.35 (Waters)

More sampled voices and explosions, this time from the 1969 movie *Battle Of Britain*, open this nostalgic homage to Britain's WWII 'Forces Sweetheart', the entertainer Vera Lynn. 'Vera' denotes Pink's return to his roots and memories of his childhood and his father's fate. Against Kamen's lush strings and brass and Gilmour's arpeggiated acoustic guitar, Roger paraphrases Lynn's famous 'We'll Meet Again': a song which, in promising that 'we'll meet again some sunny day', effectively represented a betrayal; for except in death, there was to be no such comforting reunion. Floyd had considered covering 'We'll Meet Again' for *The Wall*'s first track but were possibly dissuaded by copyright issues.

### **'Bring The Boys Back Home'** 1.21 (Waters)

Continuing his regressive journey, Pink imagines the civilian crowds demanding the return of soldiers from war. For its composer, 'Bring The Boys Back Home' is the album's key text, and far more than a simple anti-war song. '[It's] also about not allowing rock and roll, or making cars or selling soap ... or anything that anybody might do become such a jolly boys' game that it's more important than friends, wives, children, other people', Roger later said, ascribing Pink's isolation to stardom and its attendant pressures. The song continues *The Wall*'s retreat from regular rock tropes, with swirling orchestration, a rousing chorus from the New York City Opera and a martial beat thanks to 36 snare-drummers (among them Jeff Porcaro's dad, Joe) under the direction of Bleu Ocean. To the end of the song are various noises off, including Pink's manager advising 'time to go' from outside the apartment.

### **'Comfortably Numb'** 6.23 (Gilmour/Waters)

Pink's manager and road crew break into the apartment to find their errant charge unresponsive. Fearing only lost revenue, the panicked manager has a paramedic shoot his client with dope to excite a performance. Another autobiographical reference, 'Comfortably Numb' alludes to a Floyd show in Philadelphia in which Roger was sedated against hepatitis-related stomach cramps. During the gig, he was unable to focus and his hands felt 'like two balloons'. Roger said later, '[The doctor] said it was a muscular relaxant, but it rendered me almost insensible. It was so bad that at the end of the show, the audience was baying for more'. Blissfully ignorant, then, or comfortably numb.

'Comfortably Numb' is David Gilmour's main contribution to *The Wall* and one of the album's few old-school Floydian anthems. Featuring the whole band augmented by acoustic guitarist Lee Ritenour and Kamen's New York Symphony Orchestra (subsequent live performances proving the extras redundant), 'Comfortably Numb' is based on an epic and uplifting chord sequence and includes two of David's greatest solos – in performance, the second would validate hymnal rock'n'roll at its most sublime (*Guitar World* magazine declared it third-best solo of all time, behind – curiously, to this writer – Eddie van Halen on 'Eruption' and Brian May on 'Bohemian Rhapsody'). As usual, the solo root is blues, and as usual, Gilmour dissects and dismembers the Devil's Music into something thrillingly fresh and expressive.

The song also closes the curtain on the artistic collaboration between bassist and guitarist. If the Waters-Floyd partnership would stagger waywardly before collapsing under the weight of legal and sometimes nit-picking hostilities,

'Comfortably Numb' at least sees the creative partnership between Roger and David finish on a resoundingly high note. That said, the making was not without its issues. Gilmour told *Guitar World* in 1993:

> There were two recordings, which me and Roger argued about. We changed the key of the song's opening. The verse stayed exactly the same. Then we had to add a little bit, because Roger wanted to do the line, 'I have become comfortably numb'. Other than that, it was very simple to write. But the arguments on it were about how it should be mixed and which track we should use. We'd done one track with Nick on drums that I thought was too rough and sloppy. We had another go at it and I thought that the second take was better. Roger disagreed. It wound up with us taking a fill out of one version and putting it into another.

Surviving Waters' departure as a cornerstone of live gigs by Gilmour, by Waters and by Pink Floyd, 'Comfortably Numb' today tops thousands of fans' shortlists of favourite Pink Floyd songs. David had intended the original for his maiden solo record, *David Gilmour*, but ran out of time. On whether 'Comfortably Numb' would have been so revered among the Floydiscenti had it languished on a mainly underwhelming ex-Floyd solo project, one can only speculate. As it is, we've the ever-perceptive Bob Ezrin to thank for talking Waters into adapting it for *The Wall*.

### **'The Show Must Go On'** 1.36 (Waters)

Pink hits the stage under the influence, turning in a detached, hallucinatory performance. 'Ooh Ma Ooh Pa/Must the show go on?' he sings to chimeras of his mother and father, mourning the loss even of his soul as 'some mistake'. Roger wanted The Beach Boys for vocal duties, but the idea was shelved after Mike Love worried that *The Wall*'s Bible-black tones might discolour the Boys' reputedly superclean image. Bruce Johnston risked it, however, happy temporarily to swerve the 'saccharine' of his regular gig (The Beach Boys of 1979 having surfed many leagues off course from the pioneering heyday of Brian Wilson). Full of high, BB-style harmonies, a light vocal from Gilmour, Mason's dusted-off Rototoms and careful piano and synths from Ezrin and Wright, the song fulfils Waters' requirement for a sunshine-pop filler (it could equally have suited *Obscured By Clouds*) that nonetheless fits *The Wall* like a velvet mitten. Other than as writer, Roger sits this one out – ironic, perhaps, given the title and its content.

### **'In The Flesh'** 4.15 (Waters)

Following distant audience hubbub, we're back where we started, with the huge, bombastic block chords of *The Wall*'s intro. But the question-mark is gone, suggesting a totalitarian certainty about the baleful manner of Pink's rebirth. For so far down the isolationist, alienating rabbit-hole has the star descended he's now convinced he's a fascist dictator at a neo-Nazi rally, calling out minority *untermenschen* in the audience for the special attentions of his brown-shirted goon-squad. Lyrics aside, the song reprises its earlier near-namesake.

### **'Run Like Hell'** 4.20 (Gilmour/Waters)

A murderously robotic martial rhythm, tailor-forged for Scarfe's terrifyingly goosestepping hammers, accompanies Pink's continued attack on ethnic minorities. A few years later, Essex EBM band Nitzer Ebb would co-opt and speed up – indeed, pull the ring out of – a similarly mechanistic, military beat; a sound that as malevolently evokes a mob mindlessly throwing *sieg heil* salutes as any I can think of. 'Run Like Hell', snarls Pink, 'With your nerves in tatters as the cockleshell shatters/And the hammers batter down your door/You better run!' As the song ends, the strident rhythm by now almost unbearable, we hear the rabble chillingly chanting 'Pink Floyd, Pink Floyd…' in one channel and 'hammers, hammers…' in the other. Another song that would lift off in concert, as shows respectively by Waters, Floyd and Gilmour would thrillingly prove, 'Run Like Hell' is a Gilmour song also originally destined for the guitarist's solo album. Once more, *David Gilmour*'s loss is *The Wall*'s gain.

### **'Waiting For The Worms'** 4.04 (Waters)

'Eins, zwei, drei, alles', intones Pink, against the sound of marching jackboots. The spiritual decay, the mass of worms which his schoolmaster once happily ground into shape, mutates into an army of hammers, the stormtroopers bullying into submission the comfortably numb, happily lobotomised tide of humanity Waters once thought he discerned among the huge Floyd audiences that begat *The Wall*. If anything, 'Waiting For The Worms' is even more wickedly sinister than 'Run Like Hell'.

Cajoled by a bullhorn-toting Pink, inflamed with the rhetoric of hate, his audience takes to the racially-diverse streets of London. Driven by the familiar mechanistic beat and an even more intense take on the 'Another Brick' riff, the mob hears Pink again call out minorities while chillingly evoking 'showers' and 'ovens': a 'final solution' to be enacted for blessed Britannia to rise again. The mob's chanting intensifies to the point of overpowering dominion, summarily to be curtailed by a brief, single orchestral chord. Pink is Röhm, Mosley, Colin Jordan, Big Daddy Hitler himself, all condensed into one putrid Nazi shitcan.

It should by now go without saying that the horror of 'Waiting For The Worms' is all part of Pink's alienating drug delirium. He remains 'In perfect isolation here behind my wall', still haunting the war years that took his father, all reason absent without leave. The song was composed during a period of racial unrest in London, the National Front rallying too many to its repellent cause in Brixton and Lewisham. The perils of advancing fascism have rarely been addressed so unequivocally – and effectively – in a rock song.

**'Stop'** 0.30 (Waters)

Suddenly Pink stops hallucinating, although he's likely still a prisoner of his internal angst. Far now from London's totalitarian Rivers of Blood, he's alone in a cell on the comedown from the drugs, wondering if he's been guilty all along. In Roger's high voice against Ezrin's trickling piano, Pink begs to go home and 'take off this uniform'. His trial, and his accusers, judge and jury – all avatars of himself – await.

**'The Trial'** 5.13 (Waters/Bob Ezrin)

For The Wall's final epic, Waters goes full Cameron Mackintosh and lets slip the dogs of showtime. The most non-rock'n'roll song ever attributed to Pink Floyd, 'The Trial' conveys Pink's guilt-ridden human backsliding by means of huge, theatrical camp; it couldn't feel more like a *Cabaret* outtake if Roger sang it wearing pancake makeup and fishnets. It has the lot: over-enunciated vocals – complete with horrribly rrrolled rrrs from Rroger, who voices every witness in the 'trial' taking place in Pink's walled-in imagination – and Kamen's New York Symphony Orchestra, all jollying along an irritating oompah rhythm that's straight out of the Weimar Republic.

Brecht and Weill's *The Threepenny Opera* has clearly influenced Bob Ezrin's orchestral arrangement, which finally admits Floyd into its decadent portals at 3.25. David again quotes *The Wall*'s running 'we don't need no education' riff, once again more savagely and distortedly slowing it down for primo nastiness. Despite the rather comical staginess of it all, 'The Trial' (with its echoes of Kafka and/or *The Prisoner* – you choose) does provide this extraordinary record with a suitably scary false climax, in which Pink forensically dissects his own backstory, cracks under the pressure and, in accordance with his internal judgement, takes with him the wall.

**'Outside The Wall'** 1.41 (Waters)

In his 1929 surrealist painting *The Treachery of Images*, René Magritte depicted a smoker's pipe, captioned: 'This is not a pipe'. The artist's reasoning was literal: indeed, this isn't a pipe, it's a *painting* of a pipe. For *The Wall*'s coda, Roger Waters has a Magritte moment. 'Right, you've seen it now', he said. 'That's the best we can do. And that wasn't actually us. That was us performing a piece of theatre about the things that it was about and we do like you really'. And that's as far as he's been willing to go on the matter.

It's not the remit of this book to excavate every last nugget from the rich and complex seams of Roger Waters' psyche – still less attempt to interpret the work of René Magritte. But perhaps Roger was concerned that people might infer from his art a sense of exceptionalism, even isolationism: something he neither desired nor intended, despite the touchy persona. In other words, don't shoot the messenger; these things may be as they are, but we as artists can do no more than report and critique them. Gaze upon *The Wall* and understand: this is not a mental breakdown.

For the completion of the album's final line, 'Isn't this where...', you have to return to the very start of *The Wall*, where the words '…we came in?' are accompanied by a hint of the same melancholy outgoing clarinet/concertina melody. This feels like another *Prisoner* reference: having finally departed The Village after months of psychological bruising and failed escapology, Number Six finds himself in a closed loop, unavoidably returning to the same London scenes which immediately preceded his abduction and, by association, to be whisked back to The Village itself. In *The Wall*, as visualised by Scarfe's stunning animations, each end of the structure curls itself around 180 degrees to meet and form a closed circle, implying that, like Number Six, Pink is stuck on a Mobius strip of never-ending existential angst – even if 'Outside The Wall' has permitted Pink a taste of the world beyond – and, more broadly, that history is doomed to keep repeating itself.

# The Final Cut (1983)

Personnel:
Roger Waters: bass, acoustic guitar, synthesiser, keyboards, vocals
David Gilmour: lead guitar, acoustic guitar, synthesiser, vocals
Nick Mason: drums, percussion
Andy Bown: Hammond organ
Andy Newmark: drums (on 'Two Suns In The Sunset')
Ray Cooper: percussion
Raphael Ravenscroft: tenor saxophone
Doreen Chanter, Irene Chanter: backing vocals
Michael Kamen: harmonium, electric piano, orchestral conducting
National Philharmonic Orchestra
Produced at: The Billiard Room, London; Hook End Studios, Checkendon; Mayfair Recording Studios, London; Olympic Studios, London; Abbey Road Studios, London; Eel Pie Studios, London; RAK Studios, London; Audio International Studios, London by Roger Waters, James Guthrie, Michael Kamen
Engineers: James Guthrie, Andy Jackson, Andy Canelle, Mike Nocito, Jules Bowen
Released: 21 March 1983
Highest chart position: UK, France, W Germany, Sweden, Norway, New Zealand: 1, US: 6

Pink Floyd's twelfth album is a tough listen, but only if you allow it to be. If certain tracks on *Dark Side Of The Moon* famously stimulated the loins as much as the head, *The Final Cut* keeps its aphrodisiac properties hidden. Were it – mistakenly – to be consumed as background muzak, the thirteen tracks of 'A Requiem For The Post-War Dream by Roger Waters' (the album's portentous subtitle) would superficially coalesce into one glutinous 47 minutes of typical Waters misery, only rarely aroused by an impassioned David Gilmour guitar solo. As a Pink Floyd album, *The Final Cut* is dull. But as a Roger Waters album, it's brilliant.

Without being over-reverential towards a rock'n'roll record, no act of remembrance – for, make no mistake, that is what *The Final Cut* is – should pledge instant gratification. But time reveals an album of great beauty and subtlety, a massage for tear ducts as readily as synapses. Waters laments how politicians across the ideological divide have criminally reneged on the promise of lasting peace in the wake of WWII. The loss of his father in that conflict continues to haunt Roger's songwriting. But it takes another war, the 1982 Falklands campaign, to nudge the composer away from *Spare Bricks*, his original idea for a soundtrack for a movie of *The Wall*, in favour of a new anti-war concept album.

*The Final Cut*'s story is narrated by a traumatised ex-squaddie (*The Wall*'s disinterred schoolteacher) representing the British soldiers who, limping home from Europe and Asia in 1945, are betrayed by the same leaders who not only conscripted them but profited from the conflict that so damaged them. 1968's

'Corporal Clegg' was an early precursor. Firing broadsides at Leonid Brezhnev, Menachem Begin, Ian Paisley and Leopoldo Galtieri, Roger reserves his bitterest ire for Margaret Thatcher, later explaining to Floyd biographer Mark Blake:

> *The Final Cut* was about how, with the introduction of the welfare state, we felt we were moving forward into something resembling a liberal country where we would all look after one another. But I'd seen a return to an almost Dickensian society under Thatcher. I felt then, as now, that the British government should have pursued diplomatic avenues, rather than steaming in the moment that task force arrived in the South Atlantic.

Rehearsals, recording and mixdown were spread over no fewer than eight studios, all orbiting London. This accorded with the inescapable sense of fragmentation that now encircled Pink Floyd. With Rick Wright for now history, *The Final Cut* was the last studio collaboration between Waters, Gilmour and Mason. Arrangements were fleshed out by session musicians: Saxophonist Raphael Ravenscroft played on two tracks; Andy Bown stood in for Rick on keys; Ray Cooper added extra percussion; Nick was replaced for the album's difficult finale by drummer-for-hire Andy Newmark. Surprisingly absent was Bob Ezrin, Waters refusing to forgive the Canadian for prematurely releasing details of *The Wall*'s tour to the press. Michael Kamen was promoted to co-producer (with Waters and James Guthrie), as conductor with the National Philharmonic Orchestra and as mediator between Waters and Gilmour, who were rapidly transitioning to rock'n'roll's own Joan Crawford and Bette Davis. At one point, Roger was even convinced that his creative partnership was over with both David and Nick (who was weathering his own marital trials). While the two principals would sometimes meet to review progress, David's unease over both the music and what he considered his colleague's political posturing began to tell. And although the guitarist would still be paid royalties, so strained became the relationship that he had his production credit removed from the album sleeve.

Given the bassist's pre-eminence in *The Final Cut*'s fruition, and the statuses of his teammates dwindling to those of session men, it's perhaps surprising the record wasn't formally declared a Roger Waters solo album. But Pink Floyd – the brand – was flying higher than ever; having escaped the pre-*Wall* financial doldrums, no one had any appetite for taking on EMI in court – which probably would have been the next stop had the owners deemed it necessary.

Once again, Waters snubbed Hipgnosis for the sleeve design, instead doing it himself with help from his brother-in-law and *Vogue* photographer, Willie Christie. A Mondrian-style study in abstract rectilinear form proves to be a poppy and ribbons from WWII medals against a dark background. Inside the gatefold are the lyrics and photos: of more poppies and a soldier; a welder whose mask is decorated with a Japanese 'rising sun' motif; and, referencing the final track 'Two Suns In The Sunset', a nuclear mushroom cloud apparently viewed from inside a car.

Astonishingly, *The Final Cut* – the title is Shakespearean and refers to another fatal betrayal, Julius Caesar's – outdid *Dark Side Of The Moon* and *The Wall* (although both eventually sold far more) by hitting number one in the UK, while in America it peaked at number six. For David Gilmour, already unhappy at the inclusion of what he felt were rejects from *The Wall* ('Nobody thought [the tracks] were that good then; what makes them so good now?') the album's relatively poor performance in the States endorsed his contention that *The Final Cut* was a step backwards. Most pressers tended to agree: *Melody Maker* and *NME* were roundly unimpressed, while *The Village Voice* pithily saw *The Final Cut* as anti-war rock supported by 'years of self-pity'. *Rolling Stone* got it right, however, praising the album as 'a masterpiece of art-rock'; the penny had dropped that, for Pink Floyd, space rock was history, while apparently, Waters' songwriting was now the equal of Bob Dylan's. A single of 'Not Now John', coupled with 'The Hero's Return', reached number 30 in the UK.

## **'The Post War Dream'** 3.00 (Waters)

*The Final Cut* begins with a series of news soundbites: the construction of a Cambridgeshire nuclear shelter; a warship contract awarded to a Japanese firm; the illegal drug trade's effect on third-world stability. The first announcement will be echoed by the album's final track, but the most conceptually pertinent is the shipbuilding deal: for WWII veterans and their children, an example of how politicians have betrayed the post-war working class:

> If it wasn't for the Nips/Being so good at building ships
> The yards would still be open on the Clyde.
> And it can't be much fun for them/Beneath the rising sun
> With all their kids committing suicide.
> What have we done?/Maggie, what have we done?
> What have we done to England?
> Should we shout? Should we scream?
> What happened to the post-war dream?
> Oh, Maggie, Maggie, what did we do?

Viewing Roger's 40-year-old lyrics through a 2022 palantir, dismissing Japanese people as 'Nips' has long been part of the British lexicon of stereotypical insult, alongside other derogatory terms Waters has never shied from using for ironic impact. When during the 1980s 'Maggie' took on the trade unions and managed the decline of smokestack industry, working-class casualties felt little option but to aim rhetorical barbs at the Johnny Foreigners apparently plundering their jobs. Indeed, one such victim is the narrator on *The Final Cut*. Four decades on his equivalent, and the thousands abandoned due to employment 'offshoring', have been pushed not to the political left but to the far right. Less likely to support the traditional workers' allies, the Labour Party, too many accept the chilly embrace of the ultra-nationalist UK Independence

Party and its ilk. Since UKIP is home to numerous embittered Thatcherites for whom racist banter is an honour code – and who also, for different reasons, fret about the betrayal of whatever the post-war dream means to them – this is not necessarily a demographic that invites sympathy in 2022.

Today, analysis of ever-more complex international affairs demands nuance. In 1983, the Cold War offered a conveniently binary, zero-sum divide. For anti-war writers like Waters, leaders widely derided as bad actors were obvious targets. He spares none throughout *The Final Cut*. On the opening track of this superbly produced album, Roger's vocal is the most affecting element. Never the greatest singer, he makes best use of his vocal limitations to ask bleak questions, at once angrily and helplessly. Based on Kamen's orchestral horns and strings and a harmonium – an instrument that cannot help but epitomise minor-key melancholy – the hauntingly elegiac arrangement sounds in places like that archetype of working-class musical solidarity, the colliery brass band. At 2.11, 1983-model Floyd's powerful rhythm section kicks in to remind us why we're here, as Roger indignantly presses Thatcher for the answers he'll never get.

### **'Your Possible Pasts'** 4.26 (Waters)

This reworked discard from *The Wall* actually dates back to Floyd antiquity. Roger transposed the time signature, tempo and first lines from a 1968 original called 'Incarceration Of A Flower Child', which, though never recorded by Pink Floyd, would be adapted by Marianne Faithfull for her 1999 album *Vagabond Ways*.

Despite David's reservations, this fine song would have as readily matched the themes of *The Wall* as it does its resting place. With Roger's regretful vocal, the damaged narrator evokes one of the most egregious horrors of WWII – 'the cattle trucks lying in wait for the next time' (a Holocaust reference) – and implicitly warns of the potential for 'anyone still in command' to make the same vile mistakes again, just as the enclosed loop of *The Wall* posited a future doomed to repeat itself. Waters looks back in anger, fear and confusion at a past strewn with broken promises and alternate realities. He sings of the prostitute 'stood in the doorway [with] the ghost of a smile/Haunting her face like a cheap hotel sign': she's a woman fated for either her next trick or a bloody end. He recounts being taken in hand by 'the cold and religious', his independence smothered.

Lyrically the song is complex and relentlessly glum. Musically its dynamics veer from verses led by acoustic guitar and organ to the massive explosions of the choruses, Gilmour arriving at the end with a guitar solo as pained as the song's grim sentiments. As *Rolling Stone* intimated, 'Your Possible Pasts' would not have felt out of place on a Bob Dylan record.

### **'One Of The Few'** 1.11 (Waters)

In another song left off *The Wall*, the subject is a veteran returned to civvies, traumatised and unable to talk of his experiences. With the title suggesting an RAF airman, he becomes a teacher to make ends meet. Waters' intimate, slightly reverbed vocal seems to be through gritted teeth, conveying the barely-contained teacherly menace that one day will be unleashed upon the classroom. Over Roger's delicate acoustic guitar, a ticking clock marks the passing of time, while restrained synths and orchestral strings lend a distinct air of foreboding.

### **'When The Tigers Broke Free'** 3.16 (Waters)

This momentous, immensely affecting lament for Roger's father was originally intended as *The Wall*'s opening track but discarded for its personal nature at the insistence of Gilmour and Mason. 'When The Tigers Broke Free' did make it to the beginning of the feature film, but was mysteriously left off the original vinyl release of *The Final Cut*, only at last to be included on the 2004 CD reissue. The song was released as a 7-inch single in 1982 ahead of the album, backed with 'Bring The Boys Back Home' from *The Wall*.

Another song that's entirely appropriate to both albums – at this point on *The Final Cut* it's a wonder the whole album wasn't *The Wall*'s third disc – it refers to Lt Waters' death at Anzio in 1944. At the song's root is a slow, heartbreakingly sepulchral refrain. Despairingly Roger sings of King George VI's gold-leafed letter of condolence, signed by a regal but empathy-free 'rubber stamp'. Then at the end, he blows off the pent-up bitterness with a shuddering 'And that's how the High Command took my daddy from me'. With the drama heightened by a male voice choir and rousing trumpets, the sense of loss of servicemen dismissed by their superiors as 'a few hundred ordinary lives' is conveyed to eyewatering perfection.

### **'The Hero's Return'** 2.43 (Waters)

In another song discarded from *The Wall*, Roger gives voice to the airman-turned-schoolteacher, rebuking his class of 'little ingrates' with time-honoured 'Get yer 'air cut/I fought a war for you, laddie'-style clichés. In the third verse of the album's most conventional rock song yet, the former bomber pilot addresses his wife, ensuring first that she is fast asleep since 'That's the only time I can really speak to you'. He talks of how the jubilation of his return from war is tarnished by the memory of his air-gunner lost over Dresden to enemy fire, his colleague's dismembered dying words heard over a joylessly impersonal intercom. It's another track of unerring dynamic contrasts, with Gilmour's Stratocaster scrambling in towards the close like ME109s chasing a flight of Lancasters.

### **'The Gunners Dream'** 5.18 (Waters)

'The Gunners Dream' (sic – the apostrophe was mistakenly absent from both original and CD releases) equates the dying airman's ideal of peace with the broader post-war vision of a liberal world free of oppression – dreams dashed on the jagged rocks of human folly. Over Kamen's piano and tasteful orchestral strings, Roger mourns a Utopia in which everyone can enjoy food, a home and free speech, a place 'where no one ever disappears' under the heel of a tyrannical state, where its children are not sent off to die for vainglorious politicians. It's a community protected by judiciously benign laws and safe from urban terror, signified here by the urban atrocities of the Irish Republican Army. At 2.11, the singer's angst intensifies, Roger's almost primal scream picked up by Ravenscroft's expressive tenor sax solo. That the song's title might be Roger's sly reference to his favourite football team, Arsenal, does not detract from another deeply affecting track.

### 'Paranoid Eyes' 3.41 (Waters)

Over a slow, almost completely orchestral backing, the now middle-aged teacher laments how the betrayals since 1945 have fuelled his alcoholism. He tries to hide his condition from others: 'You put on your brave face and slip over the road for a jar/Fixing your grin as you casually lean on the bar/Laughing too loud at the rest of the world with the boys in the crowd/You hide hide hide behind petrified eyes'. (Nb: 'the teacher' probably shouldn't be confused with 'the gunner' who died over Dresden; while the narrative implies that the pair were crewmates, one surviving as the other perished, by this point in *The Final Cut,* the central character has become ambiguous, the two characters somehow interwoven).

### 'Get Your Filthy Hands Off My Desert' 1.17 (Waters)

The acceleration across the stereo channels of a low-level military jet (or possibly a missile) followed by a juddering explosion provides the most startling example on *The Final Cut* of holophonic recording: a 'binaural' system that stimulates the brain into reproducing immersive 3D sound images. The brief lyric here compares the respective belligerence of Soviet chairman Brezhnev, Israeli PM Begin, Argentine president Galtieri and UK PM Thatcher. Roger excoriates the latter for the sinking off the Falklands of the Argentine cruiser *Belgrano* with all hands; a decision, according to Waters, made by Thatcher over lunch. Set against Roger's plaintive vocal, the musical accompaniment, mainly orchestral cellos, is again impossibly moving and elegiac.

### 'The Fletcher Memorial Home' 4.12 (Waters)

In a song whose title explicitly refers to Waters' father, Roger gleefully imagines corralling away in a padded cell all his political bogeymen: the 'incurable tyrants and kings', among them Reagan, Brezhnev, Begin, 'the ghost of McCarthy' and 'the memories of Nixon', Paisley, the inevitable Thatcher and 'a group of anonymous Latin American meat packing glitterati'. As he introduces the list of the 'wasters of life and limb' like a major-domo at an oligarch's party, none is safe from Waters' vitriolic 'final solution' (the term lifted from Hitler's wartime ethnic-cleansing atrocities), which the bassist sets out over another sombre orchestral arrangement. At 2.16, Gilmour breaks into the happy throng and launches a laser-like solo (which may or may not be why the song was one of only three on the album to receive the guitarist's approval).

### **'Southampton Dock'** 2.10 (Waters)

The eponymous harbour looms large in the history of British conflict. From here in 1944 embarked troops bound for the Normandy landings. To here they returned in 1945, none speaking or smiling; 'There were too many spaces in the line', Waters sings, referring to the thousands lost, to a strummed acoustic guitar and doleful, slowly building strings.

37 years later, an unknown woman 'stands upon Southampton Dock/With her handkerchief and her summer frock/Clings to her wet body in the rain/In quiet desperation/Knuckles white upon the slippery reins/She bravely waves the boys goodbye again'. As the troopships leave for the Falklands, is she Margaret Thatcher, or a sorrowful wife or mother waving off a loved one? The lyric gives no clue, although 'bravely waving' plays well as a toxic gobbet of Waters irony. But there's no doubting Roger's venom as he sings:

> And still the dark stain spreads between/Their shoulder blades
> A mute reminder/Of the poppy fields and graves
> And when the fight was over/We spent what they had made
> But in the bottom of our hearts/We felt the final cut.

A few months later the troops will return to a Britain flooded with patriotic and nationalist sentiment, a fact that, given the lives lost, Waters saw as emblematic of political failure and betrayal. It's the central theme of *The Final Cut* in a nutshell.

### **'The Final Cut'** 4.45 (Waters)

'Through the fish-eyed lens of tear-stained eyes/I can barely define the shape of this moment in time'. Thus opens the album's magnificent title track, a heart-rending howl of relentless despondency. 'The Final Cut' wears its *Wall* heritage proudly. Originally intended for Floyd's previous record and narrated by Pink, the pitch-black sentiments of 'The Final Cut' are now pleaded by the teacher/gunner, struggling with his isolation and sexual dysfunction, as he spirals 'down to the hole in the ground where I hide', even contemplating ending it all.

With good reason, Waters' lyrics are often self-referential; when at 2.05 he sings 'if I show you my dark side', the first two words deliberately repeat the same conditionals on his early self-doubting masterpiece 'If'. Among the searingly negative emotions, he worries about how showing his true nature and opening 'my heart to you' will be received; by his wife and by the world. That he wavers from suicide in the final moments – 'I held the blade in trembling hands/Prepared to make it but just then the phone rang/I never had the nerve to make the final cut' – has been interpreted as an example of Waters introducing a note of positivity to an otherwise bleakly pessimistic song. Yet his 'naked feelings' by now signal such acute despair that it's hard to see any way out of his psychological gridlock.

'The Final Cut' also shows musical kinship with *The Wall*, its swirling string parts close in composition to those on 'Comfortably Numb'. Complete with a superb doubled-up guitar discourse that should lend itself to typically Gilmouresque extension, the song could have been a showstopper. That inter-band hostilities militated against Floyd touring this criminally underrated album – and caused the band to fall apart within two years – is our loss.

### **'Not Now John'** 4.56 (Waters)

Irrespective of the rights or wrongs of the Falklands war, much of the British media reported on the conflict and its aftermath with jingoistic, 'Kill an Argie and win a Metro' glee. Waters slams the news channels via a new character voiced by David's sole lead vocal on *The Final Cut*. John could be a drug-addled TV producer frantically pumping out the nationalistic line as instructed by his political masters. 'Wouldn't Maggie be pleased', he gabbles, as he ponders competing with 'the wily Japanese' and decides against taking on 'the Russian bear' for an easier target, such as 'the Swedes'. He's a political chameleon, his ideals malleable, blissfully ignorant of political and economic realities. He sets out his disparate priorities in a cokehead's litany, Roger echoing a songwriting hero, John Lennon, in a stanza similar to the stream-of-consciousness verses from the Plastic Ono Band's hit 'Give Peace A Chance'. The mask slips towards the end as this John adopts the guise of a stormtrooper hammer from *The Wall*, demanding the location of the bar, an English skinhead on the Costa del Sol.

'Not Now John' is the album's one relatively heavy rocker, rendered commercial enough for a single with a rhythmic insistence similar to 'Another Brick In The Wall pt2'. The cooing refrain from the soulful female backing vocals, 'Fuck all that', was abridged for the single to 'Stuff all that.'

### **'Two Suns In The Sunset'** 5.23 (Waters)

The final cut on *The Final Cut* is finality itself: nuclear holocaust, the inevitable consequence of a world fixated on warfare and nationalist control-freakery:

> In my rear-view mirror the sun is going down
> Sinking behind bridges in the road
> I think of all the good things/That we have left undone
> And I suffer premonitions/Confirm suspicions
> Of the holocaust to come.

'Two Suns In The Sunset' joins a noble repository of protest songs nervously predicting Armageddon, from Dylan's 'A Hard Rain's A-Gonna Fall' to Bowie's 'Five Years'. When Roger Waters wrote this disturbing finale to an extraordinary album, his crosshairs were aligned on the perpetrators of the Cold War, which in the decade before Soviet collapse came closer to an all-consuming East-West conflagration than at any time since 1962. With Brezhnev and the Warsaw Pact on one side, Reagan, Thatcher and NATO on the other, all equals in belligerent rhetoric, Waters saw no credibly responsible leader to ease the world away from incineration.

Yet, for all its doom-laden premonitions, 'Two Suns' is curiously optimistic, in the same way that *Dark Side* finished with a get-out-of-jail-free card for listeners worried that Roger had lyrically whistled up The End. In 2003 he confirmed to *Uncut* that 'Two Suns' indeed describes nuclear conflict:

> The remnants of all that paranoia from the '60s – and it's that idea that it may be at the end of life, one may have that kind of realisation that you could have when you're alive and living, and you go, hold on a minute, maybe this is what I should do.

He added that he wrote the song to encourage living in the moment. 'Don't be scared to live it. Don't be scared to take risks.'

The music itself is beautiful, not an orchestra in sight, with Andy Newmark's jazzy drumming and Ravenscroft's exquisite tenor solo (similar in feel to Jimmy Jewell's playing on Joan Armatrading's 'Love and Affection' and high enough in the register to sound like an alto) distancing the song's flavour from the rest of the album.

## A Momentary Lapse Of Reason (1987)

Personnel:
David Gilmour: guitars, vocals, keyboards, sequencers
Nick Mason: acoustic & electronic drums, sound effects
Rick Wright: piano, vocals, Kurzweil, Hammond organ
Bob Ezrin: keyboards, percussion, sequencers
Tony Levin: bass, Chapman stick
Jim Keltner: drums
Steve Forman: percussion
Jon Carin: keyboards
Tom Scott: alto & soprano saxophones
Scott Page: tenor saxophone
Carmine Appice: drums
Pat Leonard: synthesisers
Bill Payne: Hammond organ
Michael Landau: guitar
John Halliwell: saxophone
Darlene Koldenhaven, Carmen Twillie, Phyllis St James, Donnie Gerrard: backing vocals
Produced at: Astoria, Hampton; Britannia Row, London; Mayfair, London; Audio International, London; A&M, Los Angeles; The Village Recorder, Los Angeles; Can-Am, Los Angeles by Bob Ezrin, David Gilmour
Engineers: Andrew Jackson, Robert Hryeyna, Marc Desisto, Sean Katayama, Jeff Demorris, James Guthrie
Released: 7 September 1987
Highest chart positions: UK: 3, US: 3

A lot happened between Pink Floyd's twelfth and thirteenth albums. The band was dehydrated, for a start: Roger Waters quit. Then there were the 1980s: the decade in which everything suddenly went large, from hairstyles and shoulder pads to traders' bonuses and drug habits. 'My rock'n'roll is putting on weight', sang Steve Winwood in 1981. The former leader of Traffic, exact contemporaries of Floyd back in 1967, was having his music steam-cleaned by digitisation following the stoned, post-hippie analogue messiness of the 1970s. Just as big synthesisers and bigger suits began to smother Winwood's art and image, so was David Gilmour steadily pulled into the orbit of the computers and marketing men. Happily, however, David made it work. Welcome, my friends, to the Machine.

Following the bleak, high-concept chamber-pop of Floyd's previous record, the sole custodian of the Pink Floyd label was now free to return to more conventional musical tailoring. Once more, PF were a rock band, only this time they'd be a user-friendly power-Floyd, immersively programmed, drums thrust to the fore with gated reverb, everything glowing with a hygienic MIDI sheen. And apart from anything else, Gilmour could now do whatever he wanted without his bass player's permission.

But with the new album recorded and mixed between November 1986 and February 1987 in seven studios, including David's houseboat conversion *Astoria*, production was inevitably hindered by the legal squabbling that attended Waters' departure. On quitting in December 1985, Roger assumed the PF name was now obsolete, cattily dismissing whatever was left as a creative spent force. Gilmour was having none of it, although a tour to promote the guitarist's second solo album, *About Face*, drew little interest. Waters' outing for *The Pros And Cons Of Hitch Hiking* was similarly dismissed. Clearly having 'Pink Floyd' emblazoned across a concert poster meant more to the sacred markets of the 1980s than either 'David Gilmour' or 'Roger Waters'. So like cowpoke prospectors in a goldrush saloon, the pair now went head-to-head over the rights to that lucrative name.

It's the intention of this book neither to review nor to speculate about the Great Divide. Enough rainforests have been levelled, pulped and legally embossed unpicking the finer details of rock's most truculent breakup. Suffice to say that the last straw for the bassist, who finally signed over the legal entitlements to the Pink Floyd brand to Gilmour in December 1987, illustrated the absurdist depths to which the lawyerly wrangling had descended: Roger threatened to sue David should the guitarist allow Algy, the inflatable *Animals* pig, onstage for the first Waters-free Pink Floyd tour. Gilmour's response was to give Algy a giant set of porcine genitalia, legally distancing the dirigible's design from Waters' original. For many fans, including your scribe, a pig's bollocks summed up the whole sorry saga.

So Gilmour and Mason were now ready to unleash a new Pink Floyd record. But this didn't mean the keys to the executive washroom for Rick Wright. The organist returned once again as a waged journeyman, his name displayed on the album credits in a markedly smaller font than the two principals with whom he'd once been equal. Much later, Gilmour confessed that neither his employee nor his co-director of Pink Floyd Limited had contributed much to *A Momentary Lapse*: 'Nick played a few tom-toms on one track', David said in an interview, 'but for the rest, I had to get in other drummers'. (Again, it's been mooted that Nick's technique was too rusty, but it's equally likely his head was too far elsewhere, his brand loyalties now more Maserati and Bugatti than Ludwig and Paiste). David added that Rick's input was similarly minimal; 'For a lot of it, I played the keyboards and pretended it was him.'

However much he did or didn't do, Rick was in exalted company. Back as co-producer was Bob Ezrin (which stuck in Roger's craw since Ezrin was supposed to be producing Waters' second solo album, *Radio K.A.O.S.*, at the same time). Meanwhile, the studio band boasted such luminaries as bassist Tony Levin, drummers Jim Keltner and Carmine Appice, ex-Little Feat organist Bill Payne and the LA Express saxophone maestro Tom Scott.

Alongside the formidable hirelings, Floyd naturally retained David's generous talents as lead singer, instrumentalist and musical director. But Roger's departure had left Floyd's conceptual department yawningly unmanned, and the guitarist had little confidence in his own abilities as a wordsmith. After considering the Liverpool poet Roger McGough, 10cc's Eric Stewart and Carole Pope from Rough Trade, David hooked up with Anthony Moore, lately of Blackhill-signed experimentalists Slapp Happy, alongside Roxy Music's Phil Manzanera and ex-Madonna sideperson Patrick Leonard. Obviously no themed record was likely to surface from this Sargasso Sea of songwriters, sessioneers and producers – Ezrin briefly appalled Gilmour with the idea of Floyd doing an Afrika Bambaataa-style hip-hop album – while David later admitted that he found the project difficult without Roger's input.

Despite (or because of) the absence of the Great Architect, in places *A Momentary Lapse Of Reason* is the most Floydian Floyd album since *Animals*. At least two major tracks, 'On The Turning Away' and 'Sorrow', ooze with anthemic redemption, purpose-designed for instant uplift and extended, showstopping release. Yet occasionally the synthed-up production risks cosseting the songs, delivering on Waters' contention that, with Gilmour, words would always play second fiddle to the music. That the album was bereft of a consistent theme was picked up by *New York City Tribune*, which wrote of David's 'atmospheric instrumental music' lacking 'a unifying vision and Waters' lyrical direction'. *NME* decided that Floyd 'appear to have stopped', although *Uncut* would later write that the album 'announced the return of Pink Floyd'.

For the sleeve, another return was Floyd's confrère of old, Storm Thorgerson. Inspired by the song 'Yet Another Movie', Storm heroically shunned whatever passed for PhotoShopping in 1987. Instead he procured and photographed the 800 hospital beds occupying two miles of Saunton Sands in North Devon. As if to remind everyone of Floyd's new pecking order, inside is a cheesy monochrome two-shot by David Bailey of Gilmour and Mason – portraiture having been absent from every cover since *Meddle*. The album's title came about after Gilmour rejected *Signs Of Life*, *Of Promises Broken* and *Delusions Of Maturity*, any one of which would have been a gift to the ready sarcasm of his ex-bassist. He settled in the end for a line from the track 'One Slip'. Roger's take on the new record? 'A fair forgery.'

## **'Signs Of Life'** 4.24 (Gilmour/Ezrin)

Unable to concoct a unifying, *Wall*-style theme for *Momentary Lapse*, Gilmour and Ezrin focused on atmosphere, a quality noted by Bob as Floyd began work at David's Thameside studio houseboat. The tranquillity surely inspired this beautiful instrumental opener, which begins with creaking timbers and gently lapping waves – SFX now being Nick's main role – beneath layers of beguilingly spooky synths and Mason's mysterious spoken lines: 'When the childlike view of the world went, nothing replaced it/I do not like being asked to/Other people replaced it/Someone who knows'. David comes in with sky-high guitar lines over a lush chord sequence. Unquestionably Floydian – unsurprisingly, since the piece was the remnants of an early demo – its feel is that of a surrogate impressionist opener for a classic such as 'Shine On You Crazy Diamond'.

**'Learning To Fly'** 4.53 (Gilmour/Ezrin/Anthony Moore/Jon Carin)
Both lovers of aviation, David and Nick had bought a De Havilland Dove and were now taking flying lessons. Since his tuition occasionally clashed with studio duties, it seemed natural that David, helped lyrically by Moore, should recount his airborne experiences among a suite of songs unimpeded by a single theme. But there's more to 'Learning To Fly' than a millionaire thoughtfully sharing his acquisitive streak with the masses. For a rookie flier, dangling at ten thousand feet on a wing, a prayer and a worryingly recent pilot's licence must release a flood of philosophical contemplation; it's tempting to interpret the song's title and lyric as metaphors, maybe in reference to Pink Floyd's phoenix-like rebirth, more broadly for man's desire and need spiritually to take flight:

Ice is forming on the tips of my wings
Unheeded warnings, I thought I thought of everything
No navigator to find my way home
Unladened empty and turned to stone
A soul in tension that's Learning To Fly
Condition grounded but determined to try
Can't keep my eyes from the circling skies
Tongue-tied and twisted just an earth-bound misfit.

'Learning To Fly' begins with a bombastic burst of percussion and fuzzy guitar chording, quickly followed by eddying synths and Jon Carin's electric piano, all hitting a strong groove to carry David's lead vocal. Nick declared the track to be the album's most faithful to the band's spirit and sound, although long-term fans might have observed that rarely had Floyd so blatantly courted FM radio play. Also more indicative of mid-to-late period Floyd are the backing vocalists, who add a soulfully commercial depth to the choruses. On the instrumental bridge, Nick runs through a litany of pre-flight checks, all pounded along by Ezrin and Steve Forman's massive programmed drums. Radio-friendly might have been the intention, but a single of 'Learning To Fly', coupled with 'Terminal Frost', didn't trouble the UK charts and made only number 70 in the US.

**'The Dogs Of War'** 6.10 (Gilmour/Moore)
In Waters' absence, it falls to Gilmour and lyricist Moore to allow politics onto a Pink Floyd album. Here they berate 'physical and political mercenaries' as men of hate, with neither cause nor discrimination, who'll lie and deceive for hard cash. Not the most subtle of Floyd songs, although 'The Dogs Of War' does afford the opportunity to rock out with extreme prejudice. With Nick sidelined, Ezrin called up the thunderous ex-Vanilla Fudge/Jeff Beck/Rod

Stewart percussionist Carmine Appice. Since merely showing Appice a drumkit inevitably lets slip not so much the dogs of war as the hounds of hell, a suitably histrionic effect is readily achieved. The swaggering aggression continues into a blazing guitar solo from Gilmour and a skronking tenor outing by Scott Page, who succeeds in marrying the ghosts of Albert Ayler and King Curtis. 'It's a great R&B track to play live', opined Mason; Floyd's regular sticksman happily regained his chops for the tour that would realise the live album *Delicate Sound of Thunder*.

### **'One Slip'** 5.05 (Gilmour/Phil Manzanera)

Following the mercenary snarling, 'One Slip' turns out to be an upbeat pop song that feels like obvious hit material; indeed, it was released as the third single from *Momentary Lapse* along with 'Terminal Frost' or (according to territory) a live version of 'The Dogs Of War'. A number five in America, it flattened in the UK. This is unfair, since the song rattles pleasingly along on an invigorating wave of synths and MIDI programming, while the sound, punctuated with huge percussive thunderclaps from Jim Keltner, is as cleanly 1980s as Sting's aftershave. David enthusiastically vocalises the thoughts of Phil Manzanera on the law of unintended consequences, primly hinting that 'the road to ruin' awaits impulsively hasty decisions born of decadent desire. Between two people of uncertain ages, a night-time encounter, passionate and unprotected – the 'momentary lapse of reason/That binds a life for life' – leads to pregnancy; something neither party expects nor wants: 'One slip, and down the hole we fall.'

### **'On The Turning Away'** 5.42 (Gilmour/Moore)

''On The Turning Away' is about the political situations in the world. We have these rather right-wing conservative governments that don't seem to care about many things other than looking after themselves'. So explained Gilmour, in words straight from the Waters playbook. This majestic song is the album's second example of how David could as willingly embrace politics and protest as his ex-teammate. It's a big song with a big heart, imploring the strong to remember the world's less fortunate. Musically this simple, Utopian plea for tolerance and compassion has a flavour that can only be described as Celtic-hymnal, the song's steady, pacing rhythm the most archetypally Floydian on the album.

A slowly droning synth fades in on a heavily-reverbed vocal, as Gilmour intones Moore's heartfelt, though never sermonising lyrics. There's a slow build; stately keyboards play through the main theme from 0.55, before a thrilling instrumental bridge at 2.07. With all borne aloft by swirling Hammond organ, Keltner's powerhouse drumming and the backing vocalists, Gilmour's solo is agonisingly emotive, proving beyond all doubt that the guitarist believes every word he sings and that his instinctive musicianship can only emphasise the song's native optimism.

'On The Turning Away' was the second single from *Momentary Lapse*, coupled with a live version of 'Run Like Hell'. Though it stalled at number 55 in Britain, the US rightly did it proud at number one.

### **'Yet Another Movie'/'Round And Around'** 7.28 (Gilmour/Patrick Leonard)

'I don't even know what all of it means myself'. Thus Gilmour confessed to *Only Music* that 'Yet Another Movie' was likely the most 'surrealist' thing Floyd had yet done. Assuming co-conspirator Leonard felt the same way, the main difficulty, listening to the song's disparate lyrical images as they tumble around each other, is resisting comparisons with Ultravox's notorious 'Vienna': an overcooked synth opus that, while appealing by its own somewhat artificial lights, seemed to define the decade's glossy triumph of style over substance.

Whatever 'Yet Another Movie' lacks in analogue grit is compensated for in digital drama, however. Lyrical conceits aside, there's no ignoring the pervasive sense of doomy electronic theatre. Apparently opening with empty oil drums bouncing through a bombed-out refinery, the song's 'dreamlike' themes and visions are bolted into a series of heavily percussive slugs of MIDI synths, keyboards and SFX (including dialogue quotes from the films *On The Waterfront* and *Casablanca*). Layers of programming build beneath David's threatening vocal, finding brilliant release with some stratospherically bendy Gilmour soloing. At 6.18 the drums – much of which percussive effect was achieved by Mason, Foreman and Keltner playing in unison – slip away and the mood changes abruptly for 'Round And Around'. Sometimes considered a separate song, this feels more like an instrumental coda; a slowly fading loop of bass synths, with distant guitar colouring.

### **'A New Machine'** (part 1) 1.46 (Gilmour)

On this deeply strange, short, Vocodered bellow from the depths of his psyche, David offered *MOJO* only:

> Whether you want to take the song as optimistic or not… a lot of people didn't use it as an excuse to go and jump off a cliff or something, did they?

In another interview, the guitarist alluded to Rick's and Nick's supposed crises of motivation during *AMLOR*'s production. Perhaps lines such as 'Sometimes I get tired of the waiting/Sometimes I get tired of being in here/Is this the way it's always been?/Could it ever have been different?', superficially the voice of a machine, suggest that Gilmour's own patience and self-belief might be close to the red. The two parts of 'A New Machine' top and tail 'Terminal Frost'.

### **'Terminal Frost'** 6.17 (Gilmour)

The fruition of an old instrumental demo, to which David briefly considered writing lyrics, is another example of augmented Floydian atmosphere. The decoration this time comes in the shape of two saxophones, both sopranos, from the excellent John Helliwell and Tom Scott. 'Terminal Frost' has the feeling of a superior 1980s TV drama. This is apt since crack sessioneer and mood-muzak veteran Scott penned themes for two of the era's most popular cop shows: *The Streets Of San Francisco* and *Starsky & Hutch*. It's not the best track on *AMLOR*, but it's far from unpleasant. Just try to forget the image of Paul Michael Glaser's cardigan.

## **'A New Machine'** (part 2) 0.38 (Gilmour)

The first verse repeated, with a slight, inconsequential tweak to the lyric and a lot more anguish in Gilmour's treated voice.

## **'Sorrow'** 8.46 (Gilmour)

If 'On The Turning Away' hinted that Floyd still had enough juice in the tank to resonate around a giant, light show-flooded auditorium, 'Sorrow' confirmed it: a giant, irresistibly Floydian anthem, driven by the assault and battery of Gilmour's drum machine and a nourishing sonic stew of synths and MIDI programming. Said by some to refer obliquely to Roger Waters, others to the left-leaning social awareness of acclaimed novelist John Steinbeck (from whose *The Grapes of Wrath* the song's first lines are taken), lyrically 'Sorrow' feels closest to a lament for a world systematically mugged in pursuit of progress.

The huge, distorted guitar intro rasps like a broken nail on Velcro. As Ezrin recalled for *Guitar World* in 2008:

> We hired a 24-track truck and a huge PA system and brought them inside the LA Sports Arena. We had the whole venue to ourselves, and we piped Dave's guitar tracks out into the sports arena and re-recorded them in 3D. So the tracks that originally came from a teeny little Gallien-Krueger and a teeny little Fender… sound like the Guitar from Hell.

Indeed, flying over the warning synth-drones of 'Sorrow' is a symphony of guitar sounds and textures, many generated on Gilmour's new 'headless' Steinberger. 'I rather liked the sound it makes naturally', David explained later. 'And then the combination of bending up with the wang bar on whole chords while simultaneously fading in with a stereo volume pedal… that's the sound.'

David's soloing on 'Sorrow' is mesmerising. Despite all the production sorcery, his second statement, at just after six minutes, is effortlessly pure: 'Things like [that] were done on the boat', he said, 'my guitar going through a little Gallien-Krueger amp'. Still more proof that Pink Floyd grasped, better than anyone, Leonardo da Vinci's maxim 'Simplicity is the ultimate sophistication.'

# **The Division Bell** (1994)

Personnel:
David Gilmour: guitars, vocals, bass, keyboards, programming
Nick Mason: drums, percussion
Rick Wright: keyboards, vocals
Bob Ezrin: keyboards, percussion
Jon Carin: programming, keyboards
Guy Pratt: bass
Gary Wallis: played & programmed percussion
Tim Renwick: guitars
Dick Parry: tenor saxophone
Sam Brown, Durga McBroom, Carol Kenyon, Jackie Sheridon, Rebecca Leigh-White: backing vocals
Michael Kamen: orchestral conducting
Produced at: Astoria, Hampton; Britannia Row, London; Abbey Road, London; Metropolis, London; The Creek, London by Bob Ezrin, David Gilmour
Engineers: Andrew Jackson, Keith Grant, Chris Thomas, Jules Bowen, Steve McLaughlin
Released: 28 March 1994
Highest chart positions: UK, US, Canada, Netherlands, Germany: 1

Legal battling done, Pink Floyd were now buoyed by a fraternity that had been absent without leave for too long. Between 1987 and 1989, the *Momentary Lapse of Reason/Another Lapse* tour pulled down $135m worldwide, making it the highest-grossing roadshow of the 1980s. Gilmour and Mason took on side projects: David accompanied and/or produced Kate Bush, Paul McCartney, the Dream Academy, Elton John and All About Eve; Nick wrote a movie soundtrack for *The Cement Garden* and concentrated on his sports cars. By October 1991, the wealthy gadabouts were Mexico-bound, sponsored to compete in a 2,500-mile motor race, *La Carrera Panamericana*. The result (apart from eighth place for Nick and a DNF for David) was a documentary video, its instrumental soundtrack comprising portions of existing Floyd tracks and some new tunes (see final chapter).

In January 1993, Gilmour, Mason and a readmitted Wright boarded Astoria with Bob Ezrin, Andy Jackson and 65 slices of music they'd prepared in a fortnight at Britannia Row. After discarding 40, each Floyd voted on the remainder, eventually grading a shortlist of eleven songs via a points system. This alien exercise in Floydian democracy took a hit when Rick, who until 1994 was still Floyd's wage slave, awarded his employers' efforts *nul points* and his own a maximum of ten each. (Much of the rejected material, dubbed by Jackson *The Big Spliff*, would resurface as *The Endless River* in 2014).

Despite gaming the points system and his tenuous business links with Pink Floyd, Rick was pleased to be back in the inspirational fold, his name on the credits for the first time since *Wish You Were Here*. Concerned about any lingering creative torpor, however, Gilmour one day left a studio tape running while the unwitting keyboardist beavered away. The guitarist was delighted when three of Wright's improvs proved good enough to develop. Rick's return underscored what Floyd had mislaid. Although it was important that the band explored new avenues with changing times and morés and was, perhaps, inevitable under Waters' stewardship that musical exploration would be pared back to accommodate the Big Ideas – many argued that one of the few ineffably Floydian components not available from David Gilmour had been AWOL for twenty years. For much of *The Division Bell*'s soundscaping harks back to those albums on which Pink Floyd were a 'proper' band, rather than two alpha males locking horns while their lessers looked on. Two more blasts from the past were *Dark Side*'s sax player, Dick Parry, and final-mix wizard Chris Thomas. But in case anyone mistook 1994 for 1973, *The Division Bell* still featured a crack squad of sessioneers, many of whom Floyd would keep sweet for another mammoth promotional tour.

To resolve lyrical shortcomings, David signed Anthony Moore for one song, brought in Dream Academy's Nick Laird-Clowes for two and, most enduringly, introduced his new missus-to-be, the journalist and author Polly Samson, for five. Having met David in 1992, Polly had grown up in media and publishing and was no stranger to personal challenge. Following David's support during an especially testing period, she helped her fiancé forge the theme on which Floyd's new album would loosely be based: communication. This would excite much brow-furrowing that *The Division Bell* was about Floyd's relationship with Roger Waters, who now competed with Syd Barrett and Roger's dad for the title of the Allusion Most Likely To Be Found On A Pink Floyd Album. Gilmour denied this, insisting that while all interpretation was subjective, it was 'a little late at this point for us to be conjuring Roger up'. This said, Waters' shade is summoned for at least two tracks, among a suite of songs whose production unfailingly celebrates the spaciousness and clarity of Gilmour's and Ezrin's production and the expressive uplift of David's guitar. Meanwhile, the compressed drum programming of the preceding album is largely left on the MIDI-optimised hard drive.

*The Division Bell* was not named for the call to vote in the House of Commons, although 'division' chimed well with the 'communication' concept. Douglas Adams 'gave' the title to his friend Gilmour in return for a donation to the novelist's favourite charity. In fact, Adams had co-opted the line from the album closer 'High Hopes'. For the cover, Storm Thorgerson designed two heads squaring off in profile that could visually be interpreted as a third in full face. True to form, Storm dismissed namby-pamby illustration cop-outs; instead, Hipgnosis fashioned two metal sculptures the height of a double-decker bus and photographed them duking it out in a Cambridgeshire fen, Ely Cathedral a mystic presence on the distant skyline. And in case there was any doubt, Thorgerson asserted that the third face represented Syd Barrett.

*The Division Bell* went straight to number one in the UK and the US, making double platinum in Britain within six months and triple platinum in the States by 1999. Critics were split: *Entertainment Weekly* blustered that 'avarice is the only conceivable explanation for this glib, vacuous cipher'. *Rolling Stone* felt Gilmour's guitar solos were no more than 'rambling, indistinct asides'. Years later, it dawned on the media that somehow they'd been wrong all along: 'The dark horse of the Floyd canon', drooled *Uncut* in 2011. 'The opening triptych of songs is a hugely impressive return to something very close to the eternal essence of Pink Floyd, and much of the rest retains a quiet power and a meditative quality that betrays a genuine sense of unity'. Amen to that, even if seventeen years and countless youth tribes had to pass before anyone 'fessed up.

### **'Cluster One'** 5.59 (Wright/Gilmour)

'Cluster One' is an appealing six minutes of nod-out ambience based on sound effects, limpid guitar, synths and a delicate piano figure that is archetypally Wright. While the title is no more than a convenient studio categorisation for the first of several jams, the instrumental's inclusion was far from random. And although any relationship between the vaguely *kosmische* title and 1968-vintage Floyd space rock was coincidental, Bob Ezrin handily aligned with the album's theme of communication by uploading the opening SFX to an early internet server in the hope of a reply from the cosmos. He's still waiting, but it's the thought that counts.

### **'What Do You Want From Me'** 4.22 (Gilmour/Wright/Polly Samson)

The band crunch back to Earth with Guy Pratt's heavy bass, Rick's stabbing electric piano and, despite suggestions that he was tilting at fans consumed by Floyd's recent internecine firefight, David's self-doubts about his new romance. 'A lot of the lyrics were the result of a collaboration between myself and Polly', explained the guitarist. 'Some, unfortunately, came after moments of lack of communication between us'. By questioning the complexities, even viability of their own hatchling relationship, David's singing and Polly's part-contributed lyrics ably voice the potential fears of any couple, long-lived or not. With the song anchored by Pratt, Mason's powerful drumming and the dependable soul of the BVs, Gilmour's heavily reverbed playing through 'What Do You Want From Me?' is exemplary, a masterclass in emotional expression entirely in keeping with the sensitive nature of the song's content. In 1994 he told *Guitar World* of the '3D sound' in his head:

> I like to have some element of space and depth in everything we do. And I listen to a lot of records and find them two-dimensional, just in the way they're mixed. And the sad part is that it's not hard to add dimension.

This he does, with aplomb.

### **'Poles Apart'** 7.05 (Gilmour/Samson/Nick Laird-Clowes)

Yet again Syd Barrett drifts into a Pink Floyd song. Through the lyrics of Samson and Laird-Clowes we're reminded that, despite the fact that David was the band's replacement for Floyd's 'golden boy' of the first verse, Syd would 'never lose that light' in his eyes. So far, so 'Shine On'. By the second verse, however, the spectre arrives at the feast, 'Leading the blind while I stared out the steel in your eyes' – someone unlikely to be a million miles from Roger Waters.

Following synths and arpeggiated guitar motifs fading off for a muddled middle eight of church bells and hurdy-gurdy organ (a nod back at *Saucerful*'s Barrett valediction 'Jugband Blues'?), the melody returns with a third verse whose subject might be a composite of the first two. Who exactly are 'poles apart' isn't certain. Barrett and Waters? Gilmour and Barrett/Waters? At the close, perhaps David is magnanimous enough to acknowledge the importance of both very different artists to Pink Floyd. Steady-state and as beautifully produced as the whole album, 'Poles Apart' is the type of Floyd song critics would have dissed as 'plodding' in 1994. But frequent listening proves it a grower.

### **'Marooned'** 5.28 (Wright/Gilmour)

A gorgeously atmospheric instrumental which, as David averred, 'had the scent of the sea about it, probably from the sound of the guitar doing the whale-like thing'. Accompanied by an evocative film of the disporting mammals, Floyd first played 'Marooned' live on tour in Norway, a gesture that surely wasn't meant to be lost on one of the world's most notorious whaling nations. Gilmour's astounding playing is enhanced by his use of an octave-bending DigiTech Whammy pedal, the gadget that inspired the tune and its ionospheric effects: 'I think we basically wrote the first version of it the day I got the pedal.'

### **'A Great Day For Freedom'** 4.18 (Gilmour/Samson)

By 1994 the Eastern Bloc should have been a grisly memory of Wartburgs and irradiated nuclear power plants. But like the aftermath of every war supposed to end wars, the promise of peace following the collapse of the Soviet Union soon proved illusory. Here Polly Samson contrasts the euphoria of the Berlin Wall's retirement with the subsequent ethnic cleansing and conflict in the Balkans. But viewed through a more immediate prism, the structure in question looks suspiciously like a certain Pink Floyd album. Are there hints here of the shackles of totalitarianism falling away with Roger Waters' departure? Perhaps the two great events – one of global import, the other entirely personal – are juxtaposed. Equating Roger's ten-odd years of Floyd governance with Soviet Communism's ruinous five-year plans is silly, but such was the venomousness of the Waters-Gilmour standoff that any darts aimed by one at the other were likely tipped with the sweetest poison. Happier news comes with the arrangement; moved cleanly along by Rick's piano, Michael

Kamen's orchestral strings colour but never smother, allowing plenty of space for another exercise in pure Gilmour feel.

## **'Wearing The Inside Out'** 6.49 (Wright/Moore)

The first two minutes of 'Wearing The Inside Out' are unpromising. The feel is Bobby Goldsboro's 'Summer (The First Time)' – no bad thing in itself, but hardly Floyd – as Dick Parry delivers his breathy, Ben Webster-ish tenor sax over moody synth pads, tasteful guitar colouring, a stolid drumbeat and a percussionist – probably Gary Wallis – apparently piped in from a polite LA yacht-rock session.

Things improve, intensity gathering with each passing Gilmour guitar solo. Following an overly-triumphal Minimoog fanfare, at 3.09 David enters into a lovely dialogue with Dick, his consistently superb guitar finally lifting ordinary filler – if always beautifully played and produced – to a powerful and moving paean to battling isolation and depression. For the first time since *Dark Side* and, sadly, the last time ever with Pink Floyd, Rick Wright – probably Anthony Moore's lyrical subject – takes the lead vocal, on his first musical composition for the band since 'Us And Them'. Did Roger Waters play a part in Wright's post-Floyd disorder? The unassuming Rick certainly emerged from Roger's alleged *Wall*-era hectoring a damaged man. But that was then: now the loneliness, silence and self-harm are gone; he's 'creeping back to life/my nervous system all awry/I'm wearing the inside out'. The title could mean revealing one's true feelings, purging the emotions to overcome misery.

## **'Take It Back'** 6.12 (Gilmour/Ezrin/Samson/Laird-Clowes)

An appropriate title: the first few bars suggest 1968 Pink Floyd have time-jumped to a 1994 studio, no one bothering to iron out the early lumps along the way. But if the intro drifts close to space rock, it's quickly pulled back to terra firma by a shimmeringly contemporary production and the jerky guitar style The Edge utilised to pretty-up numerous songs by U2. Comparisons with the Dublin hitsters continue into subject matter to which the blessed Bono himself was no stranger: in a transcendent love song, the figure of adoration is actually Mother Earth, Gaia herself.

As Nick Laird-Clowes put it: 'David had this great idea about Gaia being a woman who could take the earth back anytime she wanted'. With her love raining 'down on me as easy as the breeze/I listen to her breathing it sounds like the waves on the sea/I was thinking all about her, burning with rage and desire/We were spinning into darkness the earth was on fire', it's clear that Gilmour, singer and joint-lyricist with Samson and Laird-Clowes, is righteously angry, fearful that the planet, if pushed too far, will simply flick our species away into oblivion. Upbeat, zeitgeisty and as commercial as hell, unsurprisingly 'Take It Back' was released as a single, coupled appropriately with a live version of 'Astronomy Dominé'.

**'Coming Back To Life'** 6.19 (Gilmour)

In the only song on the album whose lyrics are entirely his own, David asks: 'Where were you when I was burned and broken/While the days slipped by from my window watching/And where were you when I was hurt and I was helpless/Because the things you say and the things you do surround me'. This suggests he's addressing his new love, thankful that Polly has arrived to help him bury the past and, effectively, come back to life. Following a bluesy introductory solo, David's appreciation is couched in a chugging rock song that seems to have fallen out of The Eagles' LA eyrie. On 'Coming Back To Life' – the clue's in the title – David is aided and abetted by Rick on accompanying vocals and, back in the mix, swelling Hammond organ.

**'Keep Talking'** 6.11 (Gilmour/Wright/Samson)

David was so moved by Prof Stephen Hawking's voiceover for a BT TV commercial that he asked the ad agency for permission to sample the recording. Nick appreciated the relevance, even as he worried that taking a creative cue from a television ad felt 'politically incorrect'. Gilmour, however, declared it the most powerful TV advertising he'd ever seen. 'I thought it was fascinating… and I applied it to one of the pieces of music we already had.'

Strengthened by the presence of the world's most eminent populariser of science – albeit for whom motor neurone disease has obligated communication through a voice synthesiser – Floyd develop the fragment into a suitably evocative plea for people to talk to each other. Prof Hawking's dismembered tones, heard at the immaculately Floydian intro and over the middle eight, is echoed by Gilmour's guitar modified through a TalkBox. David's vocal is up close and personal, while his choppy early guitar – apparently a looped acoustic played with an Ebow (a hand-held electric bow for stringed instruments) processed through a Zoom effects pedal and run backwards – blends into spacy synths, backing vocalists answering the singer in the choruses, blattered percussion from Mason and finally Gilmour's tough rock'n'roll soloing.

A fine track, full of light and shade and tailored for rousing live performance, 'Keep Talking' was released as a US-only single in 1994, backed by a live reading of 'One Of These Days'. Quite rightly, America sent it to number one.

**'Lost For Words'** 5.15 (Gilmour/Samson)

With *The Division Bell* looking likely to be Floyd's final studio shout, David magnanimously invited Roger to contribute. The guitarist's olive branch was reportedly met with a curt 'go fuck yourself'. David replied with a vocal worthy of that master of the vitriolic put-down himself, Bob Dylan.

The mood is more than matched by Polly's lyric, observing angrily that 'While you are wasting your time on your enemies/Engulfed in a fever of spite/Beyond your tunnel vision reality fades/Like shadows into the night'. By the end, the singer wants to make peace – 'So I open my door to my enemies/

And I ask could we wipe the slate clean' – only to be decisively rebuffed. A simple acoustic strumalong with added drums, darkly dreamy synths and SFX, even the music sounds a little like Wilburys-era Dylan. The add-ins include a soundbite from a boxing match – 'winner by a knockout' – while a US-only promotional single and the CD booklet picture a pair of boxing gloves. This could be a deliberate snub, alluding to Pink Floyd's continued success compared with Roger's relatively modest solo career.

## **'High Hopes'** 8.32 (Gilmour/Samson)

So the stage is set for the latest, maybe the last, Floyd showstopper. David treks back to his Cambridge youth, touching upon Floyd's early days – the 'ragged band that followed in our footsteps' – and, once more with feeling, Syd Barrett. As if to underline its valedictory flavour, 'High Hopes' begins with familiar Floyd tropes: birdsong, a buzzing insect, a distant, comfortingly pastoral church peal, followed by a single tolling bell. Six stabs at Rick's piano arrive in gently startling counterpoint, doing for 'High Hopes' what four similarly iconic guitar notes achieved for 'Shine On'. The bell tolls throughout the song, swathed in luxuriant strings both programmed and orchestral, interrupted only by a lap-steel guitar solo by Gilmour at his most imperious.

The feeling is dignified, magisterial, a worthy final page to the Book of Floyd: one of rock music's greatest bodies of work. Despite the new lease of life taken out by the guitarist on behalf of what is now indubitably his band, it's as if Gilmour knows in his heart that Pink Floyd will make no such new statement again. 'High Hopes' ends on a slow fade, leaving only the singular bell and, after a moment, a snippet of David's stepson Charlie hanging up the phone on manager Steve O'Rourke.

So for whom *does* the bell toll? On 7 July 2006, Roger 'Syd' Barrett died of pancreatic cancer at the age of 60. Waters and Gilmour would continue their respective solo careers – and, despite the occasional truce, their war games – but other than for one-off, memorial and charity gigs (such as O'Rourke's funeral in 2003, Live 8 in 2005 and a Syd tribute in 2007), Pink Floyd were effectively done. Speculation raged that Waters, Gilmour, Wright and Mason would yet return to amaze everyone – venues from the obvious (Eden Project in Cornwall) to the borderline potty (the summit of Mount Roraima in Venezuela) were discussed – but Rick's sad passing in 2008 settled the matter. Almost.

## The Endless River (2014)

Personnel:
David Gilmour: guitars, vocals, bass, keyboards, VCS3, percussion, vocals
Nick Mason: drums, percussion
Rick Wright: Hammond & Farfisa organs, electric piano, synthesisers, Royal Albert Hall Grand Organ
Bob Ezrin: keyboards, bass, percussion
Damon Iddins: keyboards
Anthony Moore: keyboards
Jon Carin: synthesiser, percussion loop
Andy Jackson: bass
Guy Pratt: bass
Gilad Atzmon: tenor saxophone, clarinet
Durga McBroom, Louise Marshall, Sarah Brown: backing vocals
Youth: effects
Escala (Helen Nash, Honor Watson, Victoria Lyon, Chantal Leverton): strings
Produced at: Astoria, Hampton; Britannia Row, London; Medina, Hove; Abbey Road, London; Olympic, London; Royal Albert Hall, London by Bob Ezrin, David Gilmour, Phil Manzanera, Youth, Andrew Jackson
Engineers: Andrew Jackson, Damon Iddins, Phil Taylor
Released: 10 November 2014
Highest chart position: UK, Canada, France, Belgium, Netherlands, Germany: 1, US: 3

On 15 September 2008, Richard William Wright succumbed to cancer at the age of 65, seemingly bringing a poignant curtain down upon the Pink Floyd saga. Like notions of The Beatles reforming after John Lennon's death, The Grateful Dead after Jerry Garcia's or the Experience post-Hendrix, continuing without such an important sonic showrunner and close friend was self-evidently absurd.

Yet there was unfinished business. David Gilmour was keen to enshrine Rick's memory on a final Floyd album, its mainly Wright-composed content to be salvaged from twenty-odd discarded hours from *The Division Bell*. This was paradoxical; as an embattled Floyd waded through *The Final Cut*, David had sternly criticised Roger Waters for reheating leftovers from *The Wall*. But by 1983, Roger's demons were still haunting him; given his mindset, and his supremacy over Floyd's direction at the time, *Carry On Up The Wall* seemed an inevitability. Now, six years after Rick's death, building a farewell album around music the keyboardist had left behind felt only right and proper.

Half of *The Division Bell* had been pencilled as songs, the other a suite of ambient instrumentals. Part of the latter component had already been edited by Andy Jackson as *The Big Spliff*, although little would make it to the new album. In August 2012, along with engineers Jackson and Damon Iddins, Gilmour summoned to Astoria his old high-school pal Phil Manzanera, recent collaborator and co-producer of David's 2006 solo record *On An Island*.

Declining Jackson's fragrant edit, the crew instead spent six weeks combing through the source material, eventually distilling four thirteen-minute 'movements' bound by a new concept devised by Manzanera. The Roxy Music and 801 guitarist explained that the first quarter represented Gilmour, Mason and Wright arriving at Astoria to jam, after which the story became fanciful enough to warrant a goodly shot of Floyd classicism c1968: 'The boat takes off and we're in outer space', Phil raved to *Uncut* in 2015. 'They arrive on a planet that is all acoustic. Then there's this end bit, where it goes back'. David was unmoved by Manzanera's eccentric narrative, but heard value in the music. Nick agreed. David and Phil then called in Martin 'Youth' Glover (a big Floyd fan, with whom Gilmour had worked on The Orb's ambient album *Metallic Spheres*) to help shape what would become Pink Floyd's 'symphony' in honour of their departed organist.

Produced at Astoria and Medina Studios in Hove, *The Endless River* comprises the most unashamedly old-school Floyd music since the great soundscaping days of the 1960s-1970s (without, it must be said, the original band's frequent incursions into extreme musical violence). Although many tracks are under two minutes long and only two breach six minutes, they conjoin within the movements, effectively delivering four pieces each of conventionally Floyd length. Only one has lyrics, so any deeper 'concept' must be decoded from the music alone. Whether or not the music succeeds in evoking Manzanera's fevered visions is debatable; its few lyrics have little to do with cosmic galleons and acoustic planets. And no matter how atmospheric, the album's passages of moody abstraction, similar to those that once lengthily prefixed Floyd classics such as 'Shine On' and 'Echoes', risk losing direction.

Except … if only *The Endless River* wasn't so darn beautiful. Like the opening bars of 'Take It Back' from *The Division Bell*, the sense is of late-1960s Pink Floyd journeying through folded space to 2014, the years and the aggro in between dismissed, brave new studio technology just waiting to be exploited. It might have been anathema to Roger, but the album sees Floyd as born-again space rockers, unencumbered by internal quarrels or the angsty baggage of their former colleague. As suggested by the title – once again a line from 'High Hopes', possibly chosen to suggest continuity – the feeling is of timeless, linear motion, as if the listener enters not at the start but at some random point of an eternal flow, similarly departing the stream as it meanders on 52-odd minutes later. With too many other artists this apparently aimless drifting would be a negative, but Floyd are calling in favours owed by such celebrated purveyors of atmos as Tangerine Dream, Vangelis and all the electronicists inspired by PF's 1960-70s masterpieces. Even the spirit of Syd is on board, but this time without everyone feeling terribly guilty about it. 'Unapologetically, this is for the generation that wants to put its headphones on, lie in a beanbag and get off on a piece of music for an extended period of time', Gilmour told *MOJO* on its release.

Travelling back (or forward?) gives *The Endless River* an appropriately valedictory air. Offered Manzanera to *Elsewhere* in 2014:

> It was a slow cruise into the sunset rather than going out crash-bang-wallop. A sort of chill-out goodbye and very much a hybrid… almost documentary and capturing that moment in time, the last time the three of them jammed in a way they hadn't done since *Wish You Were Here* and the period before that.

Following Storm Thorgerson's death in 2013, his Hipgnosis co-founder Po Powell was retained as art director for the sleeve image, created by Ahmed Emad Eldin and design firm Stylorouge. The title-less cover depicts a lone man apparently punting a small boat across the top of a cloudbank – a trip to Cirrus Minor? – representing, according to the artist, 'the intersection of life, nature, and what is beyond the world'. It's probably closer to the mark than cosmic galleons and acoustic planets. On the reverse, the boat remains, but the man is gone. Inside the CD booklet is a series of nautically-flavoured photographs and monochrome shots of the band during the album's preparation.

As usual, the critics were divided. *The Independent*'s Andy Gill moaned about 'aimless jamming, one long thread of Dave Gilmour's guitar against Rick Wright's pastel keyboards'. *The Observer* was kinder: 'an understated affair but unmistakably the Floyd... a pretty good way to call it a day'. But David Fricke in *Rolling Stone* was bang-on: 'Wright was the steady, binding majesty in the Floyd's explorations. This album is an unexpected, welcome epitaph.'

*The Endless River* would be Amazon UK's most pre-ordered album ever, it hit number one with a bullet in several countries and its vinyl edition was the fastest-selling record in that format since 1997. The album was also released as a boxed DVD and Blu-Ray, with a 24-page book, postcards, music videos and bonus tracks culled from *The Big Spliff*, thrillingly entitled 'TBS9' and 'TBS14' (virtually identical soundscapes, with bubbling bass from Pratt and with Gilmour's guitar so reverby he might have been playing in a cave – completists/ obsessives only need apply).

*The Endless River* would be Pink Floyd's last album. A final word from David Gilmour: 'I think we have successfully commandeered the best of what there is... It's a shame, but this is the end.'

## 1st Movement

**'Things Left Unsaid'** 4.26 (Gilmour/Wright); **'It's What We Do'** 6.17 (Gilmour/Wright); **'Ebb And Flow'** 1.55 (Gilmour/Wright)

*The Endless River* opens with eerie synth pads and sampled soundbites of Floyd in introspective mood. The first words are Rick's: 'We certainly have an unspoken understanding. But a lot of things unsaid as well'. David adds, with rhythmical scansion: 'We shout and argue and fight, and work it on out'. Decides Nick: 'The sum is greater than the parts'. The synths swell mysteriously, accompanied by David's Ebowed acoustic guitar and, at the end, Rick's Hammond. The spoken sentiments could align with the previous album's theme of communication, but as an epitaph both to Rick Wright and Pink Floyd, the feel is of a greater vintage.

The title of the second piece says it all, for Floyd can achieve this effortless beauty in their sleep. Virtually the intro to 'Shine On You Crazy Diamond' v.2, the four-note guitar motif could be slotted in quite seamlessly. While we're waiting for it not to arrive, David plays a deliciously bluesy solo. The first movement ends with an elegant, abstract conversation between Rick's shimmering Fender Rhodes and David's arpeggiated and Ebowed acoustic guitar.

## 2nd Movement

**'Sum'** 4.48 (Gilmour/Wright/Mason); **'Skins'** 2.37 (Gilmour/Wright/Mason); **'Unsung'** 1.07 (Wright); **'Anisina'** 3.16 (Gilmour)

An even more transparently retrospective mood pervades the second movement. Rick shadows his iridescent Farfisa intro to 'Astronomy Dominé' before the band arrive by way of synths, David's keening lap steel and a heavy drum pattern from Nick. If the *Piper* song (and still more its live readings) memorably captured the violence of the cosmos, nearly 50 years later 'Sum' and 'Skins' – titled possibly because Mason spends much of its 2.37 bashing his to sherbet – increases the sentence, a viciously percussive section of musical waterboarding taking Floyd within a light year of 'A Saucerful Of Secrets'. After 'Unsung' and its brief chordal nod to 'Time', the second movement concludes with Gilmour's heart-wrenching, Vangelis-ish 'Anisina'. 'I found a few tracks which sounded like songs without lyrics, one became 'Louder Than Words' and one was 'Anisina'', the guitarist said. 'I thought Polly was going to write for both, but... she decided there were no words needed'. With something more still required, however, Israeli-born saxophonist Gilad Atzmon was brought in by Manzanera to play a lyrical lament for Rick.

## 3rd Movement

**'The Lost Art Of Conversation'** 1.42 (Wright); **'On Noodle Street'** 1.42 (Gilmour/Wright); **'Night Light'** 1.42 (Gilmour/Wright); **'Allons-y (1)'** 1.57 (Gilmour); **'Autumn '68'** 1.35 (Wright); **'Allons-y (2)'** 1.32 (Gilmour); **'Talkin' Hawkin'** 3.29 (Gilmour/Wright)

Rick's piano on 'The Lost Art Of Conversation' has an interestingly 'conservatoire' tone, Wright tripping pleasingly and bluesily across the top of drifting synth-pads on a piece that could have been made for a chillout lounge. With Rick remaining on vibraphone-ish Fender Rhodes, the pace picks up slightly on the bass-driven 'On Noodle Street' (which does just that). 'Night Light' returns to space, soundtracking an elegant planetary ballet. The dynamics of 'Allons-y (1)' recall parts of *The Wall*, in particular 'Run Like Hell', which outlived Roger's tenure with Floyd as a live show-closer. 'Autumn

'68' obviously refers to Rick's exquisite 'Summer '68', although musically the two songs are very different. Here Wright occupies the Royal Albert Hall pipe organ for a sepulchral passage reminiscent of Beaver & Krause's Moog odyssey *Gandharva*, punctuated by Gilmour's bluesy guitar and Mason's gong. 'Allons-y (2)' takes up the reins of its first part, before the magnificent build-up of 'Talkin' Hawkin': a natural companion to 'Keep Talking' that retains its samples of the good professor.

## 4th Movement

### **'Calling'** 3.37 (Gilmour/Moore); **'Eyes To Pearls'** 1.51 (Gilmour); **'Surfacing'** 2.46 (Gilmour); **'Louder Than Words'** 6.36 (Gilmour/Samson)

To conclude this stylish voyage through the spheres, 'Calling' is co-written by Anthony Moore, who swaps wordsmithery for his more regular gig as a composer of experimental music. While nothing here is as intimidating as his work with serial art terrorists Slapp Happy, an intoxicating darkness pervades the beginning of the last quarter of *The Endless River*. Like 'Anisina', Wright is nowhere near 'Calling'; yet with its icily Mellotron-like synth pads conveying a dramatic and oppressive sense of impending doom, the tune's a distant cousin of Rick's apocalyptic masterpiece 'Sysyphus'. 'Eyes To Pearls' is strictly filler, David's insistently simple guitar notes assaulted by the wash of Nick's gong and a battery of synths, underpinned by Andy Jackson's throbbing bass. 'Surfacing' once more sounds as if it fell off a longer classic Floyd piece, an ambient soundscape finding rhythmic form at 0.57 thanks to Nick's ever-patient timekeeping.

*The Endless River*'s concluding song, 'Louder Than Words', begins with the merest hint of the church bells from 'High Hopes', followed by David's arpeggios and Rick's crystalline piano. Polly was moved to lyricism after the all-too-brief reunion of Roger, Rick, Nick and her husband at Live 8 in 2005. As she explained in 2015 to *Entertainment Weekly*:

> They'd rehearsed, there were sound checks, lots of downtime sitting in rooms with David, Rick, Nick, and, on that occasion, Roger. And what struck me was… they don't do small talk, they don't do big talk. It's not hostile, they just don't speak. And then they step onto a stage and musically, that communication is extraordinary.

It's a triumphal lyric, speaking once again to the concept of communication: the single word which, with its caveat the dangers of misunderstanding, could be said to meld together all of Pink Floyd's albums, at least since *Dark Side*. It even throws out a rope to absent friends; the Pink Floyd achievements that are 'louder than words' and 'this thing we do' remain there for the taking – or, at any rate, should Roger Waters choose to do so. Musically Floyd's final regular song is as elegiac and uplifting as befits such a plea for tolerance and lament for lost unity. They couldn't have delivered a better signoff.

# An introduction to the live albums, compilations, waifs and strays

Where to start? Possibly only obsessive Grateful Dead fans are as willing to invest in so huge an inventory of their idols' collectables. It's inevitable that a band of Pink Floyd's stature should generate such a heaving mountain of live, remastered, unauthorised and hitherto unearthed material. But it's debatable whether the remaining Floyds do much more now than rubber-stamp legitimate product, then leave it to the managers, accountants, lawyers and record execs to sell it (often at outrageous prices) into a demographic apparently composed of retired investment bankers.

Floyd's quality-control standards are copper-bottomed. Their opinion of bootleggers who circulate, for a fast buck, what may be inferior material is famously stern. So it's hard to believe Floyd are not acutely aware of how, and at what costs to consumers, their wares are sold. Leaving aside the 'remasters' that appear in slightly modified packaging every ten years or less, a good case in point is the mammoth *The Early Years 1965-1972*: a multi-volume, 33-disc box set released in 2016. A comprehensive account of Floyd's surging creativity pre-*DSOTM*, the set contains some phenomenal music, most of it live (although even the most devoted Floyd fan might blanch at fifteen versions of 'Careful With That Axe, Eugene'). Besides the complete box set, the record company offered six of the seven volumes as separate items, each comprising three or four CDs, DVDs and Blu-ray discs. Bulked out with reproductions of printed ephemera and packaged like a small hardbacked book, each volume retailed at around £40, an average which, as I write, seems to increase exponentially. To acquire the seventh volume, which contains yet more music and DVDs from that period, obliges the consumer to buy the other six at the same time, leaving Floyd completists with potential bills of £400 and counting to plug the holes in their collections. The company has since put out a cost-reduced edition condensed to two CDs, but unsurprisingly this barely scrapes the surface of the treasures buried in the full chest. At the time of writing, and to the author's knowledge, *The Early Years* is the only legitimate (ie: non-bootleg) UK source of important and historic recordings such as 'Vegetable Man', 'Scream Thy Last Scream', *The Man/The Journey* and other fossils from Jurassic-era Floyd. As I write, single-CD editions from each volume are available relatively cheaply on Ebay. Unsurprisingly I can't verify provenance – their vendors are usually located in Russia. In 2019, a similar behemoth entitled *The Later Years* was disgorged to cover the period to date following David Gilmour's ascent to the throne in 1985. No doubt perplexingly for the wealthier Floyd collector, there is yet no equivalent for what presumably would be branded *The Middle Years*.

Unauthorised Floyd recordings abound, the stuff of market stalls, record fairs and the internet. Some are very good, others are atrocious, most are illegal and consequently way above the author's security clearance (if only because I can't be sure what I write will be safe from the bootleg police). Following Floyd's

1972 road test of *Dark Side Of The Moon* at the Rainbow Theatre, barrow-haunting record buyers chanced upon a high-quality pirate tape from one or more of the shows. Hitting the markets of Camden and Walthamstow a full year before *Dark Side*'s official release, this bootleg sold more than 100,000 and was said to have dissuaded Floyd from ever again refining unreleased work on the road.

Such forbidden fruit can also hit the pocket, as anyone who's dipped a toe into the bootleggers' murky shallows will testify. Illegitimate releases probably outnumber actual Floyd gigs: at the very moment a 1969 reading of 'Embryo' at the Royal Albert Hall was being captured, for posterity and moolah, on a cassette recorder by a bloke up in Row W, it's likely another bloke in Row Y had a mic pointed at exactly the same thing, subsequently to privately press and issue the identical music on a differently-titled bootleg. At least the authorised releases, costly as they may be, have the virtues of provenance and, often recorded straight from the soundboard, relatively decent fidelity.

# Live albums

## **Delicate Sound Of Thunder** (1988)

'Shine On You Crazy Diamond'/'Learning To Fly'/'Yet Another Movie'/'Round And Around'/'Sorrow'/'The Dogs Of War'/'On The Turning Away'/'One Of These Days'/'Time'/'Wish You Were Here'/'Us And Them'/'Money'/'Another Brick In The Wall (Part 2)'/'Comfortably Numb'/'Run Like Hell'

When the Soviet spacecraft Soyuz TM-7 was launched from Kazakhstan on 26 November 1988, two days later to dock with the space station Mir, its pilots needed some decent music to while away the journey. David and Nick, invited to attend the launch, gifted the cosmonauts a cassette of *Delicate Sound Of Thunder*. Thus Pink Floyd became the first rock'n'roll band to be played in space: pretty good, if not incredibly ironic, for a group who'd spent much of the preceding two decades denying their music had anything to do with the wretched stuff. Spared radio snooker and the Hairy Cornflake, the crew must have had a pleasant flight; recorded at the Nassau Coliseum, *Delicate Sound Of Thunder* is an excellent account of the *Momentary Lapse* tour, and a reminder that Floyd still had pulling power after Roger's departure. It sold by the bucketload, outdoing the later, more lavish *P.U.L.S.E.*.

## **P.U.L.S.E.** (1995)

'Shine On You Crazy Diamond'/'Astronomy Dominé'/'What Do You Want From Me'/'Learning To Fly'/'Keep Talking'/'Coming Back To Life'/'Hey You'/'A Great Day For Freedom'/'Sorrow'/'High Hopes'/'Another Brick In The Wall (Part 2)'/Dark Side Of The Moon: 'Speak To Me'/'Breathe'/'On The Run'/'Time'/'The Great Gig In The Sky'/'Money'/'Us And Them'/'Any Colour You Like'/'Brain Damage'/'Eclipse'/'Wish You Were Here'/'Comfortably Numb'/'Run Like Hell'

*P.U.L.S.E.* is also available as a DVD.

Probably the essential later Pink Floyd live album, at least among the official releases, even if at least three members of the 1994 touring band were hiding behind sofas from *Doctor Who* while Syd Barrett was spacehopping around UFO. Following the opener, a spine-tingling 'Shine On', the now all-powerful David Gilmour plunders the band's inventory right back to a brilliant 'Astronomy Dominé', choosing wisely from *A Momentary Lapse Of Reason* and *The Division Bell*.

Recorded in the UK and Europe and produced by Gilmour and James Guthrie, *P.U.L.S.E.* also includes a fine reading of *Dark Side Of The Moon*. Until the extra disc (recorded at Wembley Empire Pool in November 1974) that accompanied the 2011 'Experience' remix of the original, *P.U.L.S.E.* included the only official concert version of Floyd's masterpiece. The band play the whole thing fairly straightforwardly, with little instrumental stretching other than some playful extemporisation with the backing vocalists on 'Money'.

At the end, David nods at the adulatory roars with a cheery 'Takes you back, doesn't it?', as if the last 48 minutes and Floyd's thunderous delivery of rock's opus maximus has been nothing more than a relaxed Sunday afternoon stroll around Cambridge with an old girlfriend.

But worth the price of admission is the nine-minute 'Comfortably Numb'. On the definitive reading of Gilmour's stupendous main contribution to *The Wall*, he cements his place as rock's most impassioned and emotionally expressive lead guitarist. The second of his two solos will lift your heart like no other, David finding and unerringly hitting, every time, *those* notes. Those who prefer the adventurously ragged glories of early Floyd may hear and see only antiseptic sterility in *P.U.L.S.E.*'s note-perfect precision and immaculate presentation. But stick this record through a state-of-the-art sound system, kick back with a herbal remedy of your choice, then tell me your eyes haven't welled up like an overflowing grail of nectar.

## **Is There Anybody Out There? The Wall Live 1980-81** (2000)

With tracks culled from gigs at Earl's Court in August 1980 and June 1981, *Is There Anybody Out There?* transcribes faithfully Roger Waters' conceptual colossus. Performance afforded the band more room to stretch out; accordingly, a number of intros and solos are extended. As Roger originally wanted, Vera Lynn's 'We'll Meet Again' is sampled for use at the start. This is an excellent companion to *The Wall*, especially given its inclusion of two tracks left off the original for reasons of space: 'The Last Few Bricks' (a placeholding instrumental of familiar themes spanning 'Another Brick...pt3') and 'Goodbye Cruel World' and 'What Shall We Do Now?' (where Pink ponders the true value of his rock star status and possessions). Packaged on release as a slipcased 2-CD set, with a beautifully illustrated, hardbacked 66-page booklet.

## **Live At Knebworth 1990** (2021)

'Shine On You Crazy Diamond'/'The Great Gig In The Sky'/'Wish You Were Here'/'Sorrow'/'Money'/'Comfortably Numb'/'Run Like Hell'

The outdoor concert at Knebworth Park on 30 June 1990 was an opportunity for 120,000 fans to enjoy rock's deities – Pink Floyd, Paul McCartney, Eric Clapton, Genesis, Elton John, Dire Straits, Page & Plant et al – strutting their charitable stuff for the Nordoff-Robbins Centre for Music Therapy. Unfortunately, the weather gods had other ideas.

Although Floyd's performance was shortened due to rain, the resulting live record has buffed up surprisingly well. For Floyd fans who were there, it's clearly indispensable. And with the official release suppressing sales of the inevitable bootlegs, no doubt the band's accountants were happy, too. But set dispassionately against the magnificent *P.U.L.S.E.*, *Live At Knebworth 1990* is relatively inessential.

True, Floyd are joined onstage by the 21-year-old Dutch sax prodigy Candy Dulfer, who contributes good 'n' greasy alto solos on 'Shine On' and 'Money'. Floyd also have some fun on the latter, as bluesman Gilmour briefly steps out into classic Clapton territory with impromptu quotes from L. C. Frazier's

'Steppin' Out'. While cries of 'Gilmour is God' from any veterans there present of the 1960s blues club scene aren't evident on the CD, the overall balance, clarity and tightness of the musicians are much better than expected given the conditions. This said, if the 1995 set is still comparatively easy to find and money's more of an issue than completism, *P.U.L.S.E.* still has post-Waters live Pink Floyd licked.

# Compilations

## **Relics** (1971)

'Arnold Layne'/'Interstellar Overdrive'/'See Emily Play'/'Remember A Day'/'Paintbox'/'Julia Dream'/'Careful With That Axe, Eugene'/'Cirrus Minor'/'The Nile Song'/'Biding My Time'/'Bike'

Originally released on EMI's cut-price Music For Pleasure label, the placemarking 'Relics' is notable for Nick's enjoyably Heath Robinson-ish cover illustration and the inclusion of 'Biding My Time': a disposable blues that formed part of Floyd's 1969 *The Man/The Journey* suite. Lazy to start, the song features Rick's double-tracked trombone solo presaging a rowdy finish, for which most of the musicians seem to have been recorded in different studios. *Relics* was remastered for CD in 1995.

## **A Nice Pair** (1973)

*The Piper At The Gates Of Dawn* and *A Saucerful Of Secrets* bundled as a two-for-one double album. Hipgnosis's cover design featured nine visual plays on the album's title, including (inevitably – it *was* 1973) a nice pair of female breasts.

## **A Collection Of Great Dance Songs** (1981)

'One Of These Days'/'Money'/'Sheep'/'Shine On You Crazy Diamond'/'Wish You Were Here'/'Another Brick In The Wall (Part 2)'

Despite alternative mixes of 'Shine On' and 'Another Brick' and, due to licencing wars between Capitol Records and Columbia, a 'Money' makeover by David Gilmour, this is a largely pointless digest of material spanning *Meddle* and *The Wall*. Originally a single vinyl album (presumably the diktat of a record company with an eye to quick sales), subsequent CD releases saw no added tracks, despite the obvious extra available bandwidth. Floyd's 1970s oeuvre would have been better served by a double at least, but tell that to the beancounters.

## **Works** (1983)

'One Of These Days'/'Arnold Layne'/'Fearless'/'Brain Damage'/'Eclipse'/'Set The Controls For The Heart Of The Sun'/'See Emily Play'/'Several Species Of Small Furry Animals Gathered Together In A Cave And Grooving With A Pict'/'Free Four'/'Embryo'

The rebirth of 'Embryo' is welcome, but with some of their greatest work sidelined, only God and Roger Waters can explain the inclusion of 'Several Species' from *Ummagumma*.

## **Shine On** (1992)

Celebratory in shelf-presence – the spines of the nine CD jewel cases display the *Dark Side* prism when stacked – *Shine On* is a remastered, if strangely subjective compendium of *Saucerful*, *Meddle*, *Dark Side*, *Wish You Were Here*, *Animals*, *The Wall* (split over two discs) and *Momentary Lapse*, plus an extra

CD of Floyd's first five singles. The additions of a 114-page booklet, postcards and a display stand(!) demark the set as 'lavish.'

## **Echoes: The Best Of Pink Floyd** (2001)

'Astronomy Dominé'/'See Emily Play'/'The Happiest Days Of Our Lives'/'Another Brick In The Wall (Part 2)'/'Echoes'/'Hey You'/'Marooned'/'The Great Gig In The Sky'/'Set The Controls For The Heart Of The Sun'/'Money'/'Keep Talking'/'Sheep'/'Sorrow'/'Shine On You Crazy Diamond'/'Time'/'Breathe' (reprise)/'The Fletcher Memorial Home'/'Comfortably Numb'/'When the Tigers Broke Free'/'One Of These Days'/'Us And Them'/'Learning To Fly'/'Arnold Layne'/'Wish You Were Here'/'Jugband Blues'/'High Hopes'/'Bike'

Given the available space of a double CD, this self-curated set is a pretty good compilation. The programming for *Echoes* was, unsurprisingly, hotly debated among an atomised Floyd, with Roger and David especially proprietorial over their respective choices. Such was the lethal atmosphere between the two that each questioned the other's preferences almost by default. Some inclusions were obvious ('Astronomy Dominé', 'Emily', 'Another Brick', 'Echoes', etc); some glaringly evident by their absence ('Chapter 24', 'Saucerful', 'Sysyphus', 'Summer '68' – although I'll gladly concede this is the subjective view of the author). *Echoes* also highlights the perils of extracting single tracks from a larger piece of work that ought to remain uncompromised. I'm thinking here, of course, of *Dark Side Of The Moon*; while 'Money' and 'Time' are very fine standalone songs, pulling them out of their original context doesn't feel right, somehow, like taking bite-sized chunks out of an epic poem or symphony.

## **Oh, By The Way** (2007)

Scaled-down, sleeves 'n' all, to CD, a cute box-set of all official Pink Floyd albums (except, given date of release, *The Endless River*). Nothing new to report, but well received at the time.

## **Discovery** (2011)

Another CD box with the same content as the 2007 set, this time remastered by James Guthrie and Joel Plante. Each album was also made available as a standalone CD.

## **The Early Years** (2016)

A monstrous 7-volume, 33-disc compendium of music produced by Pink Floyd between 1965 and 1972. Each volume contains visual PF material recorded to DVD and Blu-Ray. However, the listings below refer only to the CD audio files, of which there are one or two per volume. Prices of these editions vary, but are usually high – up to £70 is not unusual. As I write, sellers in Estonia offer single repackaged CDs from each *Early Years* volume (music only; no DVD/Blu-Ray) for around £15 each. The Ebay ads insist these are legitimate, but usual caveats apply.

## Volume 1: 1965–1967: Cambridge St/ation

CD 1: by The Tea Set: 'Lucy Leave'/'Double O Bo'/'Remember Me'/'Walk With Me Sydney'/'Butterfly'/'I'm A King Bee'/by The Pink Floyd: 'Arnold Layne'/'See Emily Play'/'Apples And Oranges'/'Candy And A Currant Bun'/'Paintbox'/'Matilda Mother'/'Jugband Blues'/'In The Beechwoods'/'Vegetable Man'/'Scream Thy Last Scream'/CD2: by The Pink Floyd Live in Stockholm: 'Introduction'/'Reaction In G'/'Matilda Mother'/'Pow R. Toc H.'/'Scream Thy Last Scream'/'Set The Controls For The Heart Of The Sun'/'See Emily Play'/'Interstellar Overdrive'/John Latham studio recordings: 'John Latham versions 1-9'

**In 1967, five years after conceptual artist John Latham made a film called *Speak*, Roger and Nick (the director's contemporaries at Regent Street Poly) teamed with Rick and Syd to produce a soundtrack. Included here on CD2, the nine-part piece consists of an extended improvisation similar to the soundscapes of 'Interstellar Overdrive.'**

## Volume 2: 1968: Germin/ation

CD 1: Original releases: 'Point Me At The Sky'/'It Would Be So Nice'/'Julia Dream'/'Careful With That Axe, Eugene'/Capitol Studios, LA live session, 22 August 1968 (prev unreleased): 'Song 1'/'Roger's Boogie'/BBC live session 25 June 1968 (prev unreleased): 'Murderotic Woman' ('Careful With That Axe, Eugene')/'The Massed Gadgets Of Hercules' ('A Saucerful Of Secrets')/'Let There Be More Light'/'Julia Dream'/BBC live session 2 December 1968 (prev unreleased): 'Point Me At The Sky'/'Embryo'/'Interstellar Overdrive.'

## Volume 3: 1969: Dramatis/ation

CD 1: non-album tracks from More soundtrack: 'Hollywood'/'Theme'/'More Blues'/'Sea Birds'/other tracks: 'Embryo' (demo)/BBC live session 12 May 1969: 'Grantchester Meadows'/'Cymbaline'/'The Narrow Way'/'Green Is The Colour'/'Careful With That Axe, Eugene'/Live at the Paradiso, Amsterdam, 9 August 1969: 'Interstellar Overdrive'/'Set The Controls For The Heart Of The Sun'/'Careful With That Axe, Eugene'/'A Saucerful Of Secrets'/CD2: The Man/ The Journey live at Concertgebouw, Amsterdam, 17 September 1969 (prev unreleased): 'Daybreak' ('Grantchester Meadows')/'Work'/'Afternoon' ('Biding My Time')'/'Doing It'/'Sleeping'/'Nightmare' ('Cymbaline')/'Labyrinth'/'The Beginning' ('Green is the Colour')/'Beset By Creatures Of The Deep' ('Careful With That Axe, Eugene')/'The Narrow Way pt 3'/'The Pink Jungle' ('Pow R. Toc H.')/'The Labyrinths Of Auximenes'/'Footsteps'-'Doors'/'Behold The Temple of Light'/'The End Of The Beginning' ('A Saucerful Of Secrets').

## Volume 4: 1970: Devi/ation

CD 1: Live at the Casino de Montreux, 21 November 1970 (prev unreleased): 'Atom Heart Mother'/BBC live session 16 July 1970 (prev unreleased): 'Embryo'/'Fat Old Sun'/'Green Is The Colour'/'Careful With That Axe, Eugene'/'If'/'Atom Heart Mother' (with brass & choir) CD2: from Zabriskie Point soundtrack (prev unreleased): 'On The Highway'/'Auto Scene v2'/'Auto

Scene v3'/'Aeroplane'/'Explosion' ('Careful With That Axe, Eugene')/'The Riot Scene'/'Looking At Map'/'Love Scene v7'/'Love Scene v1'/'Take Off'/'Take Off v2'/'Love Scene v2'/'Love Scene (take 1)'/'Unknown Song (take 1)'/'Love Scene (take 2)'/'Crumbling Land (take 1)'/Early studio version, band only (prev unreleased): 'Atom Heart Mother'/CD3 (audio only on DVD): ***Atom Heart Mother*** (complete 1970 album 4.0 quadraphonic mix).

## Volume 5: 1971: Reverber/ation

CD 1: 'Nothing pt 14' ('Echoes' work-in-progress)/BBC live session 30 September 1971: 'Fat Old Sun'/'One Of These Days'/'Embryo'/'Echoes'/CD2 (audio only on DVD): 'Echoes' (1971 original 4.0 quadraphonic mix).

## Volume 6: 1971-2: Obfusc/ation

CD 1: ***Obscured By Clouds*** (2016 mix): 'Obscured By Clouds'/'When You're In'/'Burning Bridges'/'The Gold It's In The ...'/'Wot's... Uh, The Deal?'/'Mudmen'/'Childhood's End'/'Free Four'/'Stay'/'Absolutely Curtains'

**Before shipping, CD1 was accidentally swapped for the *Live At Pompeii* stereo CD. *Obscured By Clouds* is packaged in a separate white slipcase, advising that it is a 'Replacement CD disc for *Obfusc/ation...* (Stereo 2016 mix of *Live At Pompeii* CD supplied in error)'. The standalone edition of Volume 6 includes *Live At Pompeii* as CD2.**

## Volume 7: 1967-72: Continu/ation

**Vols 1-6 available as separate items. Vol 7 available only as part of the complete *Early Years* box set.**

CD 1: BBC live session 25 September 1967: 'Flaming'/'The Scarecrow'/'The Gnome'/'Matilda Mother'/'Reaction In G'/'Set The Controls For The Heart Of The Sun'/BBC live session 20 December 1967: 'Scream Thy Last Scream'/'Vegetable Man'/'Pow R. Toc H.'/'Jugband Blues'/Others: 'Baby Blue Shuffle In D Major' (BBC live session 2 December 1968)/'Blues' (BBC live session 2 December 1968)/US radio ad for Ummagumma/'Music From The Committee no1'/'Music From The Committee no2'/'Moonhead' (BBC live session to mark Moon landing 1969)/'Echoes' (live at Wembley 1974).

## Bonus CD: Live At Pompeii

'Careful With That Axe, Eugene'/'Set The Controls For The Heart Of The Sun'/'One Of These Days'/'A Saucerful Of Secrets'/'Echoes'/'Careful With That Axe, Eugene' (alt).

**Hitherto officially unreleased, Floyd's volcanic performance at the Pompeii amphitheatre for their 1971 film was included in *The Early Years* set. In the 2002 DVD re-release of *Live At Pompeii*, director Adrian Maben saw fit to accompany the opening bars of 'Echoes' with a fancy new montage of elegantly waltzing planets and what sounds like Dave Bowman's exaggerated breathing towards the end of *2001*. Roger Waters' comments were probably unrepeatable.**

## **The Later Years** (2019)

Got £700 to spare? A companion to *The Early Years*, this compiles Floyd's music following Gilmour's ascension. The 18 CDs and DVD/Blu-Rays of *The Later Years* comprise updated, remixed and/or surround-sound editions of *Momentary Lapse*, *Delicate Sound Of Thunder*, *The Division Bell*, *Live At Knebworth 1990*, *P.U.L.S.E.* and *The Endless River*, alongside a potpourri of restored and new contributions from Rick and Nick, unreleased live sets and demos, videos and a skipful of bells and whistles.

Of special mention is the previously unreleased concert footage of Floyd's infamous 1989 performance in Venice. The city fathers, afraid the combined impact of fandom, extreme volume and Floyd's back line would sink the Piazza and do irreparable damage to ancient buildings, instructed the band to relocate to a floating stage in the Lagoon. Angered that a pop group should dishonour the Renaissance's spiritual home, residents subsequently removed Venice's mayor. Pink Floyd helped bring down a government, then: Malcolm McLaren must have been dumbstruck.

# Waifs and Strays

## Zabriskie Point (1969)

In November 1969, Floyd were invited to Rome by Italian auteur Michelangelo Antonioni. The director wanted Floyd, then carving a reputation among makers of impenetrable European art films as go-to soundtrackers, to score his next movie, *Zabriskie Point*. A well-photographed but dull drama about right-on American students fighting the power then repairing to the desert for group ummagumma, the story didn't end well. And neither did Floyd's input, as the band discovered Antonioni impossible to please. Only three Floyd songs were retained: 'Heart Beat, Pig Meat' (an instrumental featuring the heartbeat FX later used, to much better effect, on *Dark Side*); 'Crumbling Land' (an inessential country-rocker); and 'Come in Number 51, Your Time's Up' (a rejig of 'Careful With That Axe, Eugene'). Of the discarded material, most important proved to be Rick Wright's 'The Violent Sequence', which finally came into its own as *Dark Side*'s commanding 'Us And Them'. These and other previously unreleased *ZP* discards can be found on *The Early Years Volume 4: 1970: Devi/ation* (see above).

## 'Embryo' 10.13 (Waters)

Recorded for BBC radio session, 16 July 1970
Available on *Pink Floyd: The Early Years 1967-1972 Cre/ation* (double CD edition)

For several years 'Embryo' was missing in action, apparently aborted due to impatient executives, ruffled band feathers or, possibly, boredom. Some fans believed 'Embryo' was deliberately shelved; a classic act of Floydian testiness meant to deprive the world of one of the group's best early pieces. (Presumably the band were happy enough with the song per se; Floyd audiences would continue to enjoy brilliant extended concert readings of 'Embryo' for several years).

Its incubation can be traced to live performances from 1968 and, a year later, the first sessions for *Ummagumma*, for which studio sides 'Embryo' was originally pencilled. Having demoed, however, Floyd took it no further, possibly because of the decision to populate the studio half of the 1969 double-album with individually-tailored pieces (though words and music are accredited to Roger, 'Embryo''s onstage development pointed to an evolving group collaboration). Or maybe they just couldn't be arsed; despite much superlative music pre-*Dark Side*, of that period Floyd have been their own harshest critics, as we've seen.

But whatever they might have said since, 'Embryo' is an absolute gem. Rather than allow such treasure to gather dust, Harvest had Norman Smith brush it up for inclusion on the 1970 double-sampler *Picnic: a Breath of Fresh Air*. However, the song's premature release peeved Floyd so much – perhaps because no-one at EMI had the courtesy to ask the band what they wanted – that they forced the withdrawal of the entire collection. Yet irrespective of the suits embezzling a work-in-progress and releasing it without permission, there's little immature about the original 'Embryo.'

Floyd set the controls for the heart of somewhere much closer to home than usual. The guide on this fantastic voyage is the Embryo itself: 'always need[ing] a little more room', the eponymous congeries of cells and genes waits patiently for 'the sunshine show'. What begins gently becomes transformed onstage, the lyricism of Gilmour's intro swiftly breaking out into liquid savagery. Floyd then quieten the violence for two verses, sung by David with Rick's backing. A jaunty organ figure, a baby crying, children playing and a flock of phantom gannets issuing from Wright's battery of keys celebrate the impending birth in an extended instrumental section. Here Floyd would let rip onstage; in Cincinnati in November 1971, 'Embryo' was drawn out to more than 25 minutes, due, it's said, to technical difficulties during the middle break. An ecstatic audience were none the wiser.

Presumably with a rapidly-splitting Floyd's blessing, the *Picnic* cut would reappear on the 1983 US-only collection, *Works*; on *A Breath Of Fresh Air*, reissued and expanded in 2007 to three CDs (but losing, interestingly, the *Picnic*); and eventually in various guises and lengths on the 2016 box-set *The Early Years 1967-1972*. Suppressed for too long, 'Embryo' is a small wonder, proving Pink Floyd as capable of journeying through inner space as to the farthest outer reaches.

## **La Carrera Panamericana** (1992)

'Run Like Hell'/'Pan Am Shuffle'/'Yet Another Movie'/'Sorrow'/'Signs Of Life'/'Country Theme'/'Mexico '78'/'Big Theme'/'Run Like Hell'/'One Slip'/'Small Theme'/'Pan Am Shuffle'/'Carrera Slow Blues'

Gilmour's and Mason's instrumental soundtrack for the 1991 Mexican motor race was part new pieces, part bowdlerised tracks from *The Wall* and *Momentary Lapse*. 'Pan Am Shuffle' and 'Carrera Slow Blues' are accredited to Gilmour/Mason/Wright, the first such collaboration since *Dark Side*. David wrote the balance of new material, recording with Nick and Rick augmented by Jon Carin, Tim Renwick, Guy Pratt and Gary Wallis. Heard over *Top Gear*-style visuals of muscle cars and their tough-guy drivers barrelling past bewildered locals, the new music can be striking. Needless to say the playing is exemplary, and there's the occasional surprise, such as the Roy Orbison-style intro to 'Country Theme'. But like many film scores it all otherwise fades into wallpaper. The film was shown on BBC2 that December, with an amended video released commercially.

# The Final Single: A Cry for Ukraine

## **'Hey Hey, Rise Up'** 3.45 (Gilmour/Andriy Khlyvnyuk)

On 24 February 2022, Ukraine was invaded by order of the president of the Russian Federation, Vladimir Putin. The ensuing war (which at time of writing still rages) triggered thousands of casualties, widespread destruction of Ukrainian cities and infrastructure, millions forced to seek refuge in neighbouring countries and worldwide oil and grain crises. Putin's atrocities inspired David Gilmour to reboot Pink Floyd – Gilmour, Nick Mason, bassist Guy Pratt and keyboardist Nitin Sawhney – for a benefit single to support UN humanitarian relief for Ukraine. In a media conference, David commented:

> It started after I saw an Instagram feed from a singer named Andriy Khlyvnyuk, of the Ukrainian band Boombox. He's in a square in Kyiv, wearing military fatigues and carrying a gun, and he bursts into a capella song. It struck me that this could be turned into something lovely.

With Putin's tanks stalling on the road to Kyiv, Andriy quit Boombox's American tour and returned to the capital to fight. Three days later, he posted the video of his rendering of an old Ukrainian war song, 'The Red Viburnum in the Meadow'. David (whose daughter-in-law is Ukrainian) obtained the singer's blessing for a collaboration and mapped out some ideas on turning what he'd heard online into a Pink Floyd single 'to show our anger at a superpower invading a peaceful nation.'

The result, effectively the first new Floyd music in 28 years, was recorded in David's converted barn studio and released on 8 April 2022. The song begins with a typically rousing East Slavic male voice choir, after which the band accompany a sample of Andriy singing the main theme in his native language. At 1.23 in comes Gilmour – which is, let's face it, what everyone's waiting for – and duly proves he's lost none of his chops, his soloing as crisp and incisive as an iced diamond, the bent and blue notes dancing from his Telecaster. It's actually a triptych of soloing, the three parts each differing very slightly in tone, conveying Gilmour's righteous anger and attack without losing his usual taste. The song itself is slightly lumbering; but given its good intentions, the fact it was recorded at pace and, of course, David's scintillating solos, this can be forgiven.

'Hey Hey, Rise Up' became Floyd's first Top Ten single in 43 years. And yes, there's an elephant in the room: Roger Waters was asked to contribute but declined. 'Let's just say I was disappointed and let's move on', David said. 'Read into that what you will'. But all things considered, it's good to have at least an approximation of Pink Floyd after so long – and with a protest song, no less. Damn punks.

## On a final, personal note

In 1968, my friends and I decided that our school's weekly blues club needed a boost. Elmore James and Howlin' Wolf were great, but twelve bars went a long way. And Pink Floyd? They were visionaries, the future, refreshing the parts other seers could not reach. Anyway, 'Jugband Blues' counted, right?

We were permitted one spin only of *A Saucerful Of Secrets* before the sternly orthodox fifth-form bluesologists who ran the club went full-on Taliban. They'd not be swapping Muddy Waters for Roger Waters anytime soon. But our evangelising continued apace into the following year and the relaxation of parental bans on live concerts.

Those were heady days. An anti-establishment mood still frowned upon the profit motive, and the freebie was king. For the cost of a Tube ticket, we spent a Saturday afternoon at Parliament Hill with Yes, Soft Machine and Procol Harum.

From 1968, Blackhill Enterprises occupied Hyde Park with a series of free concerts. The first featured Pink Floyd, *Saucerful* hot off the EMI presses. After similar largesse from Blind Faith and the Stones, Floyd again headlined in July 1970, introducing London to 'Atom Heart Mother'. Even as success beckoned – *Ummagumma* went top five, *Atom Heart Mother* number one – money and fame were yet to tempt Floyd from the college/club circuit that I haunted weekly. Which meant many of my gigs-to-savour back in the day had Pink Floyd all over them.

Which is a shameless way of introducing that staple of the dad-rock discourse, the favourites list. To remember every live gig five decades later is, of course, a tough call. But a recording is forever.

If you've read this far, you'll guess the author's Floydian preferences. So here are eleven Floyd tracks – in any order you like – without which life might just be intolerable:

1. 'See Emily Play'. Syd Barrett's slide intro ribboning out of my transistor radio in August 1967 was a gamechanger. 'Emily' is three minutes of psych-pop heaven, the most exquisite marriage between hit parade and the underground this side of The Beatles.

2. 'Chapter 24'. Syd quotes ancient Chinese wisdom while Rick Wright's Farfisa curls like an astral serpent around the strange and beautiful words. Parts of the 5,000-year-old I-Ching text – 'Things cannot be destroyed once and for all' – pre-date Newtonian physics, capturing Floyd's flair for esoterica with scientific, futuristic flavouring.

3. 'Set The Controls For The Heart Of The Sun'. To Roger Waters' chagrin, it defined Floyd as exemplars of space rock. An elegant promenade through the vacuum, and the first wholly successful Floyd soundscape following the bravely experimental 'Interstellar Overdrive'.

4 'A Saucerful Of Secrets'. A neutron storm in a solar graphite pile reaches criticality as a sonic approximation of Hell, before a redemptive ascent to Heaven. John Peel called this astonishing multi-part trek a 'religious experience'. Copy that.

5. 'Embryo': Floyd's homeless bouncing baby teethed from a five-minute studio demo to a fifteen-minute live epic. The band equivocated, but this glorious, archetypally-textured mood piece really should have been on *Ummagumma*.

6. 'Sysyphus'. What might have occurred had St John the Divine commissioned a soundtrack to 'The Book of Revelation'. Marshalling Bartók, Taylor and Stockhausen, Rick creates something beyond any of those worthies. It's the closest pure sound has come to a malign, sentient lifeforce. Watch and learn as 'Sysyphus' bosses the End-of-Days Brit Awards.

7. 'Summer '68'. Beatlesque hooks and on-the-road hookers. Despite early singles failures and the boulder-breaking impact of 'Sysyphus', proof that Rick had a delicious pop song in him to offset the atonal chaos.

8. 'Echoes'. A fast-maturing Floyd explore the submarine depths with one of their greatest sound paintings. It's a supremely atmospheric, 23-minute bridge between audial adenoids and post-1973 adulthood.

9. *Dark Side Of The Moon:* the whole lot; one of the vanishingly few albums – *Sergeant Pepper* and *Forever Changes* being two more – from which prising any single track defies natural laws. Everything that needs to be said has been said.

10. 'Sheep'. This almost-finale to *Animals,* or 'Shine On You Crazy Diamond'? Good as it is, the latter gets the sonic climaxing tucked up well before its lengthy instrumental coda, leaving an otherwise impeccable Floyd anthem top-heavy. 'Sheep' gets the balance right, keeping the listener on seat's edge for most of its ten minutes before David Gilmour detonates one of his most eruptive solos.

11. 'Comfortably Numb'. Bob Ezrin talked Waters into adapting this panoramic *chef-d'oeuvre* for *The Wall*. Best heard on *PULSE,* it is a perfect example of Gilmour's pre-eminence among rock guitarists and eloquent proof of the power of creative tension between two brilliant but endlessly conflicted artists.

## On Track series

Alan Parsons Project – Steve Swift 978-1-78952-154-2
Tori Amos – Lisa Torem 978-1-78952-142-9
Asia – Peter Braidis 978-1-78952-099-6
Badfinger – Robert Day-Webb 978-1-878952-176-4
Barclay James Harvest – Keith and Monica Domone 978-1-78952-067-5
The Beatles – Andrew Wild 978-1-78952-009-5
The Beatles Solo 1969-1980 – Andrew Wild 978-1-78952-030-9
Blue Oyster Cult – Jacob Holm-Lupo 978-1-78952-007-1
Blur – Matt Bishop – 978-178952-164-1
Marc Bolan and T.Rex – Peter Gallagher 978-1-78952-124-5
Kate Bush – Bill Thomas 978-1-78952-097-2
Camel – Hamish Kuzminski 978-1-78952-040-8
Caravan – Andy Boot 978-1-78952-127-6
Cardiacs – Eric Benac 978-1-78952-131-3
Eric Clapton Solo – Andrew Wild 978-1-78952-141-2
The Clash – Nick Assirati 978-1-78952-077-4
Crosby, Stills and Nash – Andrew Wild 978-1-78952-039-2
The Damned – Morgan Brown 978-1-78952-136-8
Deep Purple and Rainbow 1968-79 – Steve Pilkington 978-1-78952-002-6
Dire Straits – Andrew Wild 978-1-78952-044-6
The Doors – Tony Thompson 978-1-78952-137-5
Dream Theater – Jordan Blum 978-1-78952-050-7
Electric Light Orchestra – Barry Delve 978-1-78952-152-8
Elvis Costello and The Attractions – Georg Purvis 978-1-78952-129-0
Emerson Lake and Palmer – Mike Goode 978-1-78952-000-2
Fairport Convention – Kevan Furbank 978-1-78952-051-4
Peter Gabriel – Graeme Scarfe 978-1-78952-138-2
Genesis – Stuart MacFarlane 978-1-78952-005-7
Gentle Giant – Gary Steel 978-1-78952-058-3
Gong – Kevan Furbank 978-1-78952-082-8
Hall and Oates – Ian Abrahams 978-1-78952-167-2
Hawkwind – Duncan Harris 978-1-78952-052-1
Peter Hammill – Richard Rees Jones 978-1-78952-163-4
Roy Harper – Opher Goodwin 978-1-78952-130-6
Jimi Hendrix – Emma Stott 978-1-78952-175-7
The Hollies – Andrew Darlington 978-1-78952-159-7
Iron Maiden – Steve Pilkington 978-1-78952-061-3
Jefferson Airplane – Richard Butterworth 978-1-78952-143-6
Jethro Tull – Jordan Blum 978-1-78952-016-3
Elton John in the 1970s – Peter Kearns 978-1-78952-034-7
The Incredible String Band – Tim Moon 978-1-78952-107-8
Iron Maiden – Steve Pilkington 978-1-78952-061-3
Judas Priest – John Tucker 978-1-78952-018-7
Kansas – Kevin Cummings 978-1-78952-057-6
The Kinks – Martin Hutchinson 978-1-78952-172-6
Korn – Matt Karpe 978-1-78952-153-5
Led Zeppelin – Steve Pilkington 978-1-78952-151-1

Level 42 – Matt Philips 978-1-78952-102-3
Little Feat – 978-1-78952-168-9
Aimee Mann – Jez Rowden 978-1-78952-036-1
Joni Mitchell – Peter Kearns 978-1-78952-081-1
The Moody Blues – Geoffrey Feakes 978-1-78952-042-2
Motorhead – Duncan Harris 978-1-78952-173-3
Mike Oldfield – Ryan Yard 978-1-78952-060-6
Opeth – Jordan Blum 978-1-78-952-166-5
Tom Petty – Richard James 978-1-78952-128-3
Porcupine Tree – Nick Holmes 978-1-78952-144-3
Queen – Andrew Wild 978-1-78952-003-3
Radiohead – William Allen 978-1-78952-149-8
Renaissance – David Detmer 978-1-78952-062-0
The Rolling Stones 1963-80 – Steve Pilkington 978-1-78952-017-0
The Smiths and Morrissey – Tommy Gunnarsson 978-1-78952-140-5
Status Quo the Frantic Four Years – Richard James 978-1-78952-160-3
Steely Dan – Jez Rowden 978-1-78952-043-9
Steve Hackett – Geoffrey Feakes 978-1-78952-098-9
Thin Lizzy – Graeme Stroud 978-1-78952-064-4
Toto – Jacob Holm-Lupo 978-1-78952-019-4
U2 – Eoghan Lyng 978-1-78952-078-1
UFO – Richard James 978-1-78952-073-6
The Who – Geoffrey Feakes 978-1-78952-076-7
Roy Wood and the Move – James R Turner 978-1-78952-008-8
Van Der Graaf Generator – Dan Coffey 978-1-78952-031-6
Yes – Stephen Lambe 978-1-78952-001-9
Frank Zappa 1966 to 1979 – Eric Benac 978-1-78952-033-0
Warren Zevon – Peter Gallagher 978-1-78952-170-2
10CC – Peter Kearns 978-1-78952-054-5

## Decades Series

The Bee Gees in the 1960s – Andrew Mon Hughes et al 978-1-78952-148-1
The Bee Gees in the 1970s – Andrew Mon Hughes et al 978-1-78952-179-5
Black Sabbath in the 1970s – Chris Sutton 978-1-78952-171-9
Britpop – Peter Richard Adams and Matt Pooler 978-1-78952-169-6
Alice Cooper in the 1970s – Chris Sutton 978-1-78952-104-7
Curved Air in the 1970s – Laura Shenton 978-1-78952-069-9
Bob Dylan in the 1980s – Don Klees 978-1-78952-157-3
Fleetwood Mac in the 1970s – Andrew Wild 978-1-78952-105-4
Focus in the 1970s – Stephen Lambe 978-1-78952-079-8
Free and Bad Company in the 1970s – John Van der Kiste 978-1-78952-178-8
Genesis in the 1970s – Bill Thomas 978178952-146-7
George Harrison in the 1970s – Eoghan Lyng 978-1-78952-174-0
Marillion in the 1980s – Nathaniel Webb 978-1-78952-065-1
Mott the Hoople and Ian Hunter in the 1970s – John Van der Kiste
978-1-78-952-162-7
Pink Floyd In The 1970s – Georg Purvis 978-1-78952-072-9
Tangerine Dream in the 1970s – Stephen Palmer 978-1-78952-161-0
The Sweet in the 1970s – Darren Johnson 978-1-78952-139-9

Uriah Heep in the 1970s – Steve Pilkington 978-1-78952-103-0
Yes in the 1980s – Stephen Lambe with David Watkinson 978-1-78952-125-2

## On Screen series

Carry On… – Stephen Lambe 978-1-78952-004-0
David Cronenberg – Patrick Chapman 978-1-78952-071-2
Doctor Who: The David Tennant Years – Jamie Hailstone 978-1-78952-066-8
James Bond – Andrew Wild – 978-1-78952-010-1
Monty Python – Steve Pilkington 978-1-78952-047-7
Seinfeld Seasons 1 to 5 – Stephen Lambe 978-1-78952-012-5

## Other Books

1967: A Year In Psychedelic Rock – Kevan Furbank 978-1-78952-155-9
1970: A Year In Rock – John Van der Kiste 978-1-78952-147-4
1973: The Golden Year of Progressive Rock 978-1-78952-165-8
Babysitting A Band On The Rocks – G.D. Praetorius 978-1-78952-106-1
Eric Clapton Sessions – Andrew Wild 978-1-78952-177-1
Derek Taylor: For Your Radioactive Children – Andrew Darlington 978-1-78952-038-5
The Golden Road: The Recording History of The Grateful Dead – John Kilbride 978-1-78952-156-6
Iggy and The Stooges On Stage 1967-1974 – Per Nilsen 978-1-78952-101-6
Jon Anderson and the Warriors – the road to Yes – David Watkinson 978-1-78952-059-0
Nu Metal: A Definitive Guide – Matt Karpe 978-1-78952-063-7
Tommy Bolin: In and Out of Deep Purple – Laura Shenton 978-1-78952-070-5
Maximum Darkness – Deke Leonard 978-1-78952-048-4
Maybe I Should've Stayed In Bed – Deke Leonard 978-1-78952-053-8
The Twang Dynasty – Deke Leonard 978-1-78952-049-1

***and many more to come!***

**Would you like to write for Sonicbond Publishing?**

We are mainly a music publisher, but we also occasionally publish in other genres including film and television. At Sonicbond Publishing we are always on the look-out for authors, particularly for our two main series, On Track and Decades.

Mixing fact with in depth analysis, the On Track series examines the entire recorded work of a particular musical artist or group. All genres are considered from easy listening and jazz to 60s soul to 90s pop, via rock and metal.

The Decades series singles out a particular decade in an artist or group's history and focuses on that decade in more detail than may be allowed in the On Track series.

While professional writing experience would, of course, be an advantage, the most important qualification is to have real enthusiasm and knowledge of your subject. First-time authors are welcomed, but the ability to write well in English is essential.

Sonicbond Publishing has distribution throughout Europe and North America, and all our books are also published in E-book form. Authors will be paid a royalty based on sales of their book. Further details about our books are available from www.sonicbondpublishing.com. To contact us, complete the contact form there or email info@sonicbondpublishing.co.uk